THE ZOO

The Wild and Wonderful Tale of the
Founding of the London Zoo:
1826–1851

ISOBEL CHARMAN

PEGASUS BOOKS
NEW YORK LONDON

The Zoo

Pegasus Books Ltd
148 West 37th Street, 13th Floor
New York, NY 10018

First Pegasus Books hardcover edition April 2017

ISBN: 978-1-68177-356-8

10 9 8 7 6 5 4 3 2 1

Printed in the United States of America
Distributed by W. W. Norton & Company, Inc.

For Aaron, of course.

But also for Tommy the Chimpanzee,
whose story compelled me to write this book.

Should the Society flourish and succeed, it will . . . offer a collection of living animals such as never yet existed in ancient or in modern times.

Extract from the original prospectus of the Zoological Society of London, 1st March, 1825

This is extremely sonorous on paper; but alas for the execution of the design – is it not altogether visionary?

Extract from 'New Zoological Project' in the Literary Gazette, *Spring 1825*

We do not know how the inhabitants of the Regent's Park will like the lions, leopards and lynxes so near their neighbourhood.

Extract from 'Zoological, or Noah's Ark Society' in the Literary Gazette, *6th May, 1826*

Contents

Author's Note

This book tells the story of the first quarter-century of the Zoological Society of London and the establishment it created and developed in Regent's Park over those years. It is by no means an unknown story: there have been many thorough and fascinating accounts of the institution's establishment and development, and I owe a debt to the academics and experts who have trodden this territory before me (please see my Select Bibliography, pages 315–25, for details of some of the excellent works I have consulted). What I have tried to do is to tell that story a little differently, to bring it to life in a new, more vivid, more personal way, by relating it not as an institutional history but through the eyes of some of the people who made it happen. In this sense, it tells a factual story, but one that has been coloured in and fleshed out. (Perhaps one might say the history has been humanized, if that is an appropriate phrase for a book about a zoo.)

The extensive records in the archives of the Zoological Society of London allowed me to piece together a fairly thorough picture of the events, practices and the details of the Zoological Gardens and Museum in the Society's early decades, as well as understanding the motivations of those overseeing them. These I supplemented and contextualized with contemporaneous newspaper articles, guides, maps, weather reports, the personal correspondence and diaries, where available, of the people involved, census and parish records, and the archives of other institutions whose work and/or personnel overlapped with that of the ZSL in this period. This detailed research formed the basis for a *narrative* account of this history. In other words, on top of a factual relating of events, I have tried to recreate the atmosphere of the place and era and the emotions and ambitions of those involved in this remarkable enterprise. To this end, I have imagined details and scenarios, thoughts and reactions. When I have done so, I have always used the best available evidence: anything that is imagined is done within the confines of possibility, if not probability. Opinions of the people featured are either drawn from their own personal recordings of them, or are inspired by accounts of their personalities, or I use them to channel some of the ideas and understandings of the time. (For details of the specific sources used for each chapter, how I have used them and where I have supplemented them with a little supposition, please see Notes on the Use of Sources, pages 326–38.)

As part of my attempt to take the reader back to the spirit and mindset of these times, I have kept some of the literary conventions that were used then. For example, I have used 'the' before many proper nouns, such as in 'the Regent's Park' and 'the Queen Victoria'. I have kept the capitalizations used in cases like 'the Society' to denote importance, though for the sake of readability I have ignored the convention of capitalizing many others. With the same aim in mind I have also adopted modern, popular conventions regarding animal names (that is, I have not used capitals to denote species names as modern zoologists do, or capitalized all animal names as nineteenth-century zoologists had a tendency to do). However, although I have tried to make spellings consistent, I have not modernized all spellings (for example, I have kept 'orang utan', 'cameleopard' and 'Edgeware', all used at the time), and I have not corrected them even when they represent incorrect classifications and the biological nomenclature has been updated. In the same vein, there are many instances where the people I am writing about had ideas that we now know to be wrong or misguided but I have made no effort to amend or explain their mistakes. My priority was always to reflect scientific knowledge of the time and the protagonists' understanding of the world around them, so that the reader could share their journey as they tried to make better sense of it.

I hope that I have succeeded, and that the ride is an enjoyable one.

Isobel Charman, London, Summer 2016

1. The Ark in London

Sir Stamford and Lady Raffles,
1824–6

They could not save the animals, Tom's collection, so lovingly assembled – the pet monkeys, the bears, the tapir, the tiger. 'My Noah's ark', he'd called it – all now aflame on one great, terrible funeral pyre. Sophia knows she will never forget the hellish crescendo of the beasts' barks and cries, loud even above the cracking of the burning wood and the thunder of the hungry flames; the frantic, futile flapping of countless feathered wings against iron bars. No! She will not forget it, not for as long as she lives. However long that might be.

The human cargo has been a little more fortunate: bodies packed into two little boats the crew had managed to free in the chaos, now at a safe distance. The longboat had been aflame before they even got to it. Sophia is half naked and, as she watches the sheet of fire thrust ever higher into the abyss of the heavens, only now coming round from the daze of slumber broken by panic. The night had been thick and dark as tar but the carcass of the *Fame* is blazing more wildly with every quickened heartbeat; no longer a ship but a bonfire shifting against an unseen horizon. The surface of the ocean is seemingly alight all round them, like molten metal. Like Hell itself.

But worse is to come: the black mouth of the ocean that swallows them once the ship has eventually burned itself out, the nothingness that gnaws at them as they drift on the newly silent seas. Unseen faces, huddled together. Sophia clutches the boy to her, her nephew, as Tom in turn clutches her close. Together they float, on and endlessly on, in the total, maddening darkness. Sophia slips in and out of consciousness. All are cold without their clothes, thirsty without water, desperate without much hope. Everything they own is dancing its way to the bottom of the ocean. After all the ordeals they had already been through, a lesser woman might have wished herself there too.

But Lady Raffles is nothing if not a fighter. She has not survived the East, which snatched four of their little children from them, only to die tonight. On she clings. On and endlessly on.

It was a Sunday when they finally sailed up to the English coast: Sunday, the 22nd of August, 1824. Six months after the fateful, fiery night on the *Fame*, Sophia stood on the deck as the *Mariner* – which had borne them and their hastily assembled replacement possessions for four frightening months – made its final approach into Plymouth. It was a cool, sunny morning. Seagulls glided above, cutting between the ship's sails, and the wind tugging at Sophia's hair made her eyes water until her face was sticky with salt and tears. They were home.

And Cousin Thomas there to greet them! Sophia was giddy with a relief that dressed itself up as joy. Sir Thomas Stamford Raffles – *her* Tom – was less buoyant, and complained of a headache. He told his cousin, who had rushed to meet them after his morning sermon in Devonport, that it was *from the effects of landing*. As Tom made his formal goodbyes to Captain Young and his crew, and greeted the few friends that were gathered to meet them, Sophia confided to the minister that her husband had not been well of late.

But then, of course, he had not been well before they had even set out from Bencoolen. Failing health was the reason cited for their premature departure from that wretched place, for their forfeiture of the few more years of the Governor-General's salary they had reckoned with. Money was not enough to keep them there, with only ghosts for company, at the mercy of a climate and a land that had turned on them. No, the East India Company could keep its money. She had not been sorry to turn her back on the directors, so comfortable, so ignorant in London.

She did not speak this aloud. She did not need to: Cousin Thomas knew of their many great sorrows. Tom was more broken by it than she was, it seemed. Sophia looked over to where her husband stood a few yards away on the quayside, and the cleric's gaze followed her own. They stood a moment, watching the head with its distinctive snatch of fox-coloured hair between hat and collar. The face they both loved was turned away from them in conversation. But they observed Tom's stoop: was it more pronounced than usual? The bent back, which, he said, resulted from the ten years he had spent hunched over the clerks' desks of East India House. Then he had been just a boy, a stranger to Sophia. Now her husband of seven years had turned forty-three, had passed that milestone in the timeless, shapeless Atlantic Ocean. It was no novelty to him. He had passed other birthdays at sea and – like their first child, their poor little Charlotte – he had been born at sea. Albeit a sunnier one, a kinder one than that which had nearly snatched him back. Oh, Sir Thomas Stamford Raffles was nothing if not a man of the world.

And he was her world. Sophia could not bear to think of what
would become of her if she were to lose him too. He was the
reason she had set her jaw and clung to life as all the forces of
the earth and the heavens had conspired against them in their
battle to get home. The *Mariner* had been shaken so violently
that she had been roped to her couch for days on end, water
pouring into the cabin around her. Yes, she had clung on for her
Tom, and for Ella. How she wanted to see dear, dear Ella, who –
thank God! – they had been able to send home before she, too,
could be taken by the sickness that had so rapidly robbed them
of the other children.

And now here they were. They were home. Home and alive –
albeit barely. Tom seemed somewhat buoyed by the crowds that
were now gathering on the quayside, come to see the man and
his wife who had famously survived the terrible fire at sea. Sir
Thomas Stamford Raffles always rose to the demands of a public
occasion. Sophia thought she could see a little colour returning
to his cheeks.

When it came, the much longed-for reunion with Ella was a
subdued affair. Her parents were strangers to her. It had been
more than two years since they had hurriedly sent her home
from the unforgiving East, the sole survivor of their brood.
Then she had been just a babe in her nurse's arms. Sophia remembered the terrible countdown to the arrival of the boat that they
had decided would bear away their remaining three children
after the burial of their beloved Leopold. Yet only Ella had survived long enough to be loaded on to the *Borneo* with Nurse
Grimes when it came. The others – even the one yet to be born –
would never leave that foreign soil.

And here she was before them once again: their one small
miracle. That same bundled babe now a rosy-cheeked, healthy
little girl. Ella knew no other life than the one she had shared

these past years with her grandparents in Cheltenham. Her infant mutterings and musings betrayed no memory of the unpredictable fevers she had been saved from or the brothers and sisters who had been snatched from her, or the exotic animals with which she had shared her Sumatran home. Dove Ridge, the family's lush estate outside Bencoolen, which loomed so large in her parents' thoughts, was lost to her. She had no memory, even – save the ones Nurse Grimes had forced upon her – of the mother and father who now fussed around her, marvelling at her.

It was not only Ella who was a stranger to them. The town they knew well from the days of their courtship was near unrecognizable. It was not just that the years had changed them, Cheltenham *was* different. There was a delightful new promenade, an endless proliferation of spas and baths. A whole new estate was being built, which would rival the town centre when it was complete – *it was to have its very own pump room*, so Sophia's parents said. The traffic was incessant. The dusty roads were forever pounded by drays piled high with raw blocks of stone going one way and crates of debris the other, in addition to the carriages more liberally loaded with the better-dressed visitors and residents. They had arrived in the middle of the season, the town choked with fashionable ladies and gentlemen decamped from London.

And it was all so . . . modern! Work would soon be under way to bring piped water to the houses, and there were gas lights in the streets now – every last oil lamp gone, replaced by these new, brighter stars. It was quite remarkable to see here. Sophia remembered their arrival in London, the neat orbs lighting the sky above Westminster Bridge – it had been such a wonder! Now it was *normal*, even for a provincial town like Cheltenham. It came as a shock to those whose recent lives had been so dictated by the rise and fall of the sun. Here, at all hours of the evening, voices and footsteps and carriage wheels passed by the fine, if somewhat small, house they had taken on Wellington Place.

The Raffleses did not make use of this new release from nature's clock, or their proximity to the town and its multiplying attractions. Sophia did not feel at ease in this new, gaudy world. She did not seek out her old friends. She and her husband focused on quietly recovering themselves and on trying to become a family, of sorts, once again. They passed their days in relative isolation at their 'snug little house', save on those mornings when they ventured out to take the waters and convention demanded they stop to exchange greetings with their fellow humans. The town's healthy air and healing waters did not work any miracles on their shattered bodies overnight, but as the gentle English summer waned and the days grew shorter, their health slowly started to improve. They were well slept from nights in dry, unshaken beds and well fed. It was a relief not to be locked in constant struggle with the natural world, not to fear its teeth at every turn. And yet Sophia remained much shaken. On many mornings it took her some moments to realize, on waking, that she was no longer trapped in a dank, tossing cabin. And Tom's headaches had not disappeared.

Sir Thomas Stamford Raffles was not a man who enjoyed being idle, in good health or ill. He could not be long without an ambition, an occupation. He started speaking again of a long-held desire, one that Sophia had heard more idle talk of many times before. Her husband dreamed of setting up a society devoted to the study of the creatures on God's earth, about which they still knew little. So very little! *The time was ripe*, he said, *the nation was ready*: prosperous and at peace; at the centre of an Empire that afforded unparalleled opportunities for the discovery and collection of every bird and beast that God had put upon it. *The time was ripe*, he said, *nay, over-ripe*, to create London's very own 'Jardin des Plantes'.

Sophia well remembered the fine gardens, with so many exotic residents, that they had visited in Paris on their honeymoon in 1817. Oh, it was a magical place, quite unlike anywhere she had been before: the little rustic houses containing countless monkeys and exotic birds, a pit for the bears, a rotunda for the elephant and a giraffe, and all laid out within beautiful varied landscapes. She and Tom had been enraptured as they had walked the winding pathways that escorted visitors from one wild world to the next. How she had loved the area that emulated a Swiss garden, with its freely roaming beasts! It could not have been more different from the dingy, circus-like menageries she had come across before. This was nature, in all its Creator's intended glory.

She remembered that as they had admired the many beautiful corners of the grounds, her new husband had told her its story. The Jardin des Plantes had been born in the aftermath of the bloody Revolution, as a place where animals could be *observed* and *studied*, not just paraded and enjoyed by the rich. Tom had been so animated, saying over and over that *it was a travesty that their vanquished enemy had such a thing, and England – King and Country – did not. Why, London was the capital of the world, the metropolis of a great Empire!* An Empire of which he now knew so much, had seen so many of its beasts and plants for himself. About which he was yet hungry to know more. To *understand* more.

Now, with many more years of collecting and studying natural history behind him, he had begun to talk of it in earnest. He was sure he could do something similar – no, something *better* in London. Something worthy of an Empire of progress; something worthy of him, Sir Thomas Stamford Raffles. He was not at all deterred by the loss of his own papers, preserved specimens and live animals with the *Fame*, a collection he had so painstakingly gathered together over the years in the East Indies, intended as the beginnings of such a venture. It had been his passion, the work of his heart, the work of a lifetime. And all burned! Yet it had made him only more determined.

For now, his replacement collection of preserved specimens, hastily assembled while waiting for the *Mariner*, was still largely in boxes, waiting to find its place, its home, in this new land. As she and Tom waited, too, she thought. As Sophia listened to her husband paint a picture of the Jardin des Plantes he would build for England, she felt as if she might be ready to begin living again. For in these optimistic moments, when Tom was animated by his ambitions, the pain of their past seemed to fade a little. She dared, even, to believe that the future might hold happiness for her family. Or what remained of it.

He was anxious to get back to London. He grew restless in their cosseted world in Cheltenham. For a start, he was keen to see his East India Company colleagues to set his record of service straight. He had been away for seven years and he had a great deal of explaining to do. The months-long delay in communications between the colonial backwater of Bencoolen and his superiors in London or even Calcutta had meant he had often acted upon his own authority – even when setting up a new outpost for the Company at Singapore, at the risk of provoking the Dutch. It had suited him well at the time, but he was now worrying that he might be denied the financial compensation he surely deserved after his work, not to mention misfortunes, in his employer's name. He needed money to set up his family in a new life. He determined to venture to the capital, said he could not relax until it was done.

Sophia, as ever, refused to allow him to go anywhere without her, but for once she overestimated herself. The ordeal of the two-day journey, the filthy air and chaos of the city that met them at the end of it – so alien to them after so many years away – rendered her near useless to him, confined to their smart hotel room on Berkeley Square. Tom did what he could. He met friends at India House, managed to see the Chairman and Deputy Chairman of the Company, and glorious accounts of his conduct overseas appeared in the press. But it cost him much energy. They were both glad to get back to the relative peace of Cheltenham. They were not yet ready for the swirling metropolis, for society, for politics, for real life. Not yet.

They would, in all likelihood, move to London permanently – in time. *All in good time.* When they had both recovered themselves. Sophia entreated him to *focus on the present, for now.* Yet Tom could not stop himself looking ahead. The part of him that longed for peace and contentment said he thought he might like to farm the land, or perhaps take on a post as a country magistrate. But the hungry, ambitious part of him, a part he could never ignore for long, was fretting that he was being left behind. He was considering a career in politics, but overriding all was his passion for his own Jardin des Plantes. Before he could plan anything, however, he needed to settle his accounts with the Company. He set himself to the task.

By mid-October, the weather had turned. Hard, cold rain, propelled by churning winds, raged against the windowpanes, ever-audible, even through the thick curtains that were pulled across them. The weather was not the only thing that had turned against the Raffleses. Tom's health, which had seemed to be slowly improving, had taken a sudden battering, too. He had been in bed for some days now with an attack of his headaches. This one had rendered him more infantile, more dependent than little Ella, unable to hold a pen or sit up in bed, unable to endure even the cold, dull light of these stormy autumn days. And they had hoped to be better before the winter hit them. Sophia did what she could to nurse him, but she knew well enough, after so many years of it, that all she could do was sit and wait for it to pass. So sit and wait she did, listening to the rain clattering on the walls and windows of their little home. It gave her plenty of time to think. She was feeling a little stronger now.

Tom had been desperately writing an account of his services to the East India Company; his side of the story. He said he might need the public's support, that if people knew how hard he had worked – for the good of the nation, after all! – the directors would not dare to withhold what he was owed. It had been an ordeal, having to crawl through the recesses of his memory, with all his papers out of reach, swirling at the whims of the Indian Ocean currents. He had done some sums and had calculated a debt of at least twenty thousand pounds, lost through his efforts in Sumatra and Singapore. And yet his 'statement', as he called it, was unfinished, though it had nearly finished him.

She knew – they both did – that it was the exertion and the worry that had triggered this latest episode. And now he lay still, in the dark, helpless as a babe, as Sophia sat helpless too. How she hoped he might soon give up the idea of politics! Had it not taken enough from him already? Enough from them? The more she thought about it, the more she hoped that natural history might take priority. Was that not what made him happy? They shared so many wonderful memories of their little family's own explorations and pursuits in this field. She thought of the Animal Kingdom they'd built within their own walls at Dove Ridge, their Sumatran estate.

As the rain drummed on out of sight, she allowed her mind to return there; to lose herself in joyful memories of their children playing with the young tigers in the nursery, of Tom's daily survey of his plantations with Charlotte, Leopold and little Stamford, and how they had all traipsed through the aviary, dodging flapping wings and bullets of excrement – not always successfully! She thought of the native man of the woods who had worked for them, no more than two feet high, how they had all loved him, with his jet-black face and white surtout! And, of course, dear Mr Silvio, the monkey, who was brought into the dining room to entertain them after dinner. She had used to tease Tom that he preferred the company of that furry little creature to his own children's! It seemed a hollow joke, now. She even allowed herself to remember how, in the darker times she usually dared not think of, their ceaseless work of collecting and cataloguing specimens had provided them with much-needed distraction, comfort even.

How much good natural history had done them! How much good it might do them yet. Yes, she decided, as the rain drummed on. Yes, she would encourage him in this venture.

Little more than a month later, on the evening of Tuesday, the 30th of November, Sir Thomas Stamford Raffles was back on his feet, quite literally. He stood, glass raised, around a large table in the cavernous room of the Crown and Anchor on the Strand. The weather had not improved, but in the grand, candle-lit room, filled with the smells of their recently consumed dinner, one would never have guessed that outside the walls it was a particularly foul day.

It was St Andrew's Day and, therefore, the anniversary meeting of the Royal Society. During the proceedings earlier, just a little way down the Strand at Somerset House, Sir Stamford had been elected to its Council. It was a prestigious appointment for a man such as he; a man who had had, much to his regret, so little formal education. He was now not just a member but a *Council member* of the oldest, the most prestigious scientific institution in the world. *Look to what heights young Tom from Walworth has pulled himself!* He wanted to shout it out. Yet he had accepted the honour quietly, suppressing the childish pride beneath his practised decorum. Now, some hours later, he was no longer restrained. Now he celebrated, surrounded by almost a hundred leading men of the arts and sciences. All of them, at this moment, turned to face their re-elected President, Sir Humphry Davy, as he made the usual loyal toasts to the King. The newest Council member joined in most heartily. More than just back on his feet, Sir Stamford Raffles was back in society, back in the world – and elated to be there.

The Raffles family had arrived in London just a couple of weeks earlier, ready for what Sophia called their 'winter campaign'. Sir Stamford had recovered from his attack and, despite continued poor health, refused to delay the move any longer. *They needed to secure their future*, he insisted. To *begin* their future. Once more their possessions had been packed up – at least, those that had been unpacked in the first place. The 173 cases that contained the pieces of their lives to date, those that had not perished with the *Fame*, had been loaded onto a series of carts and dragged off in the direction of the capital. The family had followed. Tom had been impatient: *he had so much to do!*

Already things were coming together. This very man, Sir Humphry Davy, the President of the Royal Society no less, now midway through his speech – this man was helping him to make things happen. Sir Stamford and Sir Humphry had become acquainted on his previous trip home, and since he had been back this time they had had a few encouraging conversations. Most encouraging!

Sir Humphry took his seat and the rest followed, drink and age allowing them to do so with varying degrees of elegance: the Home Secretary, Mr Peel; the long-time Chancellor of the Exchequer, Lord Bexley; the President of the Royal Academy, Sir Thomas Lawrence; and the many other gentlemen, the great and good of intelligent London society who surrounded the vast table. The Treasurer of the Society remained on his feet, Mr Davies Gilbert MP. A mathematician, it was he who had first recommended Davy for work in the scientific laboratories of the newly formed Royal Institution. He turned to where his protégé now sat, most comfortably, in the top chair. The Treasurer began his customary speech in praise of their President. *Sir Humphry Davy, a man whose discoveries in analysing the alkalis and the earths were unequalled in brilliance and importance since those of Isaac Newton.* Sir Stamford made the appropriate noises of assent alongside his peers. *Yes, yes, Sir Humphry was a brilliant man. Indeed, he was a pioneer, a great thinker!*

And this man was going to help him, of that Sir Stamford was sure. They'd already shared a few tentative words about another great society: his Zoological Society.

In the first cold month of the new year, Sophia watched her husband – who she'd just ensured was suitably attired for the weather in his winter cloak – descend the steps of the house to the busy street below. He fixed his hat to his head and, with a step that was almost sprightly, he wove a course through the clattering carriages and carts, and made for the green expanse of the park. Sophia stood for a moment at the window, still watching him. He seemed well today. He did look aged, so much thinner, but Sophia knew him minutely. She studied him daily, in much the same way, she liked to think, that Tom had kept such a close eye on the plants at Dove Ridge, on the coffee and spices he had laboured over. She was a botanist, too, in her own way. She could detect change coming, gingerly, imperceptibly, just like the slow growth of a tree. She saw the energy she had always admired in her husband creeping back. She turned away from the window as he cleared the traffic.

They had been in the house on Piccadilly for two months now, but were still living in a state of disarray and packing crates. Tom had been trying to sort out his papers, but it was a task to which he had so far proved unequal; despite the superficial improvements, he was still not in good health. Besides, they were moving again very soon, taking over the lease of Sir Humphry Davy's London house on Lower Grosvenor Street. Their current residence was not adequate to their aspirations. Tom dreamed of having all his preserved animals and birds and his natural-history drawings on show, and almost as soon as they had arrived here he had declared that 104 Piccadilly *simply would not do*. There was no point settling here then, Sophia had told herself. They would sort everything out after they had moved. She hoped that in the new house they would find she could make a proper home for her little family at last.

For all the shortcomings of the present residence, its location on Piccadilly was not one: it stood directly opposite the Green Park, which Sir Stamford had now reached. The day was clear and cold, the ground frozen but free of snow – which suited him. Oh, how he valued these excursions! Sophia and his friends pressed him not to go out too much, and certainly not after sunset – his headaches still plagued him, despite the mercury he took – but whenever he could he ventured out to reacquaint himself with the capital city of the Empire he had so long served from afar. On the days he felt well, like today, he rose early, breakfasted with the family at nine – and then the morning was his, though it pained him that this was what he was reduced to. All the expeditions he had undertaken – they had both undertaken; up mountains and through rivers, knee-deep in leeches, Sophia surrounded by natives who had never seen a white woman before . . . Now he seldom went further than the other side of the park.

And yet . . . How much there was all around him to interest him! London was truly changed since the last time he had seen

it, back in 1817. Then the cloud of war – raining wretchedness
and frugality – had still lingered, hanging heavy over everything. Now Britain was booming, and quite visibly so: there
were building works in progress everywhere he looked. He felt
almost as if he was exploring a strange new land once more. The
house was just a short walk from the newly constructed
Piccadilly Circus, intersecting the grand ceremonial route from
Carlton House to Regent's Park, which was the ambitious creation of John Nash. Regent Street was almost finished now,
neatly separating the West End from the sprawling eastern side
of the city. He admired the sense of order, the planning that had
gone into it. The chaos of the old city was being tamed into a
capital that befitted a nation that now led the world. It looked
like a new Rome! He wished Napoleon could see it for himself.

On fine mornings like this, as he felt the cold, hard earth
crunch beneath his elegantly shod feet (how different from what
they had worn in the tropics!) and as the noise of the chaotic
morning streets receded behind him, he felt strong and hopeful,
in spite of his reduced physicality. He walked south through the
park, leaving Piccadilly behind him. There were many others
out that morning, taking advantage of the good weather, and he
occasionally raised his hat to his fellow walkers. He would go as
far as Buckingham House before turning back, he told himself.
He had heard that this was going to be the next project by Nash,
transforming the Queen's House into a new residence for the
King. A new King, as far as he was concerned – George IV had
been Prince Regent when he had last been in the country. Now
on the throne, he was not a popular monarch, but Sir Stamford
approved of his ambitions for rebuilding the nation, if not his
personal decadence. The parks were about to be overhauled, so
it was said, redesigned for this era of greatness and affluence. It
was hard to keep up with all that was going on – though Sir
Stamford tried his very best. He was fascinated to learn daily

from the papers about who was investing in what; the many grand schemes that were planned; the engineering marvels that would soon be set in motion.

Right now, just five miles from where he trod, they were beginning work on a tunnel that was to go beneath the Thames. How staggering to think of it! Marc Brunel had invented a cast-iron tunnelling shield for the task, and this time they must succeed, surely. Sir Stamford had unshakeable faith in the loco-motive steam engine, which would soon be taking travellers and goods – *without horses* – across the country at speeds of ten or twelve miles per hour! It was almost a reality: construction was nearly complete on a twenty-five-mile colliery railway line. He was proud to be part of the coming revolution, for he was involved in one such venture himself, as Deputy Chairman of the Norfolk, Suffolk and Essex Railroad Company, hoping to build a railway line from London to Norwich. He loved to think of himself now, in London, at the centre of a web of innovation that was transforming the nation, indeed the world, as he walked and lived and breathed. There was so much opportunity here, if only he was up to seizing it.

He could not help but wonder, too, what was happening now in all the other places he had lived, and governed: in Penang, where he had met his first, much-loved wife, Olivia; in Batavia, where he had buried her; in *his* Singapore; in Bencoolen, where his beloved children lay in the earth, now simply handed over, unbelievably, to the Dutch. He tried not to think of how he was being repaid by his employers for all he had done in their service. He still had not heard from the Company's directors about what he was to receive by way of a pension and compensation. He had had the statement he had written privately printed and circulated at the end of last year, to all the influential people he could get it to: members of the government and powerful friends. He had hoped it would force the Company's hand, making it widely known how much he had done in his nation's interest, how hard he had toiled for the best part of two decades. But Farquhar, the wretch, was now making problems for him. Farquhar, a man *he* had promoted, a man *he* had made Governor of Singapore, a man who had ignored all his orders – who had let slavery, opium and immorality flourish, the enemies of civilization he had always worked so hard to eradicate, on the newest corner of the world that he himself had claimed for the British Empire. A man now calling him, Sir Stamford Raffles, a tyrant!

But enough of that. He could feel a headache coming on, and he did not want the morning to be ruined. He paused and looked up at the trees, devoid of leaves at this time of year, yet still grand. They were plane trees, genus *Platanus* (he tried to use Linnaeus's classifications when he could). He had not quite reached Buckingham House, though he could see it ahead. He decided to take the most direct route instead, and turned east. He might even take a chaise. His head was throbbing now, and he was keen to press on before it got the better of him.

He was bound for Somerset House to meet Sir Humphry Davy. Since the night of the Royal Society dinner a few months ago, they had seen much of each other. Sir Humphry was fully committed to the idea of a society dedicated to the study of zoology, and they were now – rather wonderfully! – embarking on the joint enterprise of setting it up. They had to work out precisely what it might become, what form it might take . . . but those were just details. Sophia was always telling him not to let his hopes run away with him, but he was sure that London would have its Jardin des Plantes. And it would be a place of science, of investigation, of knowledge. They had much to discuss, he and Sir Humphry, two men with a hunger for knowledge and the spirit of discovery in their veins. On a more mundane level, there were also a few final things he wanted to ask about the house he would take over from him.

Yes, this was it: he was being welcomed into the circles he had long felt he belonged to, among the pioneering men of the age. The explorers of their day! He had almost forgotten about his headache as he hurried along in the winter sunshine.

It all began to happen fairly quickly. By the time the new leaves, shiny and green, were unfurling on the branches of the city's many plane trees, Sir Stamford Raffles's dream was also springing to life. His work had been achieved without the help of the shy March and April sunshine, for he had spent the majority of the recent weeks shut away in the study of his new home at 23 Lower Grosvenor Street. It was a prestigious address and he was pleased with it. They all were. The house – like their lives – was slowly becoming more ordered, the packing crates disappearing as the shelves and cupboards filled. It was becoming something resembling the home they had long sought. Sir Stamford was now looking for a country residence to which the household could retreat for the summer. The long-desired picture of normality for his diminished family was close enough to touch.

But that was not his prime task now. This morning, as on most others of late, he was bent over his desk, writing, writing, writing. *He had come full circle, back to his days as a young clerk*, he had joked to Sophia over breakfast. It was another wet morning, but he was oblivious to the bloated raindrops rolling down the window glass before him. The metal-nibbed pen he now used (he had thrown away his quills the moment he had discovered these modern implements on his return) scratched lightly as it moved across the paper. A rhythmic scrawl, interrupted periodically as pen was dipped into inkwell. On and on he wrote, without pause. In front of him on the desk was a proud pile of papers, copies of the prospectus for the proposed Zoological Society of London, which he had drafted and Sir Humphry had approved. Yes, it was real now.

The prospectus, dated the 1st of March, 1825 and printed just over a week later, laid out the details of the vision Sir Stamford had long had in mind: the creation of an establishment dedicated to the scientific pursuit of natural history. It would combine the study and teaching of zoology with a collection of living animals. A public menagerie, yes, but one that would allow naturalists to observe the creatures *scientifically*. There would be a collection of preserved specimens too, affording naturalists 'the correct view of the Animal Kingdom at large in as complete a series as may be practicable'. Using the knowledge so gained, the Society planned to introduce and domesticate new breeds of animal likely to be useful in common life, animals that could better serve the farmyards and dinner tables of this great nation than those that occurred naturally.

Sir Stamford wholeheartedly believed that man could control the glorious natural world bestowed on him by God. In fact, he did not just believe man could control nature but that man *should* do so. Only by studying God's creatures would mankind be able to glimpse the true wisdom and power of the Creator – and make proper use of these gifts, as He surely intended. Just to *enjoy* God's creatures, to be entertained by them without seeking to understand them, to ogle them as they performed tricks, as people did in the menageries that already existed in the nation – well, that seemed so . . . frivolous. And while Sir Stamford was many things, a frivolous man he was not. As a child he had visited and even enjoyed that most famous of all menageries, the Exeter 'Change on the Strand. How he had laughed at the monkeys gambolling in their cages! But now, to listen to grown men telling him there was no need of his proposed Zoological Collection because there were already such creatures in London – for the masses, at Edward Cross's establishment; for King and Court, at the much-diminished Tower Menagerie – well, he could scarcely hide his fury.

He had felt compelled to see for himself Chuny, the famous elephant they all spoke of with such laughter. *Chuny will take a sixpence off you with his trunk, and then he will return it, into your hand!* When he had ducked into the tall building on the Strand and climbed the stairs to the Exeter 'Change menagerie, he had walked through the rooms filled with cages, cages filled with creatures, creatures watched and goaded by little boys and girls. He had passed by them all, making his way through the Grand Hall until he stood outside the bars of its most enormous cage, ready to witness this spectacle. A finely dressed couple duly appeared and held out their hands, sixpences in their palms. And at the moment when the huge grey trunk, so coarse, so pink at the end, obligingly appeared through the bars, the absurdity of it all had struck him so he had almost laughed aloud. Just minutes away, in the Royal Institution on Albemarle Street, Sir Humphry Davy's protégé Michael Faraday was taming the elements and forces of the natural world. Here, where he could hear the roar of a lion and the chattering of monkeys and see the great hulk of an elephant in front of him, man was content just to *watch and laugh*. It was ludicrous.

Sir Stamford and Sir Humphry were not the first who believed it was time to look more closely, more scientifically, at the earth and the life that God had created. Their prospectus specifically referred to the Horticultural Society, founded just twenty years earlier: their proposed Society would do for zoology what the Horticultural Society had already done for botany. For this was an age of order, of understanding, of cataloguing, of putting everything in the world in its place, and a time when that world was increasingly within the British grasp. No longer did the Royal Society enjoy its centuries-old hegemony over knowledge and experimentation. Now gentlemen enthusiasts and those with a more professional interest in the natural sciences came together in their own associations, focusing on their specific shared pursuit.

In recent decades societies dedicated to the study of plants, geology, public science and technology had been founded. Only zoology had been neglected, apart from the attempt by the Linnean Society to set up a Zoological Club. Sir Stamford, recently elected a member of that Society himself, did not care for it. It felt too limited by the Linnaean traditions and methodologies of the last century, and its leading members – important naturalists, such as Joseph Sabine, Nicholas Aylward Vigors and Edward Turner Bennett – were all supporters of his independent plans. His bigger, grander, more modern plans.

His Society would offer 'a collection of living animals such as never yet existed in ancient or modern times'. So he had written in the prospectus. His creatures would not be 'objects of curiosity', as they were in other menageries. Neither would they be 'spectacles of wonder' and savagery, as they had been in ancient Rome. Uncivilized Rome! In his menagerie they would be 'objects of scientific research, not of vulgar admiration'. It was an opprobrium to the age and to the nation that no such undertaking already existed. He, Sir Thomas Stamford Raffles, would finally right that wrong.

Sir Humphry Davy was out of town – and, anyway, he was a man whose time must be apportioned between so many projects, from the Royal Society to the Board of Longitude to the Athenaeum Club he had established. It had been left in Sir Stamford's hands to distribute copies of the prospectus and entice subscribers in. Sir Humphry had left him with a list of potential supporters and Sir Stamford spent hours each day writing to them, and to everyone else he could think of who might be willing to lend their name or money to the endeavour. Sir Humphry and he differed somewhat as to how scientific it might eventually be: Sir Stamford was the more passionate on the point, Sir Humphry more concerned about its use to the amateur naturalists and country gentlemen who were in a position to support it financially. But they agreed in the main, and that had been enough to begin. Now the pile of prospectuses they'd had printed diminished rapidly, as Sir Stamford sat writing, writing, writing . . .

He had told Sir Humphry – had told everyone he spoke to about it – that he was confident he could attract twenty thousand members, such a need was there for this! And yet not everyone, it seemed, was quite as confident. He had yesterday's edition of the *Literary Gazette* folded next to him. Even without his looking at it, its more memorable phrases – 'altogether visionary', 'wild speculation' – seemed writ large. He was being ridiculed! Recruitment had not been as successful as he had hoped: so far, he had a mere fifty subscribers. But what did that mean? It was only a matter of more work, more time, surely. And he had some great names among them: Mr Peel, Lord Spencer, Lord Lansdowne and Lord Stanley, as well as reputable naturalists, such as Mr Vigors, Mr Bennett, Mr Sabine, and anatomists, Sir Everard Home and Mr Joshua Brookes, the latter with his own museum and anatomy school on Great Marlborough Street. Besides, Sir Stamford had never been troubled by whether something was probable or simple. Nothing had been simple in Java, or in Bencoolen, or in Singapore, and he would press on now, just as he had then. The status quo meant nothing to him. In fact, he loathed the status quo. Loathed the Exeter 'Change and its wasted opportunities.

He was busier than he had ever been, and not just the mornings, like this one, he spent in his new study: his afternoons and evenings were also increasingly occupied. Sir Stamford and Lady Raffles, now settled among the great and the good of London society, and feeling fitter than they had for a long time, were finally in a position to gorge on the feast of intellectual stimulation and pleasure available to them here. They tasted sweet after the scant offerings in the East: *he was like a bee buzzing greedily between an abundance of flowers*, he liked to say. Just last week he had been presented to the King at His Majesty's first levee of the season, surrounded by the nation's ancient nobility and new leading lights. Pall Mall had been thronged with people desperate for a glimpse of their monarch. And in his carriage he had passed them all and swept through the entrance to Carlton Palace. Such a spectacle had awaited him there! The porters at the gates in their bright liveries, the King's Guard and the Royal Horse Guard in the Palace Yard, with the booming processional music of their accompanying bands; the Grand Hall lined with a party of the Yeomen Guard, the two toweringly tall Royal Horse Guardsmen accoutred as cuirassiers . . .

He was allowing his thoughts to drift. He was, admittedly, still not quite himself. In weaker moments, he wondered if the strength would ever return to his limbs, to his head. But he banished such dispiriting thoughts when they surprised him. He had work to do, vital work for the Crown and Country of which he was so proud. He dipped his nib in the inkwell. The sound of pen scratching across paper resumed.

The new pace of life did not abate: May was even busier than April had been for Sir Stamford and Lady Raffles, now much in demand on the social circuit. Tom's work took up much of the time that was not occupied by social engagements and Sophia had hardly seen her husband take a moment's rest these past weeks. On this Thursday afternoon he was out of the house and not expected home until dinner, so when she heard a sudden agitation below she knew instantly that something was awry. She put down her pen and listened. The front door was open, allowing the rumblings of the outside world to drift up to her. The sound of voices inside, raised in alarm, brought her rushing down the stairs. The sight that greeted her in the doorway pulled a cry from her mouth and stopped her only a few steps down the staircase. Her Tom lay in the arms of a stranger, hatless, his collar roughly opened. *Was he . . . ?* She clutched her throat with one hand while the other found the banister.

One of the strangers looked up at her, read her face. *He's alive, but he's been unconscious.* She felt the breath rush out of her, and ran to her husband, who was now being manoeuvred clumsily into the drawing room.

He was in bed again. Awake, but buried somewhere within himself. He looked out at her from his shrunken face, with . . . Was it fear? A sense of his own mortality, perhaps. As if he were a frightened animal finding itself for the first time in an unfamiliar place. Not unlike when they had first brought Mr Silvio, the wild monkey, into Dove Ridge, she thought, but did not say. She had never seen that look in Tom before, had never had to be so careful with him. She thanked God he was still with her, even as she prayed silently that his usual ebullience would triumph over the strange creature that had taken hold of him.

He had collapsed when out walking and had been unconscious for almost an hour, insensible in the grime of the street. A surgeon who happened to be passing had found him, loosened his clothing and tended him where he had fallen. When he had awoken they had brought him home, conscious, just, but unreachable still. For Sophia it had seemed an age, sitting at his bedside, as she waited for him to come back to himself. Back to *her*. The doctor had suggested he be bled. She had felt as if she had been hurled into a fever-induced dream, as she so often had been out East. *Tom had been quite well that morning*, she had kept saying, when he had strode out to visit Mr Murdoch, the Scottish merchant and Fellow of the Royal Society, to talk to him about the Zoological Society, no doubt. Quite well if, on reflection, a little tired. Yes, it had been a busy few weeks for him.

If she was honest with herself now, as she sat in the quiet

dimness of Tom's chamber, curtains drawn, Sophia had known that he had been pushing himself too hard. But she had not seen him so animated for a long time, and had not wanted to dampen his ardour, the spirit that had awoken in him once more. She had been proud to sit next to her husband at dinners and watch him command the room, silence his critics, win admirers as he spoke of his great vision for the Jardin des Plantes of London. His enthusiasm was unrelenting.

Behind closed doors, things had not been as simple as he had made out over the many glittering dinner tables at which they had sat. He had been toiling on a revised prospectus, having sent out every last one of the previous batch, and had fallen out with Sir Humphry over it. Much to Tom's chagrin, Sir Humphry was wary of making the Society seem overly scientific. He had suggested that *perhaps given the low numbers of subscribers they ought to broaden its appeal*. Tom had refused to back down. They had reached a compromise, of sorts, republishing the original prospectus with a new statement attached. It had been sent to the printer on the day he had collapsed. She could not help but wonder if it was connected, though Tom had said he was happy enough with the new version.

He seemed a little better now, she thought, looking to where he lay next to her, sleeping. Yet he still spoke little. After bleeding had restored him to sensibility, a few days of bed-rest had seemed to help his body recover. She had told the newspapers that he was well again. It was not, as they had at first feared, apoplexy. She did not want word to get out that he was diminished in any way. It was bad enough that everyone knew he had collapsed. She still could not bear to think of Sir Stamford Raffles lying in the dust and dirt of the street.

Things would improve when they went to the country, she thought. Tom had found a place for them now, a fine estate not far from town in Highwood, eleven miles to the north of

London, or thereabouts. It was adjacent to one that their friends
Mr Wilberforce, the famous abolitionist, and his wife had
bought. He and Tom had long shared a hatred of the evils of
slavery, through which they had become acquainted some years
ago, and now they were set to share the lovely hill in Highwood. There were tussles over money still – the current owners
had asked twenty thousand pounds – but Tom had assured her
all would be resolved. He was still thinking about his career,
had not given up on the idea of a seat in Parliament, but perhaps
once they were in the fresh air again, with their grounds to
maintain, he would think less about that. And now that his
Zoological Society – the project closest to his heart – seemed to
be in train, perhaps he might relax. She looked at him, lying
quietly in his bed. She hoped he'd live to see his dream fulfilled.
As soon as that thought took form, she shook her head to be rid
of it. She must never think like that. Tom was strong. Tom had
so much still to do.

A little over a month later, on the 22nd of June, 1825, Sir Stamford Raffles was well enough to attend a meeting he had arranged
for the subscribers of the Zoological Society of London (at least,
those who had not yet left town for the season). The group met
in the rooms of the Horticultural Society on Regent Street. The
Earl of Darnley took the chair. Those in attendance would
appoint a committee to oversee the establishment of the Society.
Sir Stamford, hardly able to restrain his enthusiasm, was the first
to volunteer.

He was happy. It was something he had not felt in himself for a
long time, and it had taken him by surprise. He had learned to
live again after their misfortunes, but he had done that by suppressing a part of himself. Not quite his heart, but . . . Whatever
it was, that was how he had picked himself up after they had lost

their first child, their beloved little Leopold, and how he had lived through the loss of the other three. Tom had swallowed his capacity for real emotion, heartbreak and joy alike. He had lived, he had breathed; he had been stimulated by challenge and conversation; he had set himself tasks and even enjoyed achieving them . . . but he had felt nothing as intimately as he had before. He would never return to his old self, he knew — but now he felt . . . content, and even the first mutterings of joy. He had never thought he would feel it again. Indeed, after his collapse, he had wondered if he would ever feel anything again.

But here he was, out walking before breakfast on his very own farm, belonging to his new country house. It was glorious! The weather had been hot, stiflingly so, and Sophia had suffered terribly. He had not minded it so much. It was easing off now, and so early in the day, it was pleasant. He looked around where he stood. He could not see the entirety of the 111 acres he now possessed, but he surveyed as much as he could. It was a lovely piece of land. The views were wide and with enough variety to please the eye wherever it strayed. From this very spot, at the edge of the field where his men were making hay, he could see the stacks drying in the surrounding fields, the hills and dales beyond, and in the further distance, a dark green stripe of woodland. Behind him, there were extensive lawns around the house, itself solid and modern. The lawns were browning a little in this weather, but they were still perfectly delightful.

He looked at his handful of workers, moving rhythmically as they scythed the long grass, still damp with morning dew but drying in the first warmth of the day. He breathed in its strong, fragrant scent. So different from the putrid breath of London! He listened to the sounds of the birds, of the long blades swooshing through the grass, and the occasional bubble of words between the workers. He liked the clarity of the natural order of things, the lord of the manor — a position won by virtue and industry, rather than bestowed on him by birth – overseeing the happy labourers as they toiled on the land. Here he felt close to God, for surely this was the world as He had intended it.

He had taken on all the growing crops with the property, and they kept poultry, pigs, cattle and sheep, too. They had no grapes for wine, or water for fish, but the land allowed them to be near self-sufficient in everything else. The animals were his wife's domain, especially the poultry and the pigs, and she kept herself busy in the dairy. He oversaw the rest. They brewed their own beer and baked their own bread. They lived a quiet life, himself, Sophia and Ella, their nephew Charles, their few servants and labourers. It was quite unlike Dove Ridge, which, despite its remoteness, had always been so full of people: the four children and Nurse Grimes, the keepers for the monkeys, cats and tiger cubs they had kept in the house, the sultans calling in for conversations, guests from the settlement who came for the lively dinners, servants rushing to him with the poisonous snakes they had trapped . . . But he was grateful for the solitude of Highwood and he liked being tired and satisfied at the end of each day. They had found a new kind of happiness here, there was no denying it.

His friend Mr Wilberforce had not yet moved in his own family next door, but he had entrusted the laying out of the grounds to Sir Stamford. They were both becoming involved in local life, and were trying to get a chapel built – a Chapel of Ease: they were more than four miles from the nearest church. The local vicar, the vicar of Hendon – who apparently had interests in the West Indies – had not cooperated with two men known for their abolitionist ideals but neither was put off by such a trifle. They would achieve it in time. Sir Stamford also hoped to become the local magistrate; Mr Wilberforce was urging him to do so and he was happy to oblige. He liked the prospect of bringing law and morality to these lands as he had in far distant ones. He saw his future here. He liked what he saw.

That was not to say he had given up his ambitions in London. The Raffleses still had the house on Lower Grosvenor Street and would move back there in the new year. For the time being, the journey to the capital was manageable, if a little unpleasant; three miles to Edgeware, and from there eight miles along the Edgeware Road to Tyburn Turnpike. But it was summer now, and London had no need of Sir Stamford and his family nor they of it. The committee of the Zoological Society would not meet until next year, and things were in hand with that. He had already written to his friends in the East, calling for animals for the Society. He expected an orang utan skin and skeleton from Sumatra any day now. In the meantime, he had more than enough to keep him stimulated here. He was organizing his personal collections. At Highwood he finally had the Museum Room he had long craved, and was gleefully overseeing the unpacking of the specimens he had sent back to England from Sumatra, and before that from Batavia, and those he had managed to assemble after the *Fame* had gone down. He had tapirs – stuffed and preserved in spirits – a dugong skeleton, rhinoceros skins . . .

Yes, Highwood was the perfect place for his little family. There was just one problem: he could not afford it. But surely the Company would settle his claim soon. He could not believe that he had still not heard from them. In the meantime, he asked his friend Thomas McQuoid to send to him the last of his money that was in Batavia, all sixteen thousand pounds. That would cover most of it, anyway.

He was hungry. It must be breakfast time. He turned and made for the house.

It was a long and bitter winter. The first snow had fallen in October and then, in the early weeks of 1826, an unfathomably cold snap pounced. A devastating frost blinded the windows of

Highwood House and brought the estate to a sparkling stand-still. In the villages nearby it brought down the shutters of the shops, and slammed the doors of butchers, who feared for their stock. Tom was not in Town to see the chaos and frivolity brought to London by the Siberian weather, but the papers brought tales of it to his wintry seclusion, albeit somewhat delayed. The Thames, that great artery of the metropolis, gleamed with frost as its depths clotted. It fell eerily empty of its customary traffic, a blank, white path winding through the city like a ghost. The Serpentine, its tiny sister, froze solid, but she was busier than ever, her glittering surface alive with skaters, gingerbread-sellers and smartly attired ladies promenading neatly while their common counterparts more freely enjoyed its slippery surface. Those Londoners old enough to remember said it felt colder even than the winter of 1814, when the Thames herself froze solid.

The weather was not the severest blow that London had to deal with in those icy months. It was not the worst with which Tom had to contend. It was news of a graver nature that he sought in the newspapers. In December, the 'money market', which had seemed so invincible in the heady days of prosperity he had met on his return from the East, suddenly failed. The price of the stock that everyone – himself included – had bought with such confidence plummeted overnight as investors hurried to offload it. There was a run on the banks in London, which closed their doors to the endless customers wanting to withdraw their funds, and many country banks followed suit as the year staggered to a chilly close. There was no discernible reason for it: no war, no failed harvest. Though Tom sought answers in the papers, he found none. The days of optimism were over. And he still had not heard from the East India Company.

By late February, the worst of the cold weather was behind them, and Sir Stamford Raffles was drawing to a close the first ever meeting of the Committee of Proposers of the Zoological Society of London. That was now its official designation: the Zoological Society of London. It was the obvious and only choice, though including the capital city in the title was a splendid patriotic flourish. They had just agreed on it, he and his fellow Committee members gathered around the table of gleaming wood in the Horticultural Society's offices on Regent Street – the Society's Secretary, Mr Joseph Sabine, had permitted their use for this important Sunday congregation.

Sir Stamford was overseeing the proceedings from the chair, commanding the Committee that consisted of his co-conspirator, Sir Humphry Davy; his friend the Duke of Somerset; another dear friend from his days in Java, Dr Thomas Horsfield, the American physician and naturalist; the Royal Society's Treasurer, Mr Davies Gilbert MP; the famous surgeon and anatomist Sir Everard Home; the Earl of Darnley; and finally the secretary of the Linnean Society's Zoological Club, Mr Nicholas Aylward Vigors. It was a prestigious scientific committee of which its organizer was justifiably proud. The politicians Lord Auckland and Sir Robert Inglis, along with Dr Harewood, were also there, not elected to the Committee but keen to be involved with the nascent Society in the future. All had just participated in the making of history, of that Sir Stamford was sure.

He was feeling better again, despite the rough winter and the shocks it had delivered. He and his family had left Highwood in early February, to return to London for the season. He was surprised to find that he was not sorry to be back in Town, though the stinking air and incessant noise were a shock to senses soothed by the natural beauty and stillness of the English countryside. He was especially not sorry to be there today. The meeting concluded, and the distinguished company began to rise, the tone of their voices turning from formal to cordial.

Their work was well done. They had not only agreed on a name for the Society, they had started to make plans for it. Sir Stamford, with Sir Humphry, Lord Auckland and the Earl of Darnley, was to investigate the possibility of acquiring land for a menagerie in the Regent's Park. There was much to do. They agreed to meet again the following Saturday.

Sir Stamford left the building, stepping out onto the imposing Regent Street. So indescribably grand! Classical perfection. He paused to look in the direction of the park at its end, where he hoped his long-nurtured dream would become reality. The finest, newest park in the capital was the perfect spot for such a modern undertaking. He could not help but recall the words of the *Literary Gazette* article that had so angered him almost a year ago. Or, he corrected himself, which had spurred him to action: 'altogether visionary', 'wild speculation'.

No longer.

Three days later, a most distressing occurrence took place in the heart of London, on the busy Strand. Sir Stamford did not witness it but heard reports of it from newspaper-sellers, his servants, his dinner guests and, not least, his colleagues at the Royal Society, whose rooms at Somerset House were perfectly placed for them to experience, at first-hand, a struggle between man and beast.

This was what had happened, from what he could deduce, once exaggeration and speculation were removed from the story. At half past four on Wednesday afternoon, an employee of Edward Cross ran into the yard at Somerset House, and begged the soldiers on guard to follow him to the menagerie across the Strand. Chuny had started to batter the bars of his cage most violently. Cross feared the elephant would break free and tear to pieces the entire structure of Exeter 'Change and anyone in it. He begged the soldiers to put his star out of action. Quickly.

For the next hour and a half, the Strand shook with the beast's roars and thunderous kicks against the bars, and the incessant boom of the soldiers' guns as they fired into the cage, over and over again. People gathered outside, listening, blocking the traffic as their numbers swelled. Rumours flew around the crowd: *all of Cross's beasts were free and every keeper massacred!* On the commotion went. Not until the one hundred and fiftieth bullet had entered Chuny's great frame, this one just behind the ear, did the beast seem affected at all. Finally, he collapsed to the ground, rocking the building as he did so. One of his keepers had attached a sword to a pole and now rammed it into the enormous grey hulk on the floor, rammed it in right up to the hilt, again and again. He had not forgotten how Chuny had turned on a fellow keeper in October and killed him. Yet he could not help but feel a deep sadness at his demise.

Sir Stamford was appalled. It was all so unsavoury, confirming what he had long believed about the nature of establishments such as Mr Cross's. However, he read with interest the details of the elephant's care that littered the London papers; the vast quantities of food and liquid the animal had consumed, not to mention the sedative medicines they had been trying to trick him into swallowing, without success. Twenty pounds of salts at a time! Six ounces of calomel! (Sir Stamford was an habitual user of mercurous chloride for his headaches, but never took more than a single grain or two.)

The spectacle, like the endless articles in the press, did not cease with Chuny's death. Over the course of the week, thousands of people — men of science and tourists of the macabre alike — flocked to the Strand. They squeezed themselves into Exeter 'Change, waiting their turn to mount the staircase to the Great Hall, to peer into the now silent den at the far end where the bloodied carcass of unimaginable proportions lay. A number of special visitors were permitted to view it at close quarters.

One cold morning, in the darkness before dawn, a certain Mr Delville, a phrenologist, was permitted to take a cast of the head. He declared that Chuny's 'bump of fury' was exceedingly well developed, just as he had expected. Sir Humphry himself popped in to peer at the carcass. As the days wore on, the visitors had more than just the elbowing crowds to contend with: a vile stench set in, which grew so putrid that the residences of the Strand had to be evacuated.

Sir Stamford and his colleagues in the Zoological Society were more interested in what followed: a dissection of the great beast, for the purposes of comparative anatomical study. Sir Stamford followed the proceedings with fascination. So, too, did most of London. The elephant was raised from the ground with an enormous pulley, then flayed by a team of nine butchers, working through the night on Saturday. The one-ton skin they removed, three inches thick in places, was taken off the premises on Sunday morning and sold to one Mr Davis for fifty pounds. The celebrated anatomist Mr Joshua Brookes, one of the first subscribers to the Zoological Society, oversaw the dissection. He had never before worked on such a scale, but he proceeded methodically, aided by a team of eminent surgeons. First the contents of the abdomen and pelvis were removed, then the enormous heart – found to have been pierced by the sword blade – and the bullet-riddled liver. The hall was lined with green baize and filled with spectators on specially erected seats; they had paid a hefty fee to watch the show. The room was well fumigated, but still the air scratched at the backs of their throats. Hundreds more who could not get in crowded the Strand, watching the carts loaded with flesh wheeled out. Everyone wanted a piece of Chuny. A few, apparently, tried a cooked elephant rump steak, and newspapers published recipes for elephant meat, but most of it was sold by the ever-enterprising Mr Cross for cat food. More useful was the portion allowed to Sir Everard Home, an old acquaintance of Sir Stamford (he had sent Sir Everard numerous specimens from his own travels) and another subscriber to the Society, to be used in his experiments on muscle tissue.

It was a deplorable state of affairs, Sir Stamford and Sir Humphry agreed, to see the study of animals reduced to this: professional men of science chasing after the scraps thrown to them by showmen like Cross. The Zoological Society would allow dissections at the menagerie, but in a manner befitting the true study of comparative anatomy. On a more positive note, the feverish interest in the details of the dissection – as much as in the stories of the elephant's demise – proved what an insatiable appetite there was for the study of God's creatures. It confirmed Sir Stamford's belief that the day was ripe and the need urgent. He was keen to begin building the reputable, serious establishment that had now been agreed upon and to create a menagerie that befitted this great nation.

On a Thursday afternoon just a few weeks later, he came a step closer to his dream – many steps closer, to be precise. He was walking in the Regent's Park with a fellow member of the sub-committee established with the purpose of obtaining land for the Society, Lord Auckland. It was a cold March day, but Sir Stamford refused to recognize the chill. Today he saw only the sunshine. He had been permitted to enter the Regent's Park a number of times, most recently to search out possible grounds for the Zoological Society. It had impressed him on every occasion.

When he had first started work at India House in 1795, this swathe of green to the north of London had been known as the Mary-le-bone Park, or Marybone Park to the uneducated people he had grown up among in Walworth. It had been mainly farmland, with a few fine squares for wealthy townspeople at its southern tip. Young Tom had not been part of that sequestered world. But look! How quickly things changed. The park was now the crown of Nash's vision for a new London, at the northern terminus of his ceremonial street running almost all the way to Westminster. The Regent's Park was like a whole new town, with a crescent of grand white houses at its base and terraces springing up at its borders, many still being built. Sir Stamford had not seen the ruins of ancient Rome but he suspected these majestic buildings must outshine even that city's finest temples. Chester Terrace – being completed now – had almost knocked the breath from him, with its triumphal archways. It made him glad that he had lived to see this new dawn in London.

The park itself was gloriously designed, Sir Stamford thought. A huge green expanse of perfect gardens with an ornamental lake, and even a canal running around it. It was a wonder of planning, like a fine country estate – yet the din of London only a mile away! The Royal Residence that Nash had planned for it, a summer palace, had not materialized, for the King had turned his attention to Buckingham House. Many fine villas had been built within it, though, some already occupied by men of commerce and science. Men like himself, he thought, men of the new age. Indeed it was the perfect place for the Zoological Society – with its shared vision of progress, of order, of the natural beauty of God's world – to put down its roots.

He could see it now, in his mind's eye. He could picture the fine buildings he would construct on this spot and that spot in the grounds, elegant buildings that would honour and augment such a beautiful setting. Each animal would have its own accommodation – an aviary here, a paddock for deer there, the lake filled with fish and frequented by aquatic birds. He could imagine a house there for the lions from Africa, another nearby for the apes of Asia, yet another for the elephants of India. All of these beasts, from across the earth, from every corner of the endless Empire, gathered here! He could almost hear the roars.

There must be space, too, for a Museum to contain all the skins, skeletons and stuffed bodies he was already receiving for the Society from his friends out East. And rooms for the members to meet and study in. Everything would be ordered, everything in its place. There would be no poky, crowded buildings, like Exeter 'Change, filled at random. No dim corners for a huge beast like Chuny to die in. Mr Cross had already offered the Society his own animals. Ha! Cross knew that the days of such palaces of frivolity were over. A new age was upon them. Sir Stamford thought back to his visit to the Jardin des Plantes in Paris with Sophia. To the enclosures there, so suited to the outdoor setting, to the proper study of the creatures. In the Regent's Park they would be able to match it – to better it. There was so much space to build in!

Sir Stamford was happy to be making this closer acquaintance with Lord Auckland, a man of about his own age and similarly attired in a tall silk hat, high-collared shirt and cravat, a thick coat pulled around him to ward off the cold March wind. Lord Auckland was a politician from a very prestigious family. He knew well the leader of the House of Lords, the Earl of Liverpool, and had sat on many committees with him. The Society had initially hoped that Liverpool would be able to whisper the right words in the right ears, and thus procure the parcel of land upon which Sir Stamford had set his heart, upon which his mind had already built the wonders of his menagerie. It was inside the Inner Circle, near to the glorious ornamental lake, and currently cultivated by a nurseryman.

That was not where they were today. The Commission of Woods and Forests had directed them to another area, beside the newly constructed canal on the northern edge of the park. That was where they were walking now. The canal was just ten years old, a marvel of engineering, and ran all the way from Paddington, through the new village of St John's Wood, with its

Continental villas to the west of them, and on to the London
docks to the south-east. This element of Nash's grand plan had
cost the nation at least half a million pounds, he had been told.
But it was so efficient! All the speed of water transport, yet unen-
cumbered by the wind or tides, of which he knew all too much.
The two men stood on the bank, watching a laden barge move
westward, tugged along by a chestnut horse. Sir Stamford wondered how far its goods, hidden in crates, had travelled already.

*A canal would surely be useful to a Society that must rely so heavily on
London's links to the rest of the world. Indeed, but the road . . .* They
were so close to the road that they could hear its noise even now:
the constant chatter of wheels and hoofs. *That would not do, would
it?* And it was so narrow here. They would not be able to lay out
the buildings as Sir Stamford had imagined. *Why were the Commissioners reluctant to give them a finer stretch of land? Did they not
foresee the benefits the Society would bring? How magnificently it would
adorn the already magnificent park?*

No, it was not what they needed, they agreed, turning back to
the road and Lord Auckland's carriage. Sir Stamford suggested
that they go post-haste to talk to Mr Decimus Burton, a young
architect who had been recommended by Mr Bellas Greenough,
one of the subscribers to the Society and the owner of the finest
of all of the Regent's Park villas, Grove House. Mr Burton had
designed it for him, and was working with Sir Humphry too,
on the Athenaeum Club. Sir Stamford had spoken to him
already, and the young man had said he would be happy to help
the Society with its plans. He was the right man for the job, Sir
Stamford had no doubt: his father, Mr James Burton, had been
Mr Nash's builder here and had put into stone and stucco the
architect's marvellous vision. And Burton the Younger had not
only designed Mr Bellas Greenough's villa but many others in
the park – and even been given charge of some of the terraces by
Mr Nash. Sir Stamford had been most impressed, however, to

learn that the huge domed exhibition hall, the Colosseum, which was now being constructed to the east of the park, was entirely his design. A most exciting and breathtakingly modern undertaking, a purpose-built construction to house a panoramic, perspectival view of London based on exact geometrical drawings made from the dome of St Paul's. Magnificent!

Lord Auckland agreed that they should indeed talk to Mr Burton, and the two men walked briskly, both secretly glad to be getting out of the cold.

A few days later, a letter arrived for Sir Stamford at Lower Grosvenor Street, from his friend Thomas McQuoid. He had instructed McQuoid to remit his remaining money in Batavia to London so that he could pay for Highwood House. The letter contained grave news: McQuoid's company had gone bankrupt. He had lost everything – including Sir Stamford's sixteen thousand pounds. It was, more or less, the last money the family had been able to count on.

Just a few weeks later, another letter followed this most unwelcome news: a long-awaited correspondence. It was the response from the East India Company to his statement, recognizing his good service in their name. Yes, yes, he knew all of this, he thought, as he read it. But where was the detail as to how they were going to compensate him for it?

On the same day, an invoice from the Company arrived. The directors had done their own calculations. They reckoned that they were not in Sir Stamford's debt to more than twenty thousand pounds, as his own sums had indicated. Rather, he owed that amount to them. Twenty-two thousand two hundred and seventy-two pounds, to be precise.

On Saturday, the 29th of April, 1826, the first general meeting of the Zoological Society of London took place in the rooms of the

Horticultural Society. This time, it was not just the proposers of the Society who passed through the grand doorway of 21 Regent Street. On that spring afternoon, forty-eight men crossed the threshold and made their way to the meeting room. Forty-eight men who had responded to the invitation to its inaugural meeting, sent to all of the existing subscribers, and many other important and influential figures besides. There were many great men among them, professional men of science and amateur naturalists alike. Even the Lord Mayor, Mr William Venables MP, had come, Sir Stamford was gratified to see.

Sir Stamford had been called to the chair and the proceedings were under way. He was reading aloud, to those assembled, a letter from the Commission of Woods and Forests granting them a plot in the Regent's Park. The Commissioners had refused to compromise on the area they would offer, so Sir Humphry and Sir Stamford had conceded. They had taken the land by the canal, despite its drawbacks. It would do. The deal was done. They had taken on a lease for five acres, at six pounds and six shillings per acre per year. He read from the letter, in the voice he reserved for such occasions: 'The Society is to fence and lay out, plant, keep and occupy the ground within the Park in such manner as shall be previously approved by the said Commissioners, who are at liberty to require the removal of any animal which may be brought upon the premises by the Society, which may be deemed likely to become a nuisance or objectionable in the neighbourhood.'

He looked up at this point to gauge the reaction of his audience to the fact that the land was *already theirs*, and that they would soon start preparing it for the reception of the first live animals. He did not feel quite the sense of pride he had anticipated of this momentous occasion. He was, if he was honest, a little distracted. A friend who had come to the meeting, whom he had not seen for a time, had – rather unhelpfully, he thought – told him how unwell he looked. He was probably right. He certainly did not feel at full strength, as he stood there now.

Just that morning he had finally managed to sit at his desk to respond to the East India Company's devastating demand. He had written what he thought was a dignified letter, in the circumstances, to the Company Secretary, Sir Joseph Dart. He had simply asked for time to comply with their demands. Though quite what time would give him, he did not know. He felt as if he was under siege. He had nowhere to turn, no battle-winning strategy. He – a man of action, of ingenuity, of confidence – was paralysed. How would he ever pay for Highwood? It would have to go. What else they would have to part with, he dared not think. Not yet. Not while he was so busy. He would focus on the Society for now, with what energy he had left. Once that was done, he would think about money.

It was a shame that his mind kept wandering back to that, because as soon as he was elected President he would move on to a speech that he had been, mentally at least, preparing for years. A speech he had made so many times in his own mind, or shared with Sophia, and more recently with anyone who would listen. A review of the state of zoology in Great Britain, and a laying out of the objectives and details of the Society he had planned. He tried to focus on the task at hand. But he was so very tired.

It all started to come together before his very eyes, crafted with his own hands – or near enough. Sir Stamford Raffles, duly elected the first President of the Zoological Society of London at its first meeting, wasted no time in commencing the work thus assigned to him. Just a week later, he was able to report to the first Council meeting of the Society that he had taken temporary accommodation until they could build in the park itself: a townhouse on Bruton Street, the former residence of the late Royal

Academician William Owen. He took Mr Burton, the architect,
there to survey the building. It was the first occasion upon which
the two men had spent any time together, and he found Burton
eminently professional, despite his age. He reminded himself
that he had been even younger when he had been sent out to
Penang, and not much older when he had mounted an invasion
of Java and become its first Lieutenant-Governor. Mr Burton did
not betray the enthusiasm of most young men, but he seemed
appropriately interested in Sir Stamford's plans, and understood
what he wished to achieve. Sir Stamford reported back to the
Council that he thought the building entirely fit for purpose,
with a few renovations. The Museum could be installed there as
soon as the renovations – whitewashing and painting, some
repairs to the chimneys and roof – were completed.

Sub-committees were established to oversee every detail of
the forthcoming work required to accommodate the Society. Sir
Stamford volunteered to sit on four out of six, despite his wife's
concerns that he was pushing himself too hard. The subscriptions
kept coming in. Five thousand pounds were set aside for the Gardens in the Regent's Park and the President asked Mr Burton to
draw up a detailed plan. Until the menagerie was ready – which
even the ever-impatient Sir Stamford realized might take time –
they would need somewhere to keep the donations of living
animals already made to the Society. Reluctantly, he agreed with
Mr Cross of the Exeter 'Change and Mr Cops, keeper of the
Tower Menagerie, that they would have temporary care of them.
A griffon vulture and a white-headed eagle were bestowed upon
the Society by Mr Brookes, who was soon to retire. By June
1826, the Zoological Society of London had its first Council of
eminent scientists and gentlemen, its first President, a future
headquarters and Museum, its first live animals, and the land that
would boast the most magnificent menagerie ever seen.

★

Yet the venture was still mocked by the press. Sir Stamford could not believe they doubted, even now. The *Literary Gazette* called it the 'Noah's Ark' Society, claiming of its ambitions that 'there is neither wisdom nor folly new under the sun'. They compared it to the wild-beast shows of which the Romans had been so fond! Had these so-called journalists not read the prospectus, in which he had *specifically* outlined how this would be entirely different from the savagery and spectacle of ancient Rome? And the mockery hadn't ended there: they had also written that the aim was to propagate 'strange reptiles' all over the Kingdom. The absurdity! Sophia had had to calm him down when he showed it to her, almost shaking with disbelief. What he was doing *was* new! And it *was* serious. He would show them.

He wished that he did not have to expend so much energy on worrying about money. He had not yet addressed the catastrophic financial situation his family now faced. That could wait. He was Noah, if they liked, because he *was* building an ark, right here in London.

In the middle of June, the family moved back to Highwood House. Sophia hoped her husband could finally relax. He had been so terribly busy, and irritable, even – rare for Tom. The children, Ella and her cousin Charles, had been ill with whooping cough and he had suffered from it too. Back at Highwood, everyone found health and good spirits once more. Tom began to unwind. The Wilberforces moved in next door. Sophia knew there was concern over money, but surely they could sort it out. Tom's health was still poor, but she was sure it would improve now they were back in the country. They loved it there.

Just three weeks into their summer at Highwood, on the 5th of July, Sophia awoke in the first eerie light of dawn to find her husband absent from their chamber. He had come to their bed at his normal hour, and she wondered why he had risen so unusually early. She went after him. She found him at the bottom of the stairs, unconscious. The household was awoken to her screams for a doctor.

It was the day before his forty-sixth birthday.

Report made to the Family of the Late Sir T. S. Raffles of the result of the examination as to the immediate cause of his death

On inspecting the body of the late Sir Stamford Raffles in the evening of the 5th of July 1826 the following morbid appearances were observed:

Upon removing the cranium, the anterior part of the right frontal bone was twice the thickness of the left; this must be imputed to the effects of the sun in India since it is a common occurrence in those who have resided long in hot climates. The outer covering of the brain was in a highly inflamed state, which had been of long continuance, from the thickness of the coats of the vessels. In one part immediately upon the sinciput, this vasculosity exceeded any thing I had ever seen. In the right ventricle of the brain there was coagulum of the size of a pullet's egg and a quantity of bloody serum escaped, which measured six ounces. This extravasation of blood, which had been almost instantaneous, was the cause of immediate death, so far as the faculties of the brain are concerned. In the other viscera of the body there was no appearance connected with disease.

Signed, Everard Home

2. The Gardens Grow

Mr Decimus Burton, Esq., Architect,
1826–30

It was fair to say that this was one of the more curious professional situations in which Mr Decimus Burton had found himself. Naturally he did not say. With a calm manner that belied his tender age, he took an almost imperceptible step backwards while simultaneously removing his hat, which had been left teetering atop his head at a precarious angle by the animal's sudden attack. He thus prevented the distracting eventuality of it dropping to the floor.

The monkey, having lost the advantage of surprise with its first failed attempt to cause precisely that – or, better still, to claim the black silk hat for himself – swiftly retreated to the pole in the corner to which it was shackled. It swung itself onto the cross-perch atop it and there it sat, furry legs dangling, chain swinging, dark eyes glaring. The creature was clearly furious, having failed to elicit even the consolation prize of a satisfying squeal from his unwitting victim; a truly rare occurrence for uninitiated visitors to the offices of the Zoological Society of London at 33 Bruton Street.

The monkey – an infant wanderoo, it had been pointed out upon their entry to the room – now innocently stroked the impressive white beard framing its face while sizing up his peculiar adversary. Decimus Burton: tall, slim and adequately handsome, high forehead balanced by large, earnest eyes and a strong nose. Ever the professional, Mr Burton pressed on. He was determined to ignore the creature, even though it was clearly pausing only to plot its next move. He would wait to put his hat on again, thus allowing him to finish the conversation in which he was engaged with his client without further distraction. It was now apparent that he had been a trifle premature in putting it on anyway. Mr Nicholas Aylward Vigors, Secretary of the Society, had not yet finished summarizing the outcome of the previous evening's committee meeting. In short, the Marquess of Lansdowne had agreed to take over the Presidency, vacant these past nine months, and the Society was now ready to proceed with the menagerie in the Regent's Park. Mr Burton's job was to turn the designs he had drawn up for Sir Stamford Raffles last June into brick and stone, wood and iron reality.

Mr Vigors was a barrister by training and an ornithologist by passion. It was a somewhat curious marriage of interests on the surface, though the contrary deportments expected of each occupation obscured their many commonalities: the pursuit of knowledge, of truths hidden in minute detail, for frameworks to unite fragments. The somewhat dogmatic Vigors had adopted the manners demanded by his paid profession, rather than those of his hobby. He now addressed the young man as if he were in a court of law, oblivious to the rather less formal confines of an office shared with an outrageously mischievous, if temporarily vanquished, monkey. Nodding, and making the occasional note, Mr Burton silently calculated the distance he now stood from the supernaturally still creature versus the perceived length of the chain that hung loosely betwixt its leather girdle and the pole. He took a small step to the right and towards the desk that lay between himself and Mr Vigors, adorned with his own designs for the laying out of the Society's Gardens, ostensibly to study the plans more closely. Yes, that ought to do it. He was safe now.

It was many months previously that Mr Burton had first visited the building. Then he had surveyed its every empty corner with an effervescent Sir Stamford. It had been in a rather poor state of repair, devoid of inhabitants and purpose. Its last owner, the Royal Academician William Owen (whose paintings he had admired), had died there, of an accidental overdose of Barclay's Drops. It had been in sore need of a thorough whitewashing. None of that had deterred Sir Stamford. Looking back now, Mr Burton recalled not just the poor paintwork and rather offensive cornicing, but the older man's energy. Sir Stamford had expounded his vision for each room with unbridled enthusiasm, desperate to set the transformation in motion. Had he known, perhaps, that his time was short? Like most such gentlemen returned from years of service overseas, he had not looked particularly healthy; another wizened man of Empire, with exotic exploits to boast of, and the scars and pallor to prove them. But he had almost masked the weariness and wear with passion. Almost.

Mr Burton was not particularly curious about the far-flung corners of the globe of which all such men spoke, though he feigned interest as and when required. His own passions centred on older Empires, those of Greece and Rome. Nor had he much interest in animal life, preferring wonders made of stone and marble. Of course he had not shared these truths with Sir Stamford. Gladly he had agreed to work for the nascent Society: it complemented his other work in the Regent's Park so perfectly.

Besides, he had believed, as Sir Stamford had prophesied, that it would turn into something of note. It was an opportunity for an ambitious young architect; a novel commission, if nothing else. After a polite caesura engendered by its founder's death, it seemed now to be taking shape.

Mr Vigors's summary drew to a close and Mr Burton saw his chance to conclude the conversation. He was a busy man. *Yes, sir, he understood precisely what was required of him. Naturally everything would be dealt with in the most expedient manner. Of course, Mr Vigors, he very well understood that the Commission of Woods and Forests would need dealing with. He was, after all, well acquainted with the Commissioners! He was pleased to know Lady Raffles had seen the designs and had approved. Splendid! Yes, sir, please do display the plans here for the members to peruse. He would be most interested to learn of their reception.* The men eventually bade each other good day, Mr Burton assuring the client that he could see himself out.

His hat he kept clutched firmly in his hand as he made his way out of the Secretary's room, to protect himself in the (albeit unlikely) event that he had miscalculated the monkey's maximum reach. As he passed along the corridor to the front door, he was able to survey the scenes he had merely glimpsed on his arrival, and take in the activity through the open doorways at his leisure – as far as politeness allowed. He was not wholly convinced he was free from the tyranny of beasts yet for he could hear birds twittering and calling from somewhere close by, awaiting the homes he was to build for them in the menagerie. The din seemed to be emanating from the room next to the one he had just quit – thankfully, the door was firmly closed. He knew that the well-known anatomist Mr Joshua Brookes had donated a vulture, which for many years had aided in the disposal of the bodies used at his anatomy school. Mr Burton hoped he would not encounter such a gruesome creature now.

He was less concerned by the numerous animals he noticed

that were not capable of making any noise or in need of homes from him. These he saw in varying states of preservation, on desks, floors and in boxes. Earlier, in the front office he had been shown into upon his arrival, he had watched a dead fox being unwrapped by a clerk. Donated by Mr Cross of the Exeter 'Change, he had been told. (He had feigned interest, though he had been more concerned by the condition of the room: its disarray meant that it was hard to tell if all the repairs and decoration had been performed *precisely* as he had directed.) *All such creatures,* he was told, *if the condition allowed, were destined for the Museum further along the corridor and in a room upstairs, already open to members for their perusal.* The work to display the stuffed bodies, skins and skeletons in a manner appropriate to the scientific ideals of the Society was clearly . . . ongoing.

But that was not his concern. Whether or not it was of quite the standard he had prescribed, his work here at Bruton Street was long done; the Regent's Park was his domain now. Mr Decimus Burton, young and ambitious, knew he was equal to the unusual task he had taken on. As he stepped out of the door into Bruton Street, he reunited head and hat with effortless elegance. Thus appropriately attired for the cold March air, he strode off in the direction of his offices with a quick yet even pace. He was keen to begin. The Society hoped that enough might be done in time to open the Gardens this coming summer.

Decimus Burton: twenty-six years old, diligent, driven and, perhaps most importantly, born into the right family at the right time. He was the son of James Burton, the businessman, who had built much of the new London that now confronted him as he rounded the corner into Regent Street, in all its gleaming glory. (Though it was not as white as it had been a few years ago, he noted. Nothing in the city long avoided the filthy lick of the smog.) He was looking up at the façade of 9 Conduit Street – a rather fine, if somewhat conventional, three-bay, stuccoed composition with giant Ionic pilasters – when he almost collided with a pair of bonneted ladies bustling up Europe's finest shopping thoroughfare. He smiled at them, bowed and pressed on.

Regent Street was a masterpiece, but a flawed one. He couldn't see it now from where he stood at the junction of Conduit Street, but he could sense the nonsensical magnitude of All Souls' Church to the north. His unarticulated verdict was that Mr Nash rather deserved the ridicule he had received for it. The principle was sound, a terminal feature to draw the eye up from Oxford Circus, and it almost worked from a distance, but the building defied the laws of design. Its horrendously mismatched spire and Greek peristyle were an unforgivable violation of the principles of beauty and geometry. Principles that, so Mr Burton believed, must guide the pen of every architect, without exception! The god of proportion should never be sacrificed on the altar of personal ambition for the sake of . . . originality. He himself had come up with a simpler, more sympathetic design for a church in Regent Street, which he had exhibited at the Academy some years ago. Nothing had come of it.

The young man turned away from the unseen monstrosity and proceeded southwards down the busy street. Well-dressed shoppers congregated around the lavish window displays. Visible through the passing traffic – currently a pair of young men on horseback, and a rather tattered coach – was the elaborate façade of number 204, which housed the goldsmith. On his side of the street was Cramer and Co., the music publishers, where the greatest musicians of Europe flocked when they were in London. He had a fondness for music (he appreciated art in all its incarnations) but did not have time to peer in through the window to see who might be holding court there, not today. He walked on, eyes firmly forward.

Every block on this section of the street was divergent in

design. The houses with shop-fronts, which dominated, had been constructed by a number of builders and architects, and had sprung up at different times over the past decade whenever investors had appeared. His father had been the most significant of them. Since he had taken a plot in Waterloo Place when Decimus was just fifteen, he had gone on to build seventy-four houses in the street, stepping in where others had failed. He had been instrumental in getting the grand plan realized. Mr Nash's grand plan – yes, the great Nash had overseen it. Despite the lack of communion and uniformity, he had achieved a sense of balance, of sorts, with enough 'architectural' buildings – one long symmetrical frontage on every block, at least – to lend it an overall sense of grandeur. That was the young architect's verdict, anyway.

Mr Burton crossed New Burlington Street, and thus arrived at the beginning of a block that had been built by his father. He himself had had *a small hand*, he thought it fair to say, in the design of this one. They were fine buildings, with a simple, seven-bay central façade and recessed wings, buildings that stood out in the patchwork of the street through their neat and modest elegance. He had been just twenty when he had worked on them. Even then Decimus Burton had been a confident architect. Then, as now, controlled and exact, he believed that attention to detail and overall geometry could not fail to bring beautiful and appropriate results. Quite unlike Mr Nash, whose approach was famously more relaxed.

Decimus Burton, thus named because he was the tenth child to James Burton, brother to Septimus and Octavia. The devoted and obedient son (unlike some of his siblings, though one need not mention them) to a rational, precise man. To the logic he had inherited, Decimus felt that he had added artistry (though he would never boast of such a thing!). It was proving a lucrative combination. He was inundated with both

public and private commissions. His Colosseum in the Regent's
Park was nearing completion, and he had other projects in progress for the Commission of Woods and Forests. His façade at
the Hyde Park, with its Roman arches, was almost built, as was
his more monumental arch at the Green Park. The latter (modelled on the Arch of Titus) was to be the entrance to Mr Nash's
aggrandized Buckingham House, itself a triumphal commemo-
ration of Britain's victory in the recent war against the French.
On top of that he was engaged on a number of villas in the
Regent's Park and private residences elsewhere around the country, as well as a Gothic church in Tunbridge Wells, an ironworks
in Wales, and the club house for the newly formed Athenaeum
Club – though the search for a plot had proved a little troublesome. And now the work for the Zoological Society would
commence in earnest.

Despite last year's stock-market crash, which had slowed the
task of beautifying the metropolis, business was booming again.
It seemed the market for property, relatively new, was sturdier
than others. The nation was being remodelled under the patronage of its opulent king, and seemingly nothing could stop it. In
London, work was carrying on at such a pace that the city must
soon be entirely renewed. Despite his father's assertion that they
must prepare for tougher times, Mr Burton could not imagine it
any other way. Money was made in bricks and mortar and he
could not remember it ever having been different; he had grown
up with building, building, building. When he had been a boy
his father's efforts had centred on Bloomsbury, but even that was
a distant memory. For at least ten years that new artery of
London, Regent Street, had been the focus of their energies.

The road began to curve as he approached the Quadrant,
another of Nash's misjudgements and already much maligned.
Its monumental Doric colonnades, projecting over the pavements,
were a fine idea, an embellishment of the crescent tradition of

Bath, yet once again a failure in practice. It was becoming a haunt of the *less salubrious* elements of society, one might say, as colonnades were too often wont to. He had seen the painted women who flocked there each night to enjoy its gas lighting and protection from the elements as they peddled their wares. It was fast becoming somewhere a respectable man such as himself must take pains to avoid after dark, an inconvenience since his offices lay just beyond it, in Carlton Chambers on Lower Regent Street – another of his father's properties.

But it was daylight yet, and thus the domain of the better-to-do, who idled along as Decimus Burton navigated around them at his optimum walking pace, one that permitted haste while preserving decorum and style, making for his chambers.

Since Raffles's death, little has been done to disturb the remote north-eastern corner of the Regent's Park. While a year's four seasons have worked their magic on the parcel of land given over to the Zoological Society of London, mankind has not intruded, save for the digging in of a few plants and ditches. The five acres abutting the road lie dormant, waiting. It is an oasis of peace in the whirlwind of activity in this newest part of London. Scaffolds appear and disappear to reveal new jewels in the park's green crown. Near the western edge, there is much coming and going of men and carts, while barges laden with materials and debris snake along the canal. Block by block, two grand villas appear in the park, one for a marquess, one for a general, both born of the pencil of the young Mr Burton.

To the east of the park, south of the untouched plot set aside for the Zoological Society of London, new terraces are being finished, more gleaming white stucco framing the dark green. Here, a construction far grander than any of the villas is also well under way, the vast, unmissable dome of the Colosseum, piercing the smoke-streaked sky. A perfectly proportioned Grecian version of the Pantheon in Rome, its dome slightly larger than that of St Paul's Cathedral, it is now almost complete. Work is continuing on an internal apparatus, the first of its kind, to transport visitors to a viewing platform in the dome's centre, where they will be able to enjoy the view as if they are gazing out from the cathedral itself. The only divergence is that this view will be more perfect, for here there will be no weather or smog to interfere. The city is moving westwards now – even St Paul's is come to the Regent's Park.

It is not until April 1827, when workmen quit Hertford Lodge on the western side of the park – the Marquess's villa now resplendently complete and awaiting its first dinner party guests – that barrows and carts appear in the long-neglected corner belonging to the Zoological Society of London. As the year's first flashes of colour pierce the winter ground, man arrives with his tools. The land will be marked up according to Mr Burton's plans; the latest patch of the Regent's Park he is to claim from nature.

Mr Burton was there to see the work begin: the first pegging out of the grounds. It was just a few weeks after his visit to Bruton Street, and now he stood, on the green, green grass of the park, still wet with the morning's dew, watching the first lines of his design being sketched on the earth. He tried not to be bothered by the cool clutch of moisture he could feel through his (admittedly unsuitable) shoes. He focused on the small group of labourers marking out the first simple lines of boundaries and walkways. It was always a tense experience to watch one's imaginings committed to the real world, however small the early marks might be. But Mr Burton had faith in his work, had confidence that his design would work in the beautiful springtime landscape just as well as it did on the white of his paper.

The design had not yet been entirely approved. It didn't need to be. Mr Burton had created the complete, grand vision that Sir Stamford Raffles had demanded of him, but its construction would happen piecemeal, as the necessary funds accrued and the Society could acquire more land. It was a common way of working, a process with which Mr Burton was well acquainted. He had met with the officers of the Commission of Woods and Forests, and they had approved, albeit somewhat reluctantly, the overall layout for the portion of land they had so far granted the Society, south of the public drive.

It was a nuisance that they were so unenthusiastic, for this was the simplest part of the grand plan: all the main buildings would occupy another plot, north of the drive, which they would take in due course. The Commissioners' overriding concern was that the luxurious atmosphere of the new residential area was at risk of being degraded by structures designed to house animals. *'Cattle sheds' and 'kennels' were hardly likely to add to the architectural beauty of the environs*, they had said. Decimus Burton had assured them that he did not, under any circumstances, plan to build cattle sheds and kennels as they might recognize them (it pained him to have this conversation). There would not be a single unsightly structure – on that he was adamant. The Commissioners knew and trusted Mr Burton, so they agreed: the work could begin. Mr Burton wondered silently whether Mr Nash might have been behind the concerns, fearful of reducing the value of his investments in the area. If so, it was most . . . unhelpful.

Regardless, here he was, beginning yet another project in the Regent's Park. He knew it so well, now; knew its demands, its uncooperative clay soil. And he knew the men who existed there too, men of the age, with their modern tastes and desires. (The general public, of course, was not allowed in – it was a space for those who resided there, though private carriages were permitted to enjoy its pathways too.) Decimus Burton was undaunted by either. He had designed his first park villa – *the* first, in fact – when he was just eighteen, The Holme, his father's London residence. He could visualize it now, overlooking the lake in the Inner Ring, to the south of where he stood. The design was much informed by the training he was undergoing at the time at the Royal Academy (he had commenced his studies there, under John Soane, aged just seventeen, a fact of which he was rather proud). The Holme was perhaps somewhat restricted by its rigid geometry, he now conceded, with its solid rectangular mass, triangular roof and large semi-cylindrical bay dividing the principal elevation. He could admit that it was not his best work, but the experience of others pointing it out at the time had not been pleasant. John Nash, despite his best efforts to evade responsibility, was in overall charge of the developments in the park and thus had borne the brunt of the Commissioners' disapproval. Yet Decimus Burton had felt each blow himself, and had learned from the experience: he would not expose himself to such criticism again. He promised himself then that, in future, everything he designed and built would be perfect, that every client would be completely, unequivocally satisfied with his creations.

The villas that had followed were fine indeed; more sympathetic, more nuanced interpretations of the Palladian formula. The two he had just completed – Hanover Lodge, and the villa for the Marquess of Hertford – he was wholly content with, as were their owners. They stood to the west and slightly to the south of him now; tasteful displays of classical design, with the grandeur of antiquity yet entirely suited to the modern age. The real success of the properties was that, despite their proximity to one another, each felt like a country estate. And each was perfectly tailored to the individual needs of the client. He never compromised on art or comfort – one never needed to, with the right design. The two villas shared the same westward corner of the park as another he had designed some years ago for Mr Bellas Greenough. Grove House, with its iconic screen of Greek Doric columns around a semi-circular bay façade – based on the Erechtheion, though only as much as domestic comforts allowed – had won its architect no small degree of international repute. It had been a pleasure. Greenough, a geologist, was a man of the arts too, and they had spent many happy hours discussing details for the house, often during visits to the opera. He had learned from Grove House that it was the smallest things that made even such a vast building a success.

The design for the Gardens of the Zoological Society had been a new challenge altogether, quite unlike anything he had faced before, which was one of the reasons he had taken it on. Here, his task was not to create tasteful monuments to men who, by birth or by graft (both were welcome here), could afford a grand home in this newest corner of the city. It was not to integrate a single building tastefully within its setting or to conjure the illusion of purity and privacy where neither really existed. It was not to build a magnificent single monument – an archway or a colossal dome. In these five acres something very different was demanded. It was rather more like landscape gardening, he mused. Or even town planning, with the proviso that he was building for birds and beasts rather than humans. No, he corrected himself, that was not true. The challenge was to create an environment where humans could comfortably, elegantly, enjoyably observe the creatures. Of course he was building for mankind, rather than for beasts.

It was an aesthetic and, indeed, an intellectual challenge that he had relished. It was a departure for him and for architecture. Other than the Jardin des Plantes in Paris (which he had never seen), there were no precedents to follow. There might be places, individual structures, where he could turn to the columns and domes of the ancient Rome or Athens of which he was so fond, but the overall aesthetic must be different: it must be in the spirit of the picturesque. For here it was not a matter of the individual constructions but the entire composition: architect must become landscape artist, his task to render nature more pleasing, more perfect. The masterstroke of his design – yes, he might call it that – was the raised terrace, an elevated promenade that would lead visitors into the Gardens from the main entrance. From without, it would obscure the view of the Gardens, an elegant means of numbing the Commissioners' concerns about unsightliness. And the treasure was then reserved for visitors alone, who from the terrace walk could marvel at the contained world he had constructed for them, the highly ornamented Gardens with their perfect little structures, flowerbeds, curving walkways, fountains and *jets d'eau*. The terrace would hide another secret too: a colonnaded series of open dens for the wilder beasts beneath. The visitors would hear the terrifying roars of lions and tigers while surveying, in their fine clothes, the elegant vista below. Indeed, it was a masterstroke. And was it not a little . . . witty? Yes, the ever-serious Decimus Burton was indulging a not often seen side of his talents.

Here he was, a step closer to realizing the vision of which he was so (quietly) proud. Mr Burton supervised the men making their slow way along the line of the western boundary of the Society's land. This was the area in which the terrace would be built; the men were pegging out the pathway that would lead the visitors into the Gardens. Mr Burton thought of those who would walk along it. The hope was that they would soon be here. Indeed, the press was already reporting the summer opening! Mr Burton was eager to keep to his mental schedule, both in the long-term sense, and in a more immediate sense: he wanted to get to Somerset House today, to see about preparations for the year's Academy Exhibition. He planned to show two designs, rather more monumental than those he was to execute here: that for his church at Tunbridge Wells, and those for his works at Hyde Park Corner (he had heard that Mr Turner was showing five this year, but he was more excited about the section of the Elgin Marbles also to be exhibited).

He looked, very obviously, he hoped, at his pocket watch, clearing his throat. The foreman noticed. His aim achieved, Mr Burton allowed his mind to wander for a moment. He thought of Sir Stamford. He recalled the man's great enthusiasm for what was finally finding form and he felt the solemnity of the occasion. He savoured it – as much as he could, given the unpleasant sensation of damp footwear.

London is watching, waiting. The mockery in the press subsides and a genuine curiosity begins to take its place as, little by little, Decimus Burton's vision is carved into the land. First, as the sun grows higher in the sky, the walkways appear, snaking around the site, leaving empty spaces of varying sizes, awaiting their destinies. The terrace begins to rise from the earth. Soon will come the individual pieces of the puzzle. Each begins on paper, drawn by Mr Burton in his offices, then is delivered to the Committee overseeing the management of the establishment in Regent's Park, and finally placed before the men of the Society's Council for their approval. First come the designs for an aviary, with eleven compartments for the birds now confined to the Bruton Street offices and others yet to arrive. The huge dome that featured in his initial plan is not deemed practicable, but there are plenty of clever little details to make it striking. This is no basic aviary, but a beautiful, curved building with columns decorated as palm trees; a playful hint by their creator of the exotic climes whence these birds had come.

In June, the builder who has won the contract to make the designs come to life, one Mr Pettit, arrives with his men. Work begins in the first clearing between the walkways, and the first structures appear. In July – a scorching month that browns the grass and wilts the plants – Mr Burton's plans for a keeper's residence are submitted and approved, as well as a series of smaller accommodations for animals. As their homes are completed, the first animals and a keeper, Mr James Cops, are moved in. The workmen begin to fill the other empty spaces. The summer is dry, good for working, and gradually the Gardens grow.

It is a slower process than expected. The establishment's opening is pushed back until the autumn. In the meantime, a lithograph of Mr Burton's grand plan is made and distributed, to sate the appetites of those who await the real thing. Lady Raffles is delivered one as she breakfasts. The *Literary Gazette* publishes it – the ridicule of its earlier pieces has changed to excitement, anticipation. Hot days grow cooler; summer's peak passes. An additional keeper, Mr Devereux Fuller, arrives to attend to the expanding number of birds and beasts residing in the sheds and aviaries that are complete. A carpenter, Mr John Rivers, appears to help finish others. Finally, as the leaves curl and fall and the days grow shorter, the gates are opened to the Fellows of the Zoological Society of London: the five hundred or so men of science, aristocratic game breeders and amateur naturalists who have paid their three pounds' admission fee and their two pounds' subscription for the year. There are honorary members too: presidents of other notable societies, and Lady Raffles – for women are now permitted to join the Society on equal terms. All may come to the Gardens on any day they wish and bring with them two guests – the select few who may marvel at the exotic new residents of this corner of the park.

An iron cage appears and a leopard fills it, quiet and tame except at daily feeding times, when its roars echo across the park. It is soon followed by a Grecian ram, the first of its kind in England, tied to a stake in its plot nearby. The ark is filling. By the end of November, nearly two hundred animals are now on board: llamas, kangaroos, a Russian bear (acquired by the Marquess of Hertford while an envoy to Russia), emus, cranes and cormorants, in paddocks, dens and aviaries. But it is not spectacular yet. Neither is it alone in adding to its collection. That autumn, Mr Cross's menagerie in the Strand receives a new elephant and a black tiger. More wondrous than any of them is an animal that arrives on English soil as a gift to the King: a cameleopard, or giraffe – the first ever to be seen in Britain. It is Mr Cross who unloads it at Waterloo Bridge to transport to Windsor, not the men of the Zoological Society.

The trees are bare and the ground is hard. The work slows. In Covent Garden Theatre, pantomime audiences enjoy the Zoological Gardens recreated on stage in *Harlequin Number Nip*. The dancing peacock and an escaped monkey cause much laughter among the festive theatregoers. (Perhaps they have read of the Esquimaux dog that escaped and killed many other beasts in the Gardens.) But as 1827 draws to its end, that is as close as most Londoners will get to the real thing.

By March 1828, the works at the Gardens in Regent's Park were proceeding at a more rapid pace. On the last Thursday of the month, Mr Burton arrived at the site to ensure that everything was being carried out as he had ordered. This was the third time he had visited in less than two weeks. Quite how he fitted everything into his schedule, well, it was a triumph of meticulous planning. He was becoming the architect of the moment with the societies and clubs for professional men that were the fashion of the age, and had lately commenced work for the Geological Society at Somerset House. His father had just begun his greatest undertaking yet, into which his ambitious, most loyal son was inevitably drawn. Buoyed by his successes at the Regent's Park, James Burton was building an entire new town on the coast near Hastings. Mr Burton the Younger was overseeing a similar project, albeit on a smaller scale, and laying out a new estate at Calverley near Tunbridge Wells, converting it into a place of residence for genteel families. It was an interesting project, planning a whole new town. A larger, less playful version of what he had done for the Zoological Society, he liked to think.

Despite the number of commissions he was juggling, Mr Burton was all the more conscious now, if that was possible, of the need to manage each one closely – and thereby his carefully honed reputation. Mr Nash's disastrous Buckingham House had lately been revealed and had provoked unprecedented outrage among the public and in Parliament. Its immodesty in cost was one thing, but – as far as Mr Burton was concerned – its immodesty in design was unforgivable. It was a ludicrous jumble that made no sense *at all* in masonry, even if it had done on paper (and Mr Burton had never been convinced of that). Among the many bizarre features, the dome was horribly ill-judged, and seen from St James's Park, the wings appeared most incongruous. It was so appalling that Mr Nash himself had requested the funds to tear them down and start again! The situation had dragged the entire profession into disrepute. A Select Committee had now been convened to look into the matter of *all* public buildings. Mr Burton was confident that his own works – his façade at Hyde Park and his arch at the Green Park, now nearing completion – would withstand scrutiny (for he always completed his buildings as per the allotted schedule and purse, not to mention as per a *considered* design). But he was sure that such a furore would do none of them any good.

Thus, despite numerous other commitments, Mr Burton always found time to keep the necessary close eye on developments at the Gardens. Given the rate of activity at this point he deemed it prudent, for he could avert any diversions from his exact plan in good time. He was painfully aware there were still

those – some of the residents of and investors in the Regent's
Park (he suspected Nash might be among them) – who believed
the menagerie was a threat to the elegance of those fine environs, and that buildings for animals could only ever degrade the
neighbourhood. He was also more convinced than ever that the
detractors were much mistaken. He would prove it.

The architect to the Zoological Society of London had just
been deposited at the north-eastern corner of the Society's
grounds by the fine carriage of Lord Auckland, along with its
owner and Mr Joseph Sabine. Vice-President and Treasurer of
the Society respectively, they were taking a most active part in
overseeing the Gardens' development, and Mr Burton had visited with both men just the previous week. In his late fifties, Mr
Sabine was a keen amateur naturalist and a Fellow of the Linnean
and the Royal Society. Furthermore, his experience of having
been Secretary and Treasurer to the Horticultural Society for
some years, during which time he had overseen the establishment of their gardens in Chiswick, meant that the Zoological
Society now relied heavily upon him in their venture.

The three men walked from the spot on the public drive
around the park, where carriages had taken to waiting for Fellows and their guests who were visiting the Gardens. A few
were there now, horses fidgeting and snorting as the coachmen
idly stood by. Lord Auckland, Mr Sabine and Mr Burton
approached the gap in the low hedges that served as the entrance
to the Gardens. They had not been within the boundary for
more than thirty seconds when the ever-efficient Mr Johnson,
who had lately been appointed Assistant Secretary, with the
duty of looking after day-to-day matters at the growing
establishment, apprehended them. Mr Burton was now well
acquainted with the staff and – always meticulously polite to
them – bade Mr Johnson a warm good day. As the group
exchanged pleasantries, Mr Johnson noted their names in his

ledger. The chatterings of the birds and beasts that now resided in the park could be heard even from that outermost corner of the Society's grounds.

From the entrance, they were swept on to the beginning of Mr Burton's fine raised terrace. As they proceeded along it, he could see, to their left, the first hints of the impressive vista he intended to be spread out below for the visitors' visual delectation. Only a few of the large, permanent structures he planned were yet built, but those he could see were presented in a most pleasing arrangement. From where they now walked, the most prominent buildings visible were the stable for llamas, done in the Gothic style, and the elegantly curved, eleven-room aviary. He could not see the keepers' apartments he had designed, which adjoined the latter. And that was the point: the building was simpler than he had wanted. He had originally designed a many-bayed and colonnaded structure, but restrictions of space and time had been imposed upon him. And so, perfectionist – and, indeed, pragmatist – that he was, he had obscured the much-reduced version behind the aviary. Thus everything he could see from here – they were now advancing along the terrace walk – blended into the overall design, the lines of the structures in perfect harmony with the natural landscape and the artificial lines of walkways and flowerbeds. Even the temporary pens and cages (which still accommodated most of the animals) were placed at perfect intervals between the pathways that tastefully wound their way through the plot. It was obvious that his grand design would work; that it was already working. And the sight of the workers bringing further elements of it to life was most gratifying to its creator.

Unfortunately, it was difficult to enjoy it as he might wish; to absorb the splendour of the design that was now taking shape below them. For the group seemed to Mr Burton to be hurrying along the terrace, and all the while Mr Johnson was delivering an animated report on some recent occurrences. Mr Sabine was relieved to learn that the chain broken by the bear, Toby, on the previous day had been repaired, and that the beast had not succeeded in causing further damage. Lord Auckland enquired as to the delivery of the plants he had donated to the Society. *Yes, my lord, they arrived first thing this morning. The poplars donated by the Commission too. All now duly awaiting planting.* Despite his unspoken preference for silent contemplation, Mr Burton could not pretend he was less than pleased to hear of how much had been achieved even since his visit just a few days earlier.

Then he had come alone: he had wanted to peruse the site and the works in greater detail than polite company permitted. He recalled with a degree of discomfort the moment he had been introduced to Lady Raffles. He had not met her previously. Naturally, he had offered her his sincere and heartfelt condolences and told her what a fine man her husband had been. She had looked grief-stricken, though it was almost two years after his death. It was a shame, certainly, that her husband had not lived to see this taking shape. He liked to think that Sir Stamford would have approved of all he had constructed thus far. He believed he had achieved the vision they had discussed together, an educative and aesthetically pleasing little world. Lady Raffles, accompanied by her young daughter, had said they enjoyed coming here.

The party now approached the bear pit, where the terrace currently concluded – its extension, with the colonnaded open dens beneath, was not yet commenced. Work on the bear pit, on the other hand, had been under way for some months now, since his designs had been approved by the Council in January. It was close to completion. Today a number of Mr Pettit's men were at work on it. The pit itself was long since dug, and the brick walls surrounding it were nigh on finished too. The boundary wall for supporting the adjacent bank had been built a few weeks previously, and now the men had commenced a boundary wall to the terrace. All that remained was for the pole in the centre to be fitted. The bear that would soon reside there, Toby, was currently nowhere to be seen. Mr Burton preferred it that way. He was well satisfied with the pit, which was in perfect proportion with the site as he had intended.

From the bear pit, the group proceeded down the slope from the terrace to the ornamental open grounds beneath. They came almost immediately to the Llama House, which had also been under construction for some months now. It was a small double stable with two rooms for the animals, with wooden doors, plus a smaller room between them for the use of a keeper, all with Gothic detailing. A pond was now being dug in front of it. As they approached, the overall look, set against the landscape of the grounds, was neat and attractive, a fine little stable building. Oh, but it was so much more than that, too! The really rather clever feature was the path they now walked upon, leading them between the stalls so that the visitors would be able to enjoy a view of the llamas in their enclosure (once they had moved in). From there, the path led on to the rear of the building. This was where they now stood, and here one had a *completely different* view of the animals' quarters, set against the parkland behind. *That* was what elevated his designs above the ordinary, he felt: his buildings were an *experience*. He was rather pleased with this one. So, too, were his present companions: the Treasurer and Secretary of the Society were making appreciative noises.

They continued along the line of the main pathway and approached the aviary they had seen from the terrace. It had long been audible. This was one of the buildings in which the inhabitants were already accommodated, and the noise the birds made in combination was quite astonishing, though the eleven compartments did not appear to be full. From where he stood on the path, Mr Burton could make out pigeons, turkeys, pheasants, and the vulture donated by Mr Brookes, as well as some more colourful varieties, if not quite the exotic creatures he had envisaged his palm tree columns would complement. Two elderly gentlemen were intently studying the cages. They had removed their hats to lean in for a closer view through the wires. They turned, greeted Lord Auckland and his fellow visitors, then resumed their close study of the birds. Mr Burton hoped they might take a step backwards, so they could appreciate the totality of his design . . .

The emu had not yet laid another egg, they were informed by Mr Johnson, as he directed their attention to the patch of bare earth next to the structure. There, the pair of improbable creatures – most ungraceful, it could not be denied, with their bulky bodies and slender limbs contravening all laws of proportion – picked at the hard earth rather fruitlessly. Immediately behind the aviaries were the keepers' residences, though the head keeper's apartment had been occupied by Mr Johnson since Mr Cops had been dismissed. (Mr Burton had enquired on a previous visit why the head keeper had vacated the apartment he had built for him. Lord Auckland had been rather vague in response, muttering something about misconduct.) It was a cold afternoon, and Mr Johnson hurried them along. They now inspected the hedges and borders that were being planted. A double row of elms was being introduced to the centre walk and they saw the fifty poplar trees donated by the Commission of Woods and Forests, waiting to be planted.

Mr Burton knew exactly what was meant to be happening where, and it was most gratifying to see his vision for this unusual little world finding solid form. But he struggled to keep up with the animal inhabitants. They passed the tethered goats and a fearsome band of chained monkeys – he was wary of them now, after his encounter at Bruton Street – and Toby the bear, soon to be moved into his splendid new home, currently living at the end of a newly reinforced chain. He did not care for the large black bear, though it seemed to be a favourite with the visitors, a small group of whom were now clustered around it. He recalled that it supposedly had a particular taste for ale, acquired under its previous owner, the Marquess of Hertford. Mr Burton had worked for the Marquess and consequently believed it did.

They passed the temporary cages filled with animals of all kinds. And smelt them. Mr Burton silently regretted that the animal odour detracted from the experience he had so carefully created, but consoled himself that once his larger, open dens beneath the terrace had been constructed this must be somewhat reduced. The creatures they passed were mainly small ones, in small cages – the lynx and the polecat, he recalled, were not in their erstwhile homes. *Most regrettably, they are no longer with us,* Mr Johnson explained to him in hushed tones. *But Mr Burton could rest assured that now the winter was drawing to a close, the animals would be more comfortable. Less likely to sicken. And, besides, new beasts were arriving all the time!* The architect expressed sufficient interest not to appear rude; but the beasts, of course, were not really his concern.

The veracity of Johnson's claim that new creatures were being constantly acquired was soon proved. As the men were leaving the Gardens a short while later, their inspections complete, they witnessed a consignment of fowl – ducks, geese and storks, arrived from Holland – being loaded onto a small truck at the entrance. The noise the birds made as their crates were transferred from the cart to a smaller vehicle was unrelenting. Mr Burton was not unhappy to see Lord Auckland's carriage awaiting them on the other side of the road.

The work in the Gardens goes on. Another English springtime brings fresh colour to the Regent's Park. The once little-used north-eastern corner is now bursting with life, taken from across the globe and placed in the new world being constructed for it. Human life too: on six days a week men labour here as soon as there is light and until the crepuscular hour descends. Mr Burton, always immaculately attired beneath his black top hat, comes and goes. His neat figure is often seen in various corners of the gardens, observing, quietly directing. Lord Auckland, Mr Sabine, the Marquess of Lansdowne, Lord Stanley and other Council members appear and disappear. Mr Johnson is eternally present, a figure ever bustling around the five-acre space. The work stops only with the onset of evening. At night, in the pure, unadulterated darkness, the animals have the Gardens to themselves, unobserved by their slumbering keepers. Eyes flash in the cages. The cries of beasts disturb the stillness: unfamiliar calls of birds from distant lands, the barks of the wild dogs, of mischievous monkeys, the howling of wolves, the snuffling and panting of the bear, the guttural growl of the leopard, a chorus of voices of strange, foreign animals who do not belong in this fine, exclusive park; who do not belong in the city of London.

April is a lush, wet month. An ivory fence springs up to surround the paddock of the Llama House. A double row of oak trees appears in the border of the centre walk. Four East Indian sheep are delivered, soon joined by an Angora goat. A female bear arrives, and the bear pit, now finished with fine iron railings, accommodates them both. The pole is climbed – much to the delight of the goading onlookers. A little coatimundi, who rarely shows his face by day, and a peccary are introduced to small cages. Four black swans are let loose on the lake in the Inner Circle, already home to many other waterfowl belonging to the Society and now officially in their wardship.

As the days get warmer and longer, the activity increases. In May, additional labourers scurry into the grounds every morning. The walks are gravelled. A wooden barrier appears at the entrance, and a rustic hut. Fencing goes up around paddocks, some yet to be filled with animal residents. An ornamental seat appears by the bear pit, where the two bears now climb the pole for want of anything better to do. Their great bulks move up and down, hour after hour. An iron fence, five feet high, replaces the wooden fence at the entrance.

And thus the Gardens of the Zoological Society are made ready for visitors from outside its own number, finally permitted by the Commission of Woods and Forests. They will be opened to the public on six days in the week, upon the payment of one shilling per person – provided a Fellow sanctions it. Sundays – for the working masses, the only day of their own – remain the preserve of the Fellows alone. There must still be controls over who may enjoy the refined pleasures of the Gardens. Letters with the new rules arrive at the homes of the Society's Fellows all over the capital and beyond; they may sign an order of admission that allows access to the Gardens for their friends and family, when they themselves cannot be present. One signed order, presented at the Society's gate in Regent's Park with the entrance fee, will permit entry for the whole party. On the morning of the 19th of May the seat in the little hut next to the barrier is occupied by a lone figure, the money-taker. The first paying visitors hand over their signed pieces of paper and their coins and enter the world imagined by Sir Stamford Raffles and created by Decimus Burton: the menagerie of the Zoological Society of London.

A week later, it is given the ultimate seal of approval. A royal entourage arrives: Princess Victoria of Kent, escorted by her mother the Duchess, has come for her ninth-birthday treat. The party are walked around the Gardens by Lord Stanley, Mr Sabine and Mr Vigors, who call upon the keepers to better display the animals for Her Royal Highness. The young Princess is shown natural history in all its living, breathing glory: the improbable emus picking at the ground, the silver-haired rabbits vying for space in their hutches, the turkeys, the vulture, the swans and ducks and pheasants, the pretty Angora cat in its cage, the pacing dogs in their kennels, the wolves in their den, the goats and sheep tethered to their posts. She watches the monkeys playing, encouraged by the keepers. She sees the leopard pacing in its cage. She looks on as the bears climb their pole in the pit, up and down, up and down. Quite how much she – or, for that matter, the ninety-seven other finely attired gentlemen and ladies who promenade the grounds that day – grasps of the scientific purpose of the endeavour, it is hard to say. At the very least, it pleases her to see some of the more exotic residents of the Empire at such close proximity, and in such a comfortable, fashionable setting.

Mr Burton allowed himself to enjoy the glowing reports of his work in the newspapers; articles that praised his most tasteful design, which had made the Zoological Society's Gardens 'one of the most fashionable promenades' in the metropolis. And yet his work was not over. Far from it. It was an afternoon late in July, and the young architect stood in his offices, the well-worn map of the Regent's Park spread on the table before him. Alongside it was the plan of the Gardens as they now stood. Much had changed there, even in the past few months. Since kangaroos and leopards, lynxes and pumas, porcupines and tortoises, wolves, buffalo and pelicans had been moved in, numerous new cages had been constructed for them. And yet Mr Burton was confident that the plan of the grounds he was perusing was completely accurate. He made sure he was kept minutely up to date.

Like many of the newest residents of the Regent's Park, Mr Burton had also lately moved into a new home he had created. He had taken a plot on Spring Gardens for a townhouse and offices, and had created something simply and classically attractive, elegantly combining a range of influences – a fitting tribute, he liked to think, to his personal taste. The exterior of his new home was Italianate in style, with a five-bay, stucco façade, but inside he had allowed his love of the Grecian to dominate. Decorative friezes and fittings were used as generously as good taste and style allowed. Which was fairly lavishly, it seemed, from a glance at the beautifully adorned walls and cornices that greeted visitors to his living quarters, with urns on neat plinths and marble statues in custom recesses. (Mr Burton did not discriminate against Roman artefacts, however. Not long after he had moved in, he had received a delivery of casts taken from the Pantheon and the Temple of Mars Ultor, from Trajan's Forum, from the Temple of Vesta at Tivoli, and even from the Vatican.)

Spring Gardens was a fine spot, at the heart of developments presently under way in the area of the former Carlton Palace and St James's Park, an effort to continue the metropolitan improvements begun with Regent Street. Immediately to the west of Spring Gardens Mr Burton was working with Mr Nash on the site of the recently demolished palace to build a classical terrace alongside the twin clubhouses of the Athenaeum and the United Services. Immediately to the east was the new public square at the mouth of the Strand. While Regent Street had been an opportunity to develop an elegant shopping thoroughfare, Mr Burton particularly liked this new development because it focused on pursuits closer to his own heart: with its imposing classical clubhouses and fine town residences, it was to be an elegant space for men of learning and taste. He heartily approved of the newfound social status – might one even call it dominance? – of such men. Men such as himself.

Despite his commitment to these improvements, Mr Burton was relieved that the Athenaeum, soon to be crowned with a frieze of the Panathenaic procession, was finally nearing completion. Mr Nash, his supposed collaborator, had made it all rather troublesome, withholding information and designs from him. The scrutiny to which Mr Nash had been subjected earlier in the year had subsided, and he had officially been cleared of any wrongdoing. More importantly, he still had the favour of the King. The work on Buckingham House continued, at a more increased rate than ever – apparently a thousand workers toiled there every day now. And it was rumoured that plans were afoot to bring the Strand into the realm of the new London next, and that Nash was to mastermind that too.

Mr Burton, whatever his private views might be, always endeavoured to remain above the politics and to keep his focus on his own work and reputation. Currently, his business was with the Zoological Society. It was over their plans that he stood now, in shirt and waistcoat, his jacket hanging nearby because it was warm indoors. He remained a picture of perfect elegance, surprisingly unruffled given the closeness of the day. With a forefinger, he smoothed an upturned corner of the map of the park and silently wished his assistants might take better care of things. He bent down for a closer look. He knew the layout of the Gardens intricately, but now he was studying an area outside the Society's own grounds, to the north of the public drive. He had lately received word from Mr Sabine that he was negotiating with the Commission of Woods and Forests for possession of it. It had always been part of their plans – and part of Mr Burton's plans from the beginning – but only now did the Society have need of it and the means to acquire it.

The opening of the Gardens of the Zoological Society had been a tremendous success. Although the weather had been rather wet, the money-taker at the entrance now saw at least five hundred persons pass through his gate each day. In addition, live animals from every part of the globe were being donated with increasing regularity, and all had to be adequately accommodated – not to mention fairly rapidly – for the cruel English winter. The Council had decided that there was only one thing for it: expansion. Sadly, it was not as simple a matter as referring back to Mr Burton's original plans for the land they had always envisaged growing into. His design, which had originally placed aviaries and a yard north of the drive, was now some years out of date. The needs of the Society had changed. Or, rather, experience had shown that their needs were, perhaps, somewhat different from what they had originally imagined . . .

Mr Burton prided himself on being a good businessman, like his father, as well as a good architect. He knew that the client must always be satisfied. Yet he had to admit that he was somewhat concerned. There had been questions raised over the carnivores' dens, which he had long planned, in the colonnade that would be constructed under a continuation of the terrace: would the exposed dens be entirely suitable for the animals, even in the cooler months? Now on the new patch of land, north of the drive, he had been asked to design a repository in which the larger animals could pass the coming winter, as well as further accommodation for keepers, so that more of the men could sleep at the Gardens. Yes, Decimus Burton was concerned that his grand vision was going to be further modified. He did not want to say 'compromised', not yet. He would design a winter repository, naturally, but he would continue to extol the virtues of his *original* plan. To persuade his client that the beautiful centrepiece, the elegant terrace dens, need not be abandoned. Then, for the fine summer months at least, visitors could experience the Gardens just as he had intended.

He began work on the task at hand. The space he was faced with now was inconvenient. He had never liked the idea that the menagerie would be split in two by the public drive. What was sorely needed was a clever, elegant solution. Decimus Burton was, thankfully, eminently equipped to meet that demand on both counts. He had wondered how he might maintain the totality of the experience of the Gardens, when visitors had to exit one half of the grounds, cross a drive (that, thanks to the Gardens' growing popularity, was increasingly busy) and re-enter another piece of ground. He had briefly explored the prospect of a suspension bridge, but decided that that was not what he was looking for. How could he avoid the spell being broken by the noise of carriages, the sight of the busy modern world? He paused his pencil for a moment, and looked around him. One of his Grecian urns caught his eye and the closing line to the Keats poem sprang to mind:

> Beauty is truth, truth beauty – that is all
> Ye know on earth, and all ye need to know.

He had been fond of the words when they were published while he was but a teenager, and he was fond of them yet. Mr Burton looked once more to the plan in front of him.

He resumed his careful work, committing his vision for the new site to the blank page before him. He was a pragmatist as well as an artist, Decimus Burton, and if there was a shadow of doubt over the more imposing architectural features he had imagined, well, he would design others – if not as grand then at least rather clever – to replace them. He began with the space between the two plots. As Brunel had attempted to link the two banks of the great Thames so Burton would link the two gardens of the Zoological Society: with a tunnel. And what an elegance this one would be! Beauty might be truth . . . but in this instance the architect felt there should be room for a little playfulness as well, albeit most carefully considered.

Over the summer of 1828, the land to the north of the public drive remains untouched. The keeper's lodge and the winter repository placed there by Mr Burton's pen remain confined to paper. The Commission of Woods and Forests refuse to sanction the latest designs. The public drive remains the menagerie's northern limit. In summer's long days, it is ever thronged with carriages, coming and going and waiting for their owners, who weave around the increasingly ornate, increasingly inhabited site. Sometimes more than a thousand pairs of human eyes move along the pathways, peering into the cages and dens, the pits and paddocks as they go.

As the visitors exclaim at the animal attractions, the workers around them toil on, within the limits of the land. The wet weather does not stop them. Two additional keepers arrive, and a new watchman. Various other structures appear: a stable for zebras, a shed for the kangaroos, a shed for the Indian cows and sheep, an enclosure for the tortoises, a pond for the beavers, a semi-circular aviary for British birds, a house for the hawks, kennels for the dogs, and a rockery around a fountain on the lawn. The monkeys' pole acquires a cage around it to limit the inhabitants' mischief. An iron railing around the bears' den does the same. In mid-August, a fierce gale shakes the trees and makes the beasts cower in their homes. But they and the structures survive.

Autumn throws its blanket of gold over the menagerie and still the land to the north lies fallow. Despite the cooler weather, the visitors do not thin out on the pathways: they come in thousands. An alligator moves into the Gardens. Yet more change is promised. In October, newspapers sold on streets, fine and foul, carry news of grand new buildings soon to grace the Gardens: 'spacious dens for the larger quadrupeds' with an 'elevated and highly ornamental terrace extended over them'. Grand buildings, by the eminent architect Decimus Burton, as well as functional 'winter accommodation for the more delicate animals'.

If only it was that simple. If only the Commission would cooperate, rather than fuss that the Gardens might detract from the character of the park. It is October, and still they do not grant the land north of the drive. Worse, they now hesitate to sanction any building on the existing land. The designs for Mr Burton's grand terrace dens languish on the Commissioners' desks, along with those for a winter repository, hastily sketched within the present confines of the Gardens. The keepers worry that the great losses of the last winter, when so many of their beasts perished in the cold, will be repeated. Mr Burton worries that his masterpiece will be lost. And still no word comes from the Commissioners. The Council takes a desperate decision: construct the repository in the hope that it will be permitted to remain. The weather is turning. Mr Burton meets with Mr Dickson, the builder. The works commence.

Only then does the Commission respond. The answer is no. No to the dens, no to the repository, no to everything. It is Mr Maberley, who lives in St John's Lodge on the Inner Circle, who does not want to see the Gardens enlarged. His home is one of the few villas in the park that did not spring from Mr Burton's pencil – and he does not want it to create any more. The Commission will not upset him. They will upset the Zoological Society instead. So the half-built repository is torn down, the materials packed away.

Alternative measures are taken. An engineer comes to investigate installing piped-water systems to heat the dens; lamps will do it in the meantime, and curtains of sailcloth. But winter creeps into the dens and cages all the same. A stable is rented in Camden Town, on Park Street, less than half a mile away. The cages are emptied as many of the tender beasts are packed into crates and taken away, in the hope that they can live out the winter months there. Those that remain behind do not always do so for long: an alligator dies, a pheasant dies, a partridge dies, a hare dies, the sparrow hawk dies, a badger dies, the tortoise dies, a Nepal cat dies, a Tibetan dog dies. The leopards, too, are removed to Park Street to try to preserve them. The Gardens empty of animals and visitors.

And then winter comes, its yet more terrible bite arriving with the new year in all its frozen magnificence. The ground is white and solid as rock. The canal slows and sparkles. Morning after morning, animals are carried off the site, cold and hard as the ground. The keepers look on; the Council members come and go. All are powerless to save their menagerie from this painful, cold impoverishment.

It had been a full year since Mr Burton had drawn up the plans for the land north of the public drive. It had taken twelve months of negotiations – twelve months in which too much of the Society's living collection had been lost – before the Commission of Woods and Forests had finally agreed to the granting of the additional land to the Zoological Society. By the summer of 1829, Mr Maberley, the obstructive resident, had vacated St John's Lodge. Unlike his predecessor, the new tenant, the Marquess Wellesley, brother of the Duke of Wellington, did not oppose Mr Burton's work. He even employed Burton to enlarge his own home. But, most importantly, the Society had been granted a charter by His Majesty the King earlier in the year, which clarified its status as a public institution. After that, the Crown could scarcely deny it a lease. In mid-July, word was received that the Commission's objections had disappeared. Minor works had already recommenced within the boundaries of the existing land, but now the land north of the drive could be tackled too. Mr Burton had just returned from a trip to Bath, where he had been summoned by the gentlemen of the Chamber of Commerce to explore a grand renovation of the baths, when he heard the good news.

Thus a month later, in mid-August 1829, he found himself at the Gardens to supervise the laying out of the new grounds north of the drive. It had been more than two years since he had observed the same process on the original lands taken by the

Society, and on arriving at the Gardens on that August day, feeling somewhat reflective, he permitted himself a rare moment of leisure and took a stroll. It had become quite an extraordinary place. The plants and trees had matured and settled into their beds and borders. The recent addition of more ornamental features, such as rockeries and beautifully delicate wire aviaries for some of the smaller birds, augmented the already pleasing landscape. He took some time to survey the menagerie's many small wonders, each in its considered spot to sit perfectly within the beautiful grounds. The only detraction, he observed, as he perambulated the grounds, was the yet rather unsavoury odour. It emanated from the birds and beasts, and even where the dens were open, the stench hung on the air, like a rotten mist. He ruminated that the beasts themselves, with their unpleasant, *beastly* habits, were the one factor that was beyond his own control.

He wondered whether the many other visitors were as sensitive to it as he was. Despite it having been a wet summer, the Gardens had been much frequented. The same rules still applied: Fellows were allowed free rein every day and non-subscribers to the Society were permitted entry six days a week upon payment of a shilling and presentation of a written order from a Fellow. It seemed to Mr Burton's sharp eye, though, that the admissions policy was not quite as strict as it might have been: apparently it was possible to acquire a written order at the gate. However they were getting in, Londoners were making good use of the latest attraction in the capital for, despite the light drizzle, that day the grounds were thronged with people. (He learned that there had been almost a hundred thousand visitors the previous year, and that total was expected to double in this one.) Ladies with parasols paraded the walkways, gentlemen assembled in groups around the cages, talking loudly, while families and less genteel visitors crowded around the more entertaining

attractions. The leader among the latter appeared to be the bear
pit, where fathers jostled to buy buns and apples from the
sweet-seller to stick on their umbrellas and walking sticks and so
lure the bears up their pole for their children's amusement.

Mr Burton was distracted from the people, however, and
from his own leisurely study of the menagerie's attractions, by
his close inspection of the implementation of the designs he had
drawn up for the menagerie in the past year. Although his
grander plans had been frustrated, he had been almost constantly employed by the Society on one small-scale job or
another. He tried to visit them all: the emus' pond and the otters'
den, the pond for the beavers, the dens for guinea pigs, the
enclosure and house for pelicans and, more recently, a new home
for the monkeys. And, of course, he allowed himself to enjoy
some of his older structures, like the Llama House and the
palm-columned aviary for tropical birds – both now appropriately inhabited. It had all come together most satisfactorily. At
least in terms of what *had* been built. It seemed now that his
grand terrace extension would never materialize: after the heavy
losses of two winters, the keepers' preference was that the animals be kept inside, in the warmth, not exposed to the air as his
open dens would have it. Another matter sadly beyond his control, another factor he had never thought to take into account in
his work: the comfort of *beasts*.

And as Mr Burton surveyed the new buildings, cages, ornamental rockeries and flower borders, he couldn't help but notice
how many more beasts there seemed to be. There had been a
large donation of quadrupeds from the Marchioness of London-
derry, he was told, and the Society had purchased many more
from the keeper of the Tower Menagerie. These details Mr
Burton heard from Mr Johnson, who joined him partway
through his walk around the grounds, in attentive mood as ever.
Apparently Mr Cross had offered to sell his entire collection of

animals to the Society too, now that the Strand improvements were taking place and the Exeter 'Change was to be demolished. Mr Burton knew of the improvement plans, of course. Mr Nash was indeed to oversee the work there, rather surprisingly, in light of the renewed scrutiny of his conduct. Though he had officially been cleared of any wrongdoing a second time, after a second inquiry, the popular outrage at the cost of Buckingham House remained, and the great man's reputation was in tatters.

As well as pointing out the recently acquired creatures to him, Mr Johnson introduced Mr Burton to the many new humans they encountered at various stages of their circumnavigation. There were almost too many for even the meticulous Mr Burton to remember. There was, first and foremost, one Mr Miller, who had been taken on as the first Superintendent of the establishment. A former soldier, he had served in France and more recently in Portugal, but also at the Tower, and so therefore had some experience of the menagerie there. (Mr Johnson explained that his own duties were now more focused on ensuring things ran smoothly at the entrance – which made Mr Burton wonder why he wasn't there now.) There were also numerous new keepers and – armed with a small, rather tattered medical bag – one Mr Spooner, whom they bumped into as he left the enclosure that housed the kennels. He had been recently employed to keep the animals in better health – *to try to stop so many of them dying*, Mr Johnson explained, in his most serious tones. He seemed a stern, awkward man when they were introduced. *His manner with animals was better than it was with people*, Mr Johnson assured the architect.

The main purpose of Mr Burton's visit that day was not simply to perambulate the grounds, he reminded himself, or to congratulate himself on the work he had done. No, it was to add to it! Mr Burton snapped out of his moment of self-indulgence and bade Mr Johnson good day. He moved away from the crowds, the flowers and animals in his carefully created world and crossed the public drive – as always, choked with carriages – entering the newly acquired land beyond. A blank canvas, awaiting his marks upon it. A number of workmen were engaged in erecting railings to mark the extent of the new area. The focus of the work, however, was the clearing of the ground for the foundations of the winter repository. Its long-overdue commencement had been greeted with much elation from the Council and the keepers, who were desperate to avert another haemorrhage of animals such as they had endured last winter. Mr Burton's usually reserved demeanour perhaps betrayed a little of his feeling about this poor substitute for the grand terrace dens he had so long imagined. They would have been a marvel, one that could not be matched by the functional structure he was now about to commence.

He concentrated on the job at hand today, making sure the ground was dug exactly as per his detailed design, but occasionally allowing his mind to wander. He thought of the tunnel: the finely appointed tunnel that would take the visitors from one side of the road to the other, thus uniting the now fragmented landscape. It would be a consolation prize, of sorts – if the Society agreed to his design for it. Tunnels were tricky. Brunel's Thames tunnel had ended in disaster, as everyone knew, abandoned half dug – a sorry monument to failure. This, of course, was a far simpler undertaking, and Mr Burton had no doubt that he would be able to convince the Council of the benefits of such a fine addition to the Gardens. It was a clever little design, and he would persuade the Council of its merit. He had to: it offended him to think of the visitors' movement through the grounds, so carefully orchestrated by his planning, being interrupted by the busy road behind him. It would spoil the overall effect completely.

On Wednesday, the 2nd of September, 1829, Mr Burton found himself once again departing from the headquarters of the

Zoological Society of London at 33 Bruton Street; he was three years older than the first time he had done so with Sir Stamford Raffles, two years older than he had been when he had learned that his designs for the Society would be realized. Now he was soon to turn twenty-nine, already one of the most successful architects of his day. His work at the Regent's Park in particular had been much praised of late, one reviewer waxing lyrical that his 'taste in erecting domiciles appears exhaustless and inimitable' and that 'several of the dens and houses in this garden are not a whit less picturesque than the villas and mansions which we have elsewhere noticed from Mr Burton's designs'. And he had just found out that another of his fine designs for the Gardens would soon be committed to bricks and plaster.

An hour earlier, as he had entered the building, the Council had still needed convincing of his designs for the tunnel. He had gone to the bi-monthly meeting in the first-floor room at Bruton Street and done precisely that. The Council had consented, provided the Commission of Woods and Forests agreed, of course. *They need not worry on such a matter*, Mr Burton had assured them. What he did not know, as he turned and walked towards Regent Street, was that John Nash himself was resolved to prevent any further expansion of the Zoological Society in Regent's Park. He had his mind set on further building there and was trying to persuade the Commissioners that the land between the public drive and the canal should belong to *him*.

John Nash is disappointed; the work in the newest plot allotted to the Society presses on. The tunnel itself is begun in mid-September. As the air begins to cool, men and spades make the first cuts into the clay earth, a red wound in the fading summer green of the land. They dig deeper, deeper – until the white blanket of an early fall of snow stills the torn earth. With the thaw, the digging continues. The last of the leaves descend from the trees to tell us that another year in the Regent's Park is almost over. On nature's cue, the tender animals are wheeled off along the road under which the men are digging, out of the cold and towards the stables in Park Street: their sanctuary for another winter. Others are moved into the new winter repository, finally completed in the North Garden to which the tunnel will lead. It is not too soon. In November, six inches of snow cover everything: the red earth and grey stones piled up at the work site, the dark green of the hedges that mark out the winding pathways of the Gardens to the south, the fine iron railings of the bear pit, the stones of the rockery in the beavers' pond, the pointed roof and clock tower atop the Llama House. All is stillness and softness but it heralds a bleak winter. More cages, paddocks and dens are hurriedly emptied, their inhabitants rushed to Camden Town. The workmen remain behind. They must suffer the cold.

A cruel frost closes the year and begins the next, and a new decade: 1830. The Thames is covered with ice. At Greenwich, the boats and barges are trapped, motionless, in its frozen web. As they wriggle free, in the Regent's Park to the river's north, the works continue. It is a contrast to that other green expanse, St James's Park, where construction of the palace, so long mired in controversy, has ground to a halt. The King is rumoured to be gravely ill; his architect, Mr Nash, is made idle. Both their futures look uncertain. Mr Burton, meanwhile, works on. His designs for the grand entrances at either end of the tunnel are passed around the Council table at Bruton Street and approved. The first of the stones that will become the elegant archways is hauled into place as the days grow longer. The animals return in their crates and cages, loaded onto carts, as more workers arrive on foot, called in to finish the tunnel in time for the summer season. They swarm over the ground like ants. In April, the land they have been taming fights back: there is a huge slip of earth in the half-built tunnel. The men working in it escape with their lives, but Mr Burton hurriedly appears, directing the construction of a wall to support it while it is finished.

On the 17th of May, everything stops. Decimus Burton's tunnel is completed. The latest, most elegant addition to the Gardens of the Zoological Society of London is opened to visitors. Their experience of this exotic little world is interrupted no longer by the traffic on the drive. It is a tasteful, clever solution to the flaws of the landscape he has been given. It is a subtle triumph, which reflects its creator perfectly.

He was well satisfied with the finished tunnel, pleased with the details that had successfully lifted it from functional to beautiful. The lovely curve of its mouth was set in a wall crowned by a moulded balustrade, beyond which rose a roofed façade adorned with Doric columns. Rather like a *scaenae frons* behind a Roman theatre's stage, he liked to think, it gave the illusion of a perfect Palladian villa perched atop the underpass. The road was absent altogether. Visitors need not depart from the set, as one might think of it, that he had so very carefully designed for them.

The Society clearly appreciated his minute dedication to the totality of the visitors' experience of their establishment. Just two days after his tunnel was unveiled, Mr Burton was invited to become the Society's first permanent architect. He was most gratified by the offer, of course, a sure mark of the Council's appreciation of his latest achievement in their grounds. Along with the proffered appointment, the members requested another plan from him, this time detailing the Gardens as he envisaged them in their *final* incarnation, when every building and feature he dreamed of was completed. It was a most tempting

proposition, one that would allow him to retain full control of
the world he had so carefully conjured, one he could not but
accept . . . on certain entirely reasonable, well thought through
and copiously explained terms, of course. The Society agreed to
them.

In June, the arrangement was ratified: Decimus Burton
became the official architect, in the salaried employ, of the Zoological Society of London.

The summer of 1830 proved a busy one for Mr Burton, which
quickly tumbled into autumn. Now, it was an afternoon in late
October and he had just quit his home and offices on Spring
Gardens to see about yet another high-profile commission. It
had been a dusty and inconvenient few months in that part of
the city, since the improvements on the Strand had commenced
in earnest. Amongst the many buildings that had been demolished was the Exeter 'Change (though Mr Cross had been
granted the use of the former state stables for the animals, on the
square now cleared at its western end) and the road was being
widened. Mr Burton was going to look at a newly cleared plot,
on Agar Street, suggested for a hospital he was to build. Yes, it
had been a busy few months for the newly appointed architect to
the Zoological Society, but everything was moving in the right
direction for him.

The same could not be said of his former collaborator, John
Nash (if one could call their difficult working relationship a collaboration). Just before Mr Burton had taken up his new post at
the Zoological Society on the 1st of July, King George IV had
died at the age of sixty-seven. The partnership between Nash
and the King, which had remodelled so much of the capital,
came to an end. Nash would no longer be protected by his
patron from the nation's displeasure. The great architect's renovations of Buckingham House were not recommenced, though

he had continued to involve himself in other building projects in the capital. He had taken a particular interest in stymieing the Zoological Society of London's plans for their grounds in the Regent's Park, putting up endless objections to their proposal via the Commission of Woods and Forests.

But Mr Burton dared hope that the troubles might now be over. Finally – just this past week – Nash had been officially dismissed from the Buckingham House project by the Board of Works, on grounds of profligacy. His authority over the Commission, over the Crown's redevelopment of the capital, must surely also end. The architect of the Zoological Society of London would be allowed to work unimpeded.

Spring Gardens adjoined the Mall, which Mr Burton now reached. Nash's abandoned project was at the other end, to his left. The trees that lined the Mall had shed their leaves, and as he looked down the long, straight avenue he caught a glimpse of the building at the end, devoid of the scurrying workers who had adorned it for so long. A poem sprang to mind, recently republished after the death of its author, Percy Shelley: 'Ozymandias'. Looking towards Nash's unfinished monstrosity, he recalled the 'colossal wreck' of which Shelley had written; the shattered monument to a fallen ruler. Mr Burton was surprised that he detected a note of triumph in his breast. He found that a little distasteful. He reprimanded himself that his own creations – his grand archways, his Colosseum, the Athenaeum, the elegant tunnel and the lovely Gothic Llama House, even, in the Regent's Park – might well be colossal wrecks themselves, one day. Though privately, fiercely, he hoped that his designs would endure, that it would be Decimus Burton and not John Nash who would be remembered by history. He turned on his heel and headed for the Strand.

3. The Solitary Surgeon

Mr Charles Spooner, Medical Attendant,
1829–33

Charles Spooner arrived at the Zoological Society's Gardens one Tuesday morning in mid-July to be met with the news that there were injuries among the kangaroos, some of them severe. Walking tall as he clutched a leather case, filled with the tools and drugs of his trade, Mr Spooner was neatly clad in comparison to Mr Fuller, the head keeper, who was escorting him: the other was in his working dress and stank of his early-morning labours in the dens. Spooner's youthful face betrayed his bewilderment. He had commenced his employment only the previous week and still did not know how he had ended up there. How, aged twenty-two, after less than a year in London, he found himself medical attendant to the menagerie of the Zoological Society at the Regent's Park.

Quite a few men had care of the animals when they were well. When they were ill, just one man was responsible: himself. In addition to Fuller, there were a couple of assistant keepers, numerous under-keepers and keepers' helpers. Spooner did not know their names; he was too serious a man to be easily sociable and, besides, he sensed that the men were somewhat suspicious of him. Fuller, leading him briskly along, explained the situation with the kangaroos: *The night watchman heard them. Kept running at the fence, throwing themselves at it. I was woken but it was too late. They'd done themselves quite a bit of hurt.* Spooner said nothing, but followed.

That morning he had already treated a llama. A llama! A llama with cutaneous eruptions, no less: that was how he had diagnosed the irritated skin revealed by the thinning of its woolly coat. Such strange, rather sad creatures, he thought, in their fancy little house. (And, besides, what an odd place for an animal to reside, with its unnecessarily pointed doorways and ornate windows.) He had been treating the white one for a few days already. He had prescribed, and the keepers had been duly administering, nitrated mercurial ointment to the affected areas of the skin (often used to treat venereal disease in humans, he knew it well from his days with Mr Jervis, the druggist-chemist). Spooner had been hugely relieved to see this morning that it seemed to be working and made sure that the head keeper was well aware of that fact too. Spooner was employed on a trial – the first man to fill the post – and he knew he had much to prove.

Currently, he was hurrying to keep up with Fuller as he crossed from the lawn in front of the Llama House into the courtyard. Nearby there were several temporary kennels for dogs and the noise of barking was tremendous. It lifted Spooner's spirits. Opposite were the dens for the larger quadrupeds, but this morning they were making for the yard behind, where the reindeer and the kangaroos were separated into enclosures. Spooner's business, of course, was with the kangaroos. He had looked them over before, out of curiosity. There were several, bred in captivity at Windsor menagerie and by the Marquess of Hertford; gentle creatures despite their size and the strength

that Spooner saw in their hindquarters. He had observed that
the keepers were not afraid of them, but cautious with the larger
ones. He allowed himself to be guided by them. He knew animals well enough, for he had grown up on a farm, so he respected
their power.

As they neared the fence, most of the kangaroos looked
towards the sound of approaching footsteps, for the day was
young and the animals had been largely undisturbed since the
early-morning rituals. The last of the night's dew sparkled on
the grass and the air was still cool. Spooner had on his overcoat.
He could see immediately the veracity of what the keeper had
told him about the animals' injuries. He stood at the fence and
watched them for some moments. None was animated. A few
lay splayed on their sides beneath their shelter, others hopped
unenthusiastically around the small paddock, bent double on to
all four unevenly matched limbs. Many had visible injuries; one
animal in particular had very large contusions on its head, its
eyes barely open. Spooner was surprised. Had they really done
this to themselves? Not for the first time he wished that the animals might speak to tell him what was wrong. He supposed all
that was expected of him, however, was to treat them, not to
understand them.

He told Fuller he would need hot water and two men to help
restrain the creatures. He would administer fomentations to
their wounds. What else could he do? Fuller sent the paddock's
keeper away to boil some water, and stood silently next to the
new medical attendant. While they waited, Spooner reached
into his pocket for his snuff box. He was surprised to find he was
quite moved by the sight of the strange, foreign animals, bearing the marks of what must have been a failed bid for freedom.
He took a pinch of the brown powder between thumb and forefinger, savouring the sensation as he inhaled. He had been using
more since he had been in London. To suppress the stench of the

city, he told himself, though here that was masked by the smell of the beasts and their muck, which he didn't mind. The thought occurred to him that the animals might have been trying deliberately to harm themselves. He hoped it was nothing so sinister.

He asked himself, yet again, what on earth he was doing there. It certainly wasn't what he had intended when he had moved to London and enrolled at the Veterinary College, just eight months ago.

Spooner had not found the post: it had found him. The Society's Council had approached the Veterinary College, and the assistant to Professor Coleman had picked Charles Spooner out of the fifty students in attendance that year. The young man thus plucked from his peers had been honoured and not a little surprised. He supposed he was one of the more disciplined among them (and if medical students had a bad reputation, veterinary students' far exceeded it), and as good a student as any. He had greater experience than most, too, thanks to his apprenticeship as a druggist. For one or all of these reasons, twenty-two-year-old Charles Spooner, who had not even completed his studies, had been recommended by the Veterinary College as the first ever medical attendant to the Zoological Society of London. He wondered if there was another post like it elsewhere, or if he was the very first. (Perhaps he had a predecessor in Paris, he mused, where they were decades ahead in the veterinary arts. Here, it was still such a new science.)

'Medical attendant' was his official title. Spooner preferred the more professional term, 'veterinary surgeon'. That was what they now were called in the Cavalry, and that was what he would call himself. However you might designate it, the post had been created for one reason only: as an attempt to stop the high incidence of animal mortality. He was to visit the Gardens

at the Regent's Park three times a week, more often when necessary, to care for the sick and injured animals as directed by Fuller
and the other keepers. The animals at the Society's farm in
Kingston, recently acquired for the purposes of breeding and
experimentation, were not to be his concern (mostly game and
other 'useful' creatures, as far as he knew). Those were the terms
of his contract. He had agreed to come on Tuesdays, Thursdays
and Saturdays.

He was honoured, yes, and he was daunted. How could he
not be? There were more than six hundred animals in residence,
of almost two hundred different species, the vast majority of
which he had never seen the like of before, other than in passing
glimpses at travelling menageries, let alone had any experience
of treating! In fact, his experience was very limited indeed.
He had helped with the cattle he had grown up with; he had
learned about horses at the college and a little about dogs at some
private classes he'd attended. Now the list of animals in his care
was formidable: a lion, a pair of leopards, a puma, a beaver, a
raccoon, a coatimundi, countless species of monkeys, porcupines,
sloth bears, an Arctic bear, a black bear, kangaroos, sables, llamas,
falcons, eagles, owls, ostriches, emus, macaws, a pelican, reindeer, Australian dogs, a jackal, wolves . . . All were at varying
stages of acclimatization to captivity and the British weather.
Many of them he had seen only in the *Guide to the Gardens* he'd
been studying, but in less than two weeks in the post he had
already treated a reindeer for cutaneous eruptions, as well as the
white llama, a leopard with indigestion, an emaciated tiger cat,
a wolf with mange, a sloth bear with vomition, a raccoon with
inflamed eyes . . .

And now kangaroos with self-inflicted contusions. He
noticed that the keeper was returning with a large basin. He had
better prepare himself. He knelt down on the courtyard stones,
still cool, and opened his case to remove some cloths he might

use for poultices. As he did so, he noticed that the kangaroos had all turned towards a small group of visitors who were approaching the enclosures. He recognized Mr Sabine among them: the Society's Treasurer and the man who had interviewed him for the post. It was the last thing he might have asked for, to be supervised as he worked.

Spooner couldn't resist coming in on the following Monday. He didn't have any private clients that afternoon so he had a few hours to spare, and he was eager to see how the kangaroos were getting on – especially the large female. He had examined them quite a few times the preceding week and he was very pleased to see that most were making good progress. Most, but not her. He had suggested that the keepers feed them green food – fresh grass and green plants – as was often given to horses in the summer months. Perhaps it would help them to recover their vitality. As to what had caused such erratic behaviour, he simply did not know. He had observed that many animals in the Gardens frequently injured their companions, and he had treated several – jackals and baboons in the main – for their wounds. But injuring *themselves*? It seemed so unnatural.

It was a fine day, and the Gardens were choked with people – in this high season there were sometimes two thousand each day. Spooner usually tried to arrive early, to enter the grounds before the visitors did, but that morning he had been engaged at a private stables and had decided to call in only when he was on the way home to his rooms in Camden Town. He had been somewhat dismayed to see the carriages clogging the public drive around the park as he had approached, a clue to what he would be met with inside: the crowds around the bear pit, the many enclosures and cages, chattering couples blocking the pathways, older gentlemen perched on the chairs dotted around the lawns, roaring and laughing. That was quite apart from the many workers, the carpenters, gardeners and tradesmen, who were perpetually buzzing around. There was always something being built. Spooner found it almost overwhelming. That they irritated him was not his prime concern; more importantly, they irritated the animals. Walking sticks and parasols were banged against bars to attract them – sometimes even pushed through to prod them. The woman who kept a little stall next to the bear pit was always busy, always shouting at the bears and goading them up the pole, selling sticky buns, nuts and fruit for the visitors to feed to the pit's ever-greedy inhabitants. They had not a moment's peace while the gates were open.

Spooner was coming to the end of the raised terrace and saw the woman ahead of him now, encouraging the squawks of delight from the gathered crowds as the bears obligingly climbed for her wares. He hurried past, following the path from the terrace to the enclosures below and the worst-affected kangaroo. The keeper was busy talking to two bonneted ladies who were asking about the animals, something about what they ate. Spooner interrupted to ask a far more pertinent question: *how were they today?* He could see all too clearly for himself: the female who had been most seriously injured was not recovering. She looked worse, in fact, lying in the shelter, moving very little. He had spent enough time watching the creatures over the past week to know a little of what was normal, even for such exotic animals. Even from a distance he could see how strangely she held her very swollen head, with one eye now permanently closed, the other partially so. The keeper confirmed that she was in a poor way. Spooner ordered warm water prepared once again, and told him to fetch Fuller urgently. He prepared his equipment as he waited.

Fuller arrived, clearly a little disgruntled at having been disturbed, along with the kangaroo keeper and one of the keepers' helpers, carrying the requested basin of water. Fuller was little older than himself, Spooner presumed, but he was a confident man and much respected by those beneath him. He had just been sworn in as a special constable by the local magistrate, empowered to control the summer crowds at the Gardens if the need ever arose. Spooner had not had much to do with him – Fuller generally sent one of his assistants on the rounds with him now – but sensed that the head keeper felt his appointment had encroached upon his own authority. But Spooner was not a man to be cowed. As Fuller drew near, he explained that he was very concerned, and wanted Fuller to make sure a careful watch was kept over the animal from now on.

Doing away with pleasantries on his side, too, Fuller silently opened the paddock and they all went in. Fuller stood guard as his men moved the other animals away from the shelter where the injured one lay, then held her down. She was very weak. She struggled feebly. Spooner, cautiously, leaned over her. Up close, he could see that a discharge was coming from her nostrils – like a horse with strangles, he thought. The eye that she could still open was dull, and looked around weakly. He ordered the men to be gentle but firm, to hold her as still as they could. He removed a cloth from his case, soaked it in the hot water, and held it as tenderly as he could to her swollen head. She tried to resist him, pathetically. Spooner hoped he was relieving her pain more than he was causing her to suffer. After a few minutes he ordered her released. He felt miserable as he walked away, Fuller talking to the men as they secured the enclosure again. He could hear the cries of the spectators around the bear pit on the terrace above, the sticks rattling the railings, the shrieks of delight, and reached into his pocket for his snuff box.

The next day, she was dead.

He learned upon his arrival that she hadn't survived the night. Spooner was surprised by how uneasy he felt as he went about his rounds that morning. He had seen endless beasts die on the dairy farm his father managed, and since his arrival just two weeks ago plenty of rather more exotic species had perished: an alligator, a seal, two woodpeckers and a cat. The kangaroo weighed heavily on him, perhaps because he could not understand it. His workload for the day distracted him somewhat. The llama now had constipation as well as cutaneous eruptions (he prescribed Glauber's Salt, powdered aloes and nitre, to be given in warm water). He inspected the wolf's mange (and ordered the tar liniment repeated), and ministered to the swelling on the jackal's leg (with calomel and powdered digitalis). He had been told he was to conduct a post-mortem on the kangaroo when his work there was done, and it dominated his thoughts. He was troubled by the animal's death, yes. But he could not wait to get beneath its skin.

The carcasses of the exotic residents of the Regent's Park were much in demand; the menagerie was a veritable treasure trove for the comparative anatomists who sought the secrets of the natural order beneath the shells, furs and feathers of the many creatures who made it up. Spooner would not be allowed to examine every animal that died there. It had been made very clear to him that a system was in place: the more interesting corpses would be sent to the Fellows, such as Mr Owen at the Royal College of Surgeons, who worked with the Hunterian collection of anatomical specimens, or the anatomist Mr Brookes, for dissection. Many were ultimately destined for preservation for the Museum, and he would have to be careful with his knife. But Spooner had in turn made clear to the Superintendent, Mr Miller, that if he were to find out why these animals were dying he had to be allowed to look inside them. He had already conducted a post-mortem on a peccary and a seal.

Just a month ago, when he was still a full-time student, he'd been lucky to get a seat in the cramped lecture theatre close enough to see anything at all of the anatomical demonstrations performed by (the unpopular) Mr Vines. The stink and the stuffiness made it hard to concentrate on anything, and usually the students were only ever allowed to work on donkey meat, even though they were supposedly studying the horse. The operations performed in the open ground outside the horse infirmary had been few and far between. Such scraps had never sated Spooner's appetite. He'd gone to knackers' yards, like his fellow students, not far from the college at Belle Isle, to try to learn more, but had struggled there. Despite his having grown up on a farm he had found the industrial scale of the slaughter, the needless suffering and the blood flowing around his feet too much to stomach. He had attended private classes outside the college at Mr Youatt's infirmary at Nassau Street, and even done some work for him there, where he had seen a little more of the inner workings of horses and dogs. He had been to lectures and demonstrations at the various medical schools across the city – at St Bartholomew's, St George's, Guy's and St Thomas's, and at private medical schools, like Hunter's on Great Windmill Street. In short, he had done everything he could to arm himself with knowledge, but still he was ignorant. Now, having the carcasses of exotic beasts to examine, alone and in peace, he was achingly aware of what a choice opportunity he had been given.

Where practicable, this unsightly work was done in the stable building on Park Street. It had been taken on by the Society last winter to accommodate the delicate creatures, and it was also where they macerated the bodies of those they had no further use for, or whose skeletons were being prepared for preservation for the Museum. Unsurprisingly, it reeked. The stench surprised even Spooner when he entered, a man well used to the odour of beasts and death. It filled his mouth. Yet as he stood, scalpel in hand, before the carcass of the kangaroo, laid out upon a large wooden table in a corner of the small, dark room, he ceased to notice anything else, not even the foul air that seeped from the very fabric of the building. His focus was minute: on the grey-brown, furry head before him. It was horribly misshapen. As he made the first incision, Spooner knew he did not really need to do so – it was obvious that her injuries had killed her. But he wanted to. He relished peeling back the skin, even if all he could see beneath was a smashed mass of bones.

Those were the moments he treasured, the moments when he felt as if he had time to do more than rush around, reacting to the problems that arose daily. When he was alone with a carcass, he was shut away from the meandering and muttering gentlemen, the prodding and provoking crowds, lost in his intricate work. Each time his blade cut into a new creature he felt a surge of excitement, a sense of the uncharted territory he was entering. He wanted to find out why they had died, of course, but he could not deny that he had an ulterior motive: his own thirst for understanding. For himself, yes, but also for his profession. It was a glorious era for science, when so much was being discovered, the mysteries of life revealed in the organs, even the tiniest components of living beings. Comparative anatomy was such an invaluable, exciting route to knowledge. He remembered Professor Coleman's very first lecture to the new students, talking of the grand tradition begun by pioneers like Dr Hunter. A tradition he now followed in! Spooner himself was not so much interested in the great debates – what these details disclosed about man's relationship to other creatures, the Continental ideas that questioned man's uniqueness and seemed to frighten the Establishment so. He wanted to know how these creatures functioned for their own sake, so that he could better treat them. He detested experiments and researches on live animals, was sorry that some thought it the surest way to new knowledge. This had seemed to be changing of late, thanks to the work of other like-minded professionals, and the Society for the Prevention of Cruelty to Animals, which had been founded a few years ago.

Not vivisection: *this* was the way to learn. Spooner looked down at the bloodied mess he was working on. Most of the bones within the head and face were broken. There was no more he could find out here, no buried answer as to why the creature had done this to itself. As he wrote his findings in his journal and prepared to make his way home to his lodgings, he could not help but ruminate on how little he still knew. It was unfortunate to be so coldly reminded of this, when he would sit his final examination for his diploma that very evening. He really must go home and prepare. He lived only a mile away, just the other side of Camden Town, between Pancras Workhouse and Old Church, in front of the River Fleet. He told the under-keeper who was attending at the stables that he had finished, and stepped out of the dark stench into the bright, hazy daylight of the smoky city.

That evening, Charles Spooner was seated before the examining committee, in a dimly lit room in a hotel on Conduit Street. Professor Coleman and his assistant, Mr Sewell, were the only veterinarians on a panel of prominent medical men, presided over by the eminent surgeon Sir Astley Cooper. Spooner sat opposite the predominantly white-haired, elderly gentlemen, who were questioning him on the subjects he had learned in his nine months at the college: the principles of anatomy, pathology and *materia medica*. There was no practical element to the examination, sadly, for that was the one area in which he was confident he had gained the upper hand over his fellow students during the past month. But, then, the whole affair was no more than a formality: the questions were familiar, he was well rehearsed and, besides, no one failed. There was just the polite suggestion that the student continue in their studies a little longer.

Spooner was well aware of the growing tension within the veterinary community over precisely what he was now participating in: the antiquated system of the granting of the diploma he sought. Indeed, the college was being scrutinized as never before: the incredibly short course, the paucity of anatomical demonstrations and the dominance of the old medical elite over the fledgling sister profession. Just a few weeks earlier (the day after he had commenced his work for the Zoological Society), there had been an open meeting of veterinarians, which had descended into such a row that it had been adjourned. Spooner followed it all with interest. Times were changing. The profession even had its own journal now, the *Veterinarian*, edited by Mr Youatt, who promoted a scientific, specialist approach to the veterinary art and was a vocal advocate for reform at the college. Slowly but surely, veterinarians were proving they were not simply jumped-up farriers. He liked to think he was contributing, too: was not his recent appointment symbolic?

At that moment, though, he concentrated on the task at hand – even if it was one of the most flawed parts of the outdated education his peers were, justly, up in arms about. He would pass this examination, receive his diploma, and then the real learning could begin.

In the cool, damp days of early August, Spooner spent much time at the new Monkey House, towards the eastern edge of the Gardens. It was only just completed. When he had started work there, the simple, squat building had been teeming with workmen, busy converting it from its original use as a repository for various mammals. He remembered the puma had been kept there, a sloth bear, and many more, all crowded into small cages, seemingly at random. Now it was the sole preserve of the monkeys – and one of the Gardens' favoured attractions. People loved to watch the little creatures inside doing their tricks (though sometimes they were horrified by the monkeys' more scandalous acts). Spooner enjoyed watching them, too. Monkeys were not an uncommon sight in London, often accompanying street musicians and the like, and a staple in any travelling menagerie. But it was different being able to observe so many living together, and to observe them over time. He was getting to know them.

The building was an elegant construction, as even Spooner could see, now that the workmen had left it, with wire-fronted, open cages around which visitors were always crowded. At the back of the building there were indoor apartments, protected from the cold, which he found dark and short of air. Spooner had learned recently that the architect's father had built the Veterinary College back in 1791. Mr Burton, who seemed a permanent feature here, had been making small-talk with him – which Spooner loathed when he was trying to work. He had only just stopped himself telling the fellow what he thought of the mean, cramped building he had studied in – and that he found the atmosphere of the interior of the Monkey House not hugely dissimilar.

Quite what the monkeys thought of their new home, he did not know. They were not well, in any event. The long-armed monkey had had strange convulsive fits and was now severely constipated. He hoped the Epsom salts he was giving him would relieve him in time. More worrying, however, was that the other monkeys kept biting each other. When Spooner stopped here on his rounds, the keepers removed them from the cage and held them as still as they could so he could apply tincture of myrrh to their wounds, which were quite fearsome (though not as fearsome as the angry, writhing creatures themselves). He ordered the keepers to repeat this every morning when he was not there to do it himself. Once treated, the victims could only be returned to the cages and possible further attacks. Nearby the Monkey House there were some poles with little boxes on top, to which some of the more playful, hardy animals were chained in the daytime. But they were always returned to the crowded cages at dusk. He supposed they were rather like slum dwellers, crowded together. Perhaps it was unsurprising that they behaved with the same roughness.

Oh, this city! Sometimes he was surprised by the extent to which he missed the space and light of his boyhood home in Essex, especially in the summer. Even when it was cold and wet, as it was this August. He longed for fresh air, scented only by cut hay and animal dung. There was plenty of both here, of course, and the city's stench was masked somewhat. Perhaps that was one of the reasons he didn't feel the same claustrophobia in the park as he did on the streets beyond it. The crowds were the same, though. Just better attired and better spoken here, a playground of the privileged. (He had seen some more 'ordinary' types in here too, this summer: it seemed it was possible to get entrance to the Gardens simply by arriving at the gates – but the shilling fee and exclusive Sunday policy meant that it remained out of bounds for the labouring masses.) Almost everywhere in London, the cramming together of human beings was an accepted part of life. He had seen the new 'omnibuses' that had appeared on the capital's streets this summer. People were packed in like cattle. He wondered if the monkeys felt like that, too, in their new home.

He was used to the sounds of their shrieking now, as each in turn was held down to be treated, and he was duly cautious of them. They were vicious to humans as well as each other – he had seen a lady's sleeve pulled through the wire one morning, torn in two by the quick paws of one of the more mischievous creatures. (He felt strangely encouraged by that. And at least the monkeys weren't injuring themselves, he thought. Not like the poor kangaroos.) One morning, as he was battling to apply the tincture to a nasty wound upon a particularly determined animal, a well-dressed tradesman approached with the carpenter. He was obviously rather entertained by the noisy scene he had walked into. He remarked upon it, and Spooner was forced into perfunctory conversation, just as soon as he had returned the monkey to its keeper. He learned from the man that the cages were to be heated with hot water for the coming winter and he was there to oversee the installation. Some of the aviaries were already thus heated, he was told. Despite Spooner's vehement dislike of the carpenter (a rough fellow who always had the look of drink about him), he was curious to learn about this, and spoke with him and his companion for some minutes upon the subject.

Professor Coleman from the college had been most adamantly opposed to the heating of stables – indeed, heating in general – and had taught them that warm stables gave horses pneumonia, not their going out into the cold. But surely it was very different for these creatures, accustomed to tropical climes. As the medical attendant packed up his supplies, the heating man and the carpenter disappeared into the rooms at the rear of the Monkey House. He wondered what effect their engineering would have on the creatures. He would try to keep an eye on it, if he could. If he had the time.

As it currently stood, the new medical attendant could barely keep track of all the creatures he had in his care and *where* they were housed, let alone *how*. There seemed to be a constant flow of new animals into the Gardens that summer – almost as constant, Spooner thought gloomily, as the flow of carcasses out. In mid-August, when he was tending the injured monkeys, a lion cub arrived, transported from Africa by one General Reid. (It was quite common, Spooner had gathered, for diplomats and naval officers to bring back exotic creatures they encountered overseas.) Nelson, as the cub was known, was the second lion to arrive in the summer of 1829. The Society had also purchased a young male Cape lion from the Tower Menagerie, Nero. There was a panther, too, which had arrived in the middle of July. Suddenly the medical attendant (just a month in the job, but now officially qualified, at least) had quite a few rather formidable and very prestigious beasts to care for. Only if they fell ill, of course, which most duly did. Otherwise they were Fuller's business.

Spooner was just finishing his work with the larger quadrupeds, housed in newly constructed dens on the edge of the lawn. Alongside the puma, suffering from vomition, that he had just attended to (he had prescribed opium and antimony), other cages contained Nero, and the young tigress he had treated for emaciation (with calomel). The visitors adored the spectacular beasts, and finally having some for them to marvel at was a coup for the Society. Their dens, as far as Spooner understood, were only temporary accommodation. The plan was to build a series of fine open chambers for the carnivores beneath an extension of the terrace, as well as suitable permanent accommodation for the smaller creatures, though something had held up the start of the works.

The lion cub, Nelson, had been placed in a small, movable cage, one of many the carpenter had made in recent months because the arrangements for accommodation changed so frequently. Many were currently situated in the space beyond the kangaroo and deer yards. When he reached the area, he saw Nelson immediately. Spooner was not a sentimental man, but he was much moved by the first sight of the small creature, not much bigger than a large household cat, cowering alone, with only the strange noises of the other beasts nearby – civet cats and coatimundis, and further away, the dogs – to comfort him. Spooner asked the keeper stationed there how old he was. *The man who had had care of the animal for its passage to England had guessed four or five months.* Spooner was sure, anyway, that if little Nelson was at liberty he would still be with his mother. He knelt down, and leaned in against the bars of the cage; the creature's fur was surprisingly fluffy – where he had it. On his legs and feet he had sores that looked like mange. He would need to be let into the cage with him, he told the keeper. A few visitors noticed and stopped to watch.

The cub was not big enough to be dangerous, and the keeper held and petted it as Spooner applied tar liniment to the sores (they had been taught to use it on horses' feet at the college, and he hoped the effect would be the same). As he rubbed it into the bare patches of the young lion's legs, Spooner could not but wonder quite what his relationship was to it: a vulnerable little creature that would soon grow into a much more ferocious beast. He had chosen to care for animals over humans, giving up his apprenticeship as a chemist, because of a desire to decrease the suffering and improve the lives of innocent beasts, the horses, dogs and cattle that so willingly, so obediently served their masters. And now he was caring for lions. Not the dutiful slave of man, they were savage and wild, even if majestic. But this one was dependent on him now and he felt sorry for it.

Nelson got worse. As well as the skin condition, he just wasn't quite right. Spooner tried alternatives, calomel and jalap, to try to purify and rebalance the blood. Then he noticed that the animal's teeth, which were only just pushing through his gums, were irritating him. The keepers were not optimistic of his chances. They told Spooner that this was a very common cause of mortality in lion cubs. One said that only one cub at Exeter 'Change – out of ten or more, he thought – had survived teething. Spooner was a determined man. He would do what he could, even if the odds were against him. He would come to see him whenever he could find the time.

But at such moments, he couldn't help but wonder whether

one young man, working just three days a week, was ever going to be an adequate match for so many different animals, with so many different anatomies, with their wounds and their illnesses and their mystifying behaviour.

Four monkeys were dead by the middle of the month. The long-armed monkey went first, then a rhesus monkey. The last three went within two days. Jabins, a favourite of the crowds and keepers, was among the dead. How could Spooner know what was killing them? He did the only thing he could do: he cut the bodies up. Two of them had already had their brains removed for examination by a Mr Gold. The fight over carcasses was beginning to infuriate him. How was he ever going to learn anything about these creatures? And if he couldn't learn, how could he stop them perishing?

Mr Gold told him that Jabins's brain was much inflamed, so he could only presume that that had been the cause of his death. Spooner had himself found small tubercles on the membranes of the (highly inflamed) lungs, liver and spleen he had examined. In the carcasses of the other two monkeys upon which he had conducted post-mortems, he found much bigger tubercles, covering all of the abdominal and thoracic viscera, saving the kidneys, and especially the lungs, liver and spleen, just as in Jabins's corpse. It was worrying to see such diseased organs in all three creatures. Something must be causing it. He just didn't know what. An impure atmosphere? Perhaps it was true what the keepers said about the bad air that rose up from the damp clay soil. Perhaps it was the cool weather.

The preparations for the coming winter were already in hand; a winter that he felt in his bones already. He noticed that fewer visitors were blocking the pathways and, instead, it was workmen in his way. The land north of the road was finally being granted to the Society and the work on a permanent repository began. For now, temporary barriers went up against the ravages of the impending winter. The carpenter began constructing a shelter before the dens for large quadrupeds and another over the small, movable cages. In September, the Monkey House was fitted with porches before the doors to guard against the cold. Soon, he saw that even some of the plants were being dug up, to be moved to the greenhouses of the farm at Kingston for the winter. He remembered, with no little anxiety, what he had been told of the dramatic rates of mortality among the animals the previous year.

Nelson got worse. By the end of September, Spooner couldn't help but share the keepers' pessimism about the teething cub. His cage had been moved out of the cold and into the chamber under the terrace, along with some of the other less hardy animals. Since the bison had died, it had been used as a storeroom. He had treated the bison without success; to his dismay, the failure had been much reported in the newspapers. Spooner did not dwell on that now as he knelt in the lion cub's cage, surrounded in turn by the cages of his companions. Nelson was feeble and thin, and clearly in discomfort. When the keeper had prised open his mouth at his bidding, he could see that the gums were visibly swollen. Spooner opened his case and hoped that his chemist's knowledge would help him to save Nelson.

He had been apprenticed after his schooling to Mr Jervis. In the shop on the busy Westbar, across the river from the chimneys of the Sheaf Works, and alongside the dressmakers, confectioners, furniture brokers and greengrocers, the young Spooner had served endless customers with calomel and laudanum, jalap, and jars of leeches for bleeding. He had been confident in the dispensary with drugs and doses. He was confident now. There was one minor problem: many of the drugs and chemicals available had different effects on humans and animals, had different effects, even, on different animals. At the college, he had been taught a little of how drugs worked on horses, a little less on how they worked on dogs by Mr Youatt. But since he had been treating bison, baboons and hyenas, well, it had been a case of trial and error. Professor Coleman had told them that that was all they might do, and 'If you should err you would know better next time.' He had erred in the past; he hoped he would not err this time.

Now he searched through the treatments that he had at his disposal: the trocar he plunged into abdomens to relieve gas (unsuccessfully, in the bison's case), the fleam and basin he used for blood-letting when the heart needed relief. The laxatives he used for constipation and indigestion: Glauber's Salt, Epsom salts and castor oil. The stimulating and soothing ointments and liniments he used for skin complaints, many of which he had made up himself with ingredients purchased from the Apothecaries' Hall: tar liniment, turpentine liniment, sulphur liniment, nitrated mercurial ointment, tincture of myrrh, camphor, the powdered opium he used in cases of vomition (he had treated the sloth bear with it of late, to good effect). Then there were the emetics and purgatives, the powerful substances, like jalap and tartarized antimony, to which he had turned to rid the animals' systems of whatever was doing them harm. And the alteratives: powdered antimonials and the ever-reliable calomel, with its powerful influence over the entire system, its ability to check and alter anything out of balance. It was this that Spooner now removed from its place in his neatly arranged case: the bottle of calomel. He also took out the tartarized antimony – a good emetic in dogs, he knew. He measured out two grains of calomel, one of the emetic tartar.

He had just given calomel and powdered antimonials to the older lion Nero, too. Nero was suffering from a badly contused eye, a wound – it made his blood boil to think of it! – that had been inflicted by a lady's parasol. And it was the beasts that were accused of being vicious and uncivilized! He increasingly despaired of his task here. The thought that the Society might lose both lions in their collection entered his mind, but he refused to let it linger. He told the keeper to hold little Nelson firm, and prayed that the drugs would work their wonders.

The keeper later reported that the vomition had come first, weak streams of warm liquid. Then the purgative effect had taken hold. Spooner was pleased, and hoped that this would put the little creature's system back into balance.

When he returned to check him on his next visit, however, he was disappointed to find that Nelson was worse, much weakened. Spooner believed now that he would lose him. He tried two grains of powdered antimonials and this time he took a risk and prescribed digitalis too: foxglove. He would also administer a clyster to the anus: Nelson must be flushed out. The medical attendant had warm water prepared. The cub was removed from the cage. The creature was small, and so weak that it was not difficult for two keepers to hold him almost completely still. Spooner sucked the water into his brass clyster pump. He lifted the limp tail and inserted it as gently as he could. The cub snarled.

Oh, he did not want this creature to die!

Nelson, it became apparent by his next visit, did not want to die either. Spooner found him somewhat improved, moving around more, eating again. Nero's eye was better too. Judging Nelson to be out of mortal danger, he could now focus on treating the cause of his problems: his teething. Spooner had decided that he must perform some minor dental surgery – he could delay it no longer. He did not like operating when he could avoid it, and wished there was some way he could numb the pain when he had to. There wasn't, of course: humans and beasts alike had to suffer the excruciating agony of surgery, though at least humans might have a little whisky. He could only be as swift as accuracy permitted. It still took a good few minutes – of obvious suffering for little Nelson – for him to cut away part of the troublesome tooth.

On his next visit, he lanced Nelson's swollen gums. Spooner did not enjoy doing that either. But by the following Tuesday, the 6th of October, the lion cub was well enough that Spooner was able to write in his records, *Better. No medicine ordered.* And he had feared he would be writing the findings of a post-mortem examination. He must report it to the Veterinary Medical Society, he thought. It might be a breakthrough of sorts or, at the very least, some additional knowledge on the workings of the drugs in any veterinarian's pharmacopoeia.

That night, he took his evening meal in the Elephant and Castle Tavern just by the college, surrounded by his successors, the latest students there. He was proud of himself. He had just saved a lion. A lion! Yes, the burden of his work at the Gardens was exhausting. Yes, he often wondered if he was making any difference at all. And yet, he realized, he was beginning to take pleasure in his work. He looked at the men he had been among just a few months ago – students, drunk, some of them, he was sorry to see – and felt aloof. He was like an explorer, embarking on a great voyage.

Like all adventurers, he would meet with hard times on the journey. The very next day an inch of snow fell on the capital. Spooner was not on duty at the Gardens, where stoves were hurriedly lit in the various dens and beneath the temporary shelters. As he walked home to his lodgings on Cook's Row from the stables of a private client, he watched the snowflakes spiralling out of the grey sky with a quiet sense of dread.

★

Summer, 1830. The first medical attendant to the Zoological Society of London had survived his first winter at the Gardens in the Regent's Park; it had been bitter, with much snow and even ice on the Thames. Many of his charges had not been so fortunate. Losses had been worryingly high, as last year, despite the myriad precautions taken, despite even the ministrations of the new medical attendant. The Council, though, was optimistic that the situation would now improve, for on the land north of the drive the repository was finished, complete with heating apparatus designed to keep the interior temperature at seventy-five degrees, even during a frost. (The idea of open dens beneath the terrace had been dismissed, deemed too exposed for most of the year.) In early July, the animals who had resided in the repository since its completion were moved out by the keepers through the fine, new tunnel to the South Garden and its habitations, which were more conducive to their exhibition. The parrots and small animals that had spent the winter in the warmth of the Bruton Street offices took their place in the repository.

The beginning of the summer season in the much-improved Gardens should have been a time of excitement yet the mood was sombre. It was not due to the death of the King a few days earlier, for no one had paid much heed to that. Spooner, for one, was pleased that the age of decadence presided over by George IV might now be relegated to history, and hoped that William IV would be better suited to the modern, more professional spirit that he sensed taking hold around him. No, the mood at the Gardens was sombre because of the death of one of their own: Josiah Graves had died of injuries sustained in an attack by the big Arctic bear. His fellow keepers had been much shaken. Spooner was less surprised, given the amount of goading the animal endured, day in, day out, not to mention the rough manner many of the keepers used with the animals. Over the winter they had killed one of the llamas, by suffocation, while he was trying to treat it. His relations with them had never been good but thereafter had grown frostier still. The funeral of Josiah Graves reminded everyone that they were all risking their lives with these beasts. Spooner hoped that his own gentle, wary approach would serve him better.

He had been employed by the Society for a year now. Although he had little to show for it in terms of the mortality rates, his confidence was growing. He was learning slowly. He was making a name for himself within the profession, too – he had been sharing his experiences with his peers in the Veterinary Medical Society, his remarks often then published by Mr Youatt in the *Veterinarian*. As he had watched the tunnel and the other new structures erected, he imagined a building that might more directly benefit his own work: a dedicated infirmary. He wondered about the efficacy of treating sick animals among the others, and of leaving those who were suffering to the attentions and whims of the visitors. There had been such an infirmary at the Veterinary College. He mentioned it to Mr Burton, who said he would suggest it to the Council of the Society. As the official architect, he now attended their meetings regularly. He reported back to Spooner in late July that the idea would be considered. The medical attendant was pleased: he felt he was being taken seriously.

One morning in mid-September, Spooner arrived at the Gardens (he had walked the mile from his rooms in Camden Town, as he always did) to be informed by the boy on the gate that Superintendent Miller wanted to speak with him. That was most unusual. The Superintendent normally greeted him in passing, but on the rare occasions he had a message for him, it was passed on through Fuller. As Spooner made his way past the entrance lodges and ascended the terrace, with its ornately planted flowerbeds in late-summer bloom either side, he wondered what the summons might concern. Perhaps the infirmary was to be built. He had heard nothing more of it since it had been mentioned to the Council at least a month before, though a great deal of building work had been undertaken: an eagle house, a seal house, an enclosure for wolves, an ostrich house, a new house for the peccaries, a house for tapirs, one for wapiti deer, a cage for squirrels . . . There were many new creatures to accommodate, for, on top of the usual donations and purchases, the King had donated all of the animals in his predecessor's personal menagerie at Windsor to the Society. He was a man of greater modesty and believed the royal collection should be at the disposal of the nation rather than the monarch alone. Such patronage was a huge boost to the Society's status as an institution of national import. Spooner found it hard to celebrate, though, when an additional antelope, two zebras, a mule, a wild boar, a Cape ram and countless smaller creatures arrived at the Gardens (luckily some others had gone to the farm at Kingston). A hospital was needed now more than ever: his workload had expanded dramatically these past few months.

The day was young, the morning bright. Spooner descended from the terrace, avoiding the bear pit. He had come to hate the sight of it. On a busy day the crowds that gathered around it were little better than those at a bear-baiting, only better clad. Mr Burton had altered it, after Graves's mauling, but only to make it more secure for the keepers, not to protect the animals from the braying crowds. That morning, it was yet quiet. The woman was setting up her stall selling the items with which the creatures would be harassed later. He followed the pathway that led him behind the Llama House, past the ornate cage where the macaws usually resided. The removal of animals from the South Garden for the winter had already begun, and the parrots had been first to go.

The Superintendent's office was in the apartment that the head keeper, Fuller, had recently taken over from Mr Johnson, which was situated behind the large aviary. (Spooner did not fail to notice the increasing esteem in which Fuller was held.) As he approached, he could hear the birds on the waterfowl's lawn before it, the cranes and wading birds having already been turned out from the aviary for the day. He skirted the aviary, the curassows, guans and other birds it still contained, and entered the apartment at its rear. He knocked at the door to the sitting room, which served as Mr Miller's office, and presented himself to the Superintendent when he heard the shout to enter. The medical attendant, who received so little attention here, as a rule, was pleased that he had come to his notice now.

The news that Miller greeted him with, rather brusquely, was unexpected. He had in front of him on his desk a letter from the Council. *They had demanded a report on the subject of the great level of mortality among the animals.* Miller, a veteran of the Napoleonic Wars and a rather dull man, read the missive aloud to him without emotion, and it felt to Spooner rather like an exercise in humiliation: *what causes could be assigned for such a mortality and whether he could suggest any mode by which it could be lessened in future . . .*

Spooner began to reply. Miller cut him off: *They expect a report in writing.* Spooner composed himself, answering that he could have it ready within two weeks. *Good. That is all.* Miller returned to the papers on his desk as Spooner showed himself out of the sitting room, out of the apartment and back into the cacophony of the Gardens.

He felt it deeply. It was a criticism. He had been employed to curb the mortality rates among the animals and he had failed to do so. He was livid. The keepers had managed to kill a zebra just a few weeks ago while transporting it – and he was the one being criticized! He was not a miracle-worker! Spooner had a temper and he wrestled with it now, trying to focus his energies on what he might write.

He was busy, as usual. The monkeys were troubled again: the wanderoo had died, the green monkey was not feeding well, the dog-faced monkey had a lacerated back and the palliated monkey was constipated. His post-mortem investigations revealed highly diseased lungs. Many of the remaining monkeys began to exhibit symptoms of the same. Even Nero, the lion, had breathing difficulties. Was it the onset of the cold weather that was causing it? The new heated building had not helped, it seemed. He had begun, where he could, to make suggestions that he felt might mitigate the effects of captivity and a strange climate; a change of diet (which he tried for the leopard when it was unwell) or more exercise (which he had done for the dogs), but he simply did not have the time to look into anything scientifically, as he would have liked to do. He was kept so busy with the immediate needs of the animals. That week he had had to treat a beaver with a tumour under its throat (he lanced it) and a zebra with dental problems (he filed the edges of its teeth, which he hoped would prevent further laceration of its cheek . . .).

What but that could he write in his report for the Council? He worked on it in the evenings, in his rooms in Camden Town, as September waned and October – with its sharper bite – came into view. He wondered, even if the Council agreed to the hospital, would that really change things? He needed to understand the animals better so that he could know what they needed. Was it the cold that was to blame? Or the bad atmosphere in the Gardens? Did the animals' accommodation need ventilating, perhaps? He hoped, in his more optimistic moments, that his careful post-mortem work would, over time, reveal the answers to him. In the meantime, he submitted his report and waited for the response. Was he to lose his job? Or might he finally be given the extra resources he needed? The hospital, even. He could only wait and see.

Neither happened. The Council was obviously satisfied, and the medical attendant worked on, just as before. The preparations for the coming winter went on around him. He was familiar now with the yearly cycle of the Gardens. The heated, enclosed repository in the North Garden filled as the more exposed cages in the South Garden emptied. In the middle of October, the kangaroos were removed from their paddock and taken through the tunnel to the North Garden. That night, they started behaving erratically again. Spooner was shaken to hear the news, when he came into the Gardens two days later, that one of the kangaroos had actually killed itself, so hard had it run against the paddock fence. Again, he was troubled by such behaviour. He wanted to know why they did this to themselves. Was it the effects of confinement? The stress of the relocation? But his time was so limited! In that same single day a greyhound and a seal had died suddenly, too, and he had had to go and see the beaver whose jaw he had operated on, the lion Nero with his breathing problems, a constipated dromedary, a zebra with catarrh, the sloth bear, which wasn't feeding well . . .

Of greater significance, if not mystery, was the death of an orang utan at the end of October. It would have been the star attraction, the most exciting, novel creature the Society's collection had yet contained – had it ever reached the Gardens. A gift from one Captain Swinton of the East India Company, it only got as far as Bruton Street, where it lived out its last few days in a sadly debilitated condition. Spooner only heard of it; he didn't see the animal. The post-mortem examination was carried out at Bruton Street by Mr Owen. He presented his report with much fanfare to the inaugural meeting of the Zoological Society's new Committee of Science and Correspondence in early

November, set up to further the investigation and discussion of animal physiology and zoology (as well as to communicate the Society's needs, in terms of animals they most wished to acquire, with corresponding members overseas). Owen concluded that the animal had perished from exhaustion of the system caused by the long voyage from Calcutta, improper food and diarrhoea. Spooner was left to read about it.

It did not surprise him that he had been denied the glory. He was accustomed to choice specimens or body parts being sent to more esteemed scientists; it happened often. He had even had to endure dissections performed by others before assembled Fellows in the Gardens, on occasion. The previous winter, Mr Brookes had spent two days delighting visitors with his anatomical examination of the male ostrich that had died in the menagerie. But that the orang utan's body had gone to Owen made it worse, somehow. The Royal College of Surgeons was part of the old guard of the medical world, as he saw it, maintaining the orthodoxies of patronage and conservatism, rather than the new meritocracy that challenged it, the men who worked their way to the top by learning and excellence rather than money and networks. It was a new meritocracy that he liked to think he was part of. He was encouraged by this show of the Society's commitment to serious science, at least, if not their choice of favoured anatomist. He thirsted to make proper scientific study at the Gardens, to show his employers that he was progressing. The Council had not responded to his report of last month so Spooner decided that the time had come to take matters into his own hands. Wasn't that what men like him did now? Men like Mr Youatt with his journal, refusing to toe the line.

One night in early November, he sat by candlelight at his desk in his rooms in Cook's Row, a fire ablaze in the grate. He wrote a letter to the Council, explaining that he needed more time

with the animals. And more time meant more money, to pay for
more working days at the Gardens. He wanted to make himself
a respectable, useful career there, to do good work for the Society and for his much-derided profession. (Besides, he was no
great fan of the private practice with which he had to supple-
ment the sixty pounds per annum salary he received if he was to
make a decent future for himself.) He simply explained that,
because of the great increase in the number of animals in the collection of late, *his time was necessarily more taken up than was at first*
agreed upon and that his present salary was too limited to allow him to
devote the additional attention which was now required.

It wasn't long before word was returned to him: *The Council see*
no reason for making any alteration in the salary hitherto allowed to the
surgeon of the establishment. At least now they were referring to
him as the surgeon rather than the medical attendant, he noticed.
It was a small sweetener for a bitter pill. He was disappointed, of
course, but he was not ready to give up yet, he knew that much.
Even if he did not get the pick of the specimens, where else could
he explore the inner design of so many creatures? There was no
Burke or Hare to snatch the bodies of monkeys and opossums
for him to work on. He would press on.

But change was in the cool November air, if not in the Zoological Society then certainly in the world beyond it. Two weeks
after the Council had given Spooner their curt response, the
Tory government fell, replaced by the Whigs who were calling
for electoral reform. First a new, more sober king on the throne,
and now a reforming government in Westminster. Spooner
observed it with some interest. Men such as he, without property but with some education and a profession, had something
to gain from the promised political reform. And this new spirit
of reform reached wider, sweeping through so many of the old
aristocratic worlds. The London University, now in its fifth

year, was a case in point, was it not? Much despised by the old medical schools and the Church, completely secular and run as a company, it was opening new doors for utilitarian, scientific men. It had a chair in comparative anatomy, and it was rumoured that Mr Youatt was soon to start a course on veterinary science. And private medical schools were being established to challenge the hegemony of the old aristocratic hospital schools, with their unfair systems of patronage, not to mention their old ideas. The more radical, uncontrolled energies scared him – that month there had been riots in rural communities not far from where he had grown up – but he wholeheartedly supported the more rational reform.

It was in this spirit that an idea began to take shape in Spooner's mind. If he couldn't set himself up purely through his work for the Society, he would have to be more creative in making his name. Why not establish a private school of veterinary anatomy himself? If he succeeded, it would be the first of its kind in London. Spooner did not have a radical agenda, like many of the new private medical schools, he just wanted to advance the knowledge of veterinarians, and make a little money while he did so. He wondered if he might even be able to acquire some specimens from the Gardens. That would certainly make his school unique. Over the winter of 1830, Charles Spooner set about making change a reality, as those around him – the Whigs, their followers, and the disgruntled workers alike – did their best to enforce it in a wider sense.

The Society might not have deemed it necessary to expend more money on the medical attendant in the care of the animals it already possessed, but there was no shortage of money to buy new ones. The miserable end of the orang utan had not quelled the enthusiasm for the acquisition of the globe's more exotic species; on the contrary, it meant that the thirst of the Fellows for such specimens to study – and to entertain their guests – had not been slaked. The Society's efforts to change how animals were exhibited in Britain had been a huge success: a quarter of a million visitors had passed through the Gardens' gates over the previous year to see the collection for themselves. It was such a success, indeed, that it was now faced with a rival. As well as a sister organization in Dublin, the ever-enterprising Mr Cross was in the process of establishing his own Zoological Society just south of the river. The hunt for more exciting attractions thus gained new impetus. Spooner was keenly aware of what it meant for him. His workload, already nigh on unmanageable, would increase. In May 1831, it got very big indeed: the Zoological Society of London acquired its first elephant.

It was purchased rather suddenly, at the bidding of the Society's anniversary meeting. The auction took place while the beast was aboard the ship that had transported it from Madras, by way of China, and the servants of the Establishment had just a few days to prepare for its arrival. Fuller collected it from the docks on a Friday evening, walking the giant beast through the darkened streets of London in just two hours, all the way to the Regent's Park. It had been quite a spectacle, judging from the accounts Spooner had read in the papers: 'His paces were so active as to compel the keepers who accompanied him to run frequently to keep up with him.' No wonder, when it had been cooped up in a ship's hold for nine long months! He read the enthusiastic reports with a pang of bitterness. Fuller was quite arrogant enough, he mused, and such celebrity could only make him worse.

And now Fuller was engaged to be married. The head keeper must be in receipt of a salary much larger than his own. Spooner wondered when he might be able to think of marriage and a family. He certainly couldn't on his sixty pounds a year. He reassured himself that he was on his way now, since he had taken

matters into his own hands. His school of anatomy had progressed so far that now he was acquiring his first pupils. It was
just a start, but he dared be optimistic: he knew how eager the
students of the college were for anatomical instruction. All the
same, for three days in the week his energies remained focused
on the animals he cared for at the Regent's Park.

When Spooner came into the Gardens on the Saturday after
the elephant's arrival, he made his way straight to the temporary
enclosure that had been prepared for it, against his better judge-
ment. He felt it somewhat unprofessional to take an interest in
the animal, as if it was any old menagerie attraction. As he made
his way through the manicured grounds in the early-summer
sunshine, he reassured himself that it was natural to want to
acquaint himself with an animal he might have to care for. It
had had an incredibly long journey, after all, and was unlikely to
be in good health, like so many of the animals when they arrived
from far-flung corners of the globe. As he approached the temporary home it had been accorded, in the North Garden, it
became clear that he need not have troubled himself: he would
not even be able to get close to it.

His view was almost completely obscured by admirers: people of all ages and sizes pressed firmly against the bars and each
other; children pushed handfuls of grass through the iron bars
and squealed with delight as a grey trunk stretched to receive
them. The newspaper articles about the elephant's arrival had
excited the citizens of London, a many-armed, many-voiced
mass of people who had found they could afford a shilling to see
the new attraction. Spooner did not wait his turn to get close to
the beast, but walked on. The time would come when it needed
his care.

When he was in early enough, before the crowds descended,
Spooner enjoyed watching the elephant. A 'noble' male, so the

papers said (and indeed he was), affectionately known as Jack. Such an odd creature, really, with its long, wrinkly trunk and its face that betrayed gentleness – sagacity, even – despite its great size. Jack instantly became the Gardens' star attraction and, as such, no care was spared it. Special accommodations were put into progress right away; a pond was begun in its enclosure in early July, to be ten feet deep and much wider, set in a turfed paddock with an appropriately large stable. The Elephant House was to be heated, like many others had been, and various means of accomplishing it were explored. The importance of natural light was also being taken into account by Mr Burton in his designs now. Conditions for the animals seemed to be improving and with the elephant a real sense of its natural habitation had been taken into account.

And yet Spooner could not help but fixate on the incongruity of those endeavours with the stall that had been set up next to the elephant's paddock by Mrs Fidd, the wife of one of the keepers. The buns, cakes and fruit she sold to eager visitors to feed to Jack could hardly be said to emulate the creature's life in a state of nature. At least, that was not how Spooner imagined the wilds of the Indian continent to be . . . *The Council must have sanctioned it*, he was told, when he made enquiries of the elephant's keeper, who had had the care of the beast during its passage, and was now attired in a dirt-coloured cloth jacket and trousers, with a fur cap, so that he looked the part. *Well, Mrs Fidd was not permitted to sell any liquors*, Spooner was informed, when he questioned whether such an excessive amount of unnatural food was appropriate.

Fuller, too, would hear none of it when Spooner mentioned it to him: *Did he know how much food the animal required? A few cakes made no difference!* He taunted Spooner with tales of the beast's appetite, the hats he had plucked from the heads of onlookers on the journey through London, the brooms the sailors had informed him Jack had consumed during the passage. Spooner wondered what the beast would look like inside. Somewhat akin to the bison he had dissected? He remembered reading about the dissection of Chuny, when Spooner was in Sheffield with Mr Jervis, how he had pored over the details even then. He wanted this elephant to stay alive.

Spooner kept thinking of Mr Youatt's first lecture at the London University, back in February, printed in full in the *Veterinarian*. Youatt had spoken of the influence of food on the production and modification of disease. He had also spoken of the impact of the removal of animals from natural situations and habitats, and 'the absurd practices' to which they were then subjected. That had stuck in Spooner's mind, especially as he watched, summer's day after day, the constant movement of cakes and buns from the hands of children or the ends of walking sticks and parasols into the elephant's greedy, ever-accepting trunk.

In the middle of July, Spooner learned that Fuller had been called in front of the Council to explain a complaint that had been reported to them, that the animals at the park suffered from the food given to them by the visitors. He had been thoroughly interrogated on the subject, by all accounts. Spooner was angry to learn that Fuller had apparently satisfied them that in no case had any injury been caused (how could *he* know when injury might not be immediately apparent?) and irritated that the Council set such store by the head keeper's word and not his own.

At least, Spooner was pleased to see, something was being done about the other ways in which the visitors so clearly mistreated the animals. One day he came in to see a sign being placed on boards situated around the grounds, asking that ladies did not touch the animals with their parasols, 'considerable injury having arisen from this practice'. He thought of the lion, Nero, who in January had succumbed to the breathing problems that had been plaguing him over the winter. The sign did not stop the prodding and poking altogether, but Spooner did notice a slight improvement. And something was also being done about the visitors themselves that summer. In August, it was ordered by the Council that the admissions policy be more strictly adhered to, that only Fellows of the Society and their guests, or those who really did have the written permission of a Fellow, be permitted through the gates. It seemed rather at odds with the mood of the day, Spooner thought, given the widespread calls for widening of the franchise, but at least it might stop the Gardens becoming such a circus.

That same month another order from the Council brought most welcome news to the medical attendant: a committee had been established to investigate the possibility of building a hospital on land newly acquired in the South Garden.

Spooner had not thought much further on the issue of the animals' diet, until he was dissecting a leopard one Saturday afternoon in late November. The animal was splayed on the table in front of him, its abdomen opened. The smell was not too unpleasant for it had not been long dead. His tools were laid out neatly on the bench next to him, just as he liked them. The room was well lit. It was a far cry from his usual working conditions. Today he was not hidden in a corner of the Gardens, or in the suffocating stable on Park Street: he was in his very own dissecting room.

His school of anatomy was now a reality. He'd found and taken eminently suitable premises, a house nearly opposite the Veterinary College, with a yard and building, formerly used as a stable, adjoining it. The Dissecting Room was at the heart of everything: it was where he gave his lectures and demonstrations. It had a large table at its centre, with benches for the students placed around it – carefully, so everyone had a good view. The school was in its infancy, but Spooner was attracting many students from the latest intake at the Veterinary College. He was talking to his friend Mr Morton, who worked as a dispenser at the college, about offering some lectures on *materia medica* there too.

Now, as he made the first midline incision into the leopard's beautifully spotted belly, he was watched intently by a group of his students and helped by another, who held the splayed limbs wide. The men were not much younger than himself (he had just turned twenty-five) yet were so far removed from him. Now they sat transfixed, in total silence as his knife cut through the skin and he pulled the abdomen apart to reveal its secrets. He knew those gathered around him could not quite believe their luck to be observing the dissection of an exotic carnivore at such close range. Spooner could not quite believe his own. An erstwhile inhabitant of the Gardens, the leopard had been very obviously dying, and Spooner had asked if he might see if it could be revived under his personal care, in the warmth of his premises in Camden Town. To his utter astonishment, it had been agreed that he could take it. Of course, no one expected it to live, and there were plenty of carnivores on display now, so one leopard was no longer of much consequence. The creature had died at the very moment the crate it had been lifted into was removed from the heated den into the cold November air. But Spooner had the body, which he now explored with his knife. He confidently explained to his students what he was doing as he examined the contents of the abdomen, even though he was rather surprised by what he had just found.

He had assumed that the leopard was suffering from ascites,

that that was the cause of its visibly swollen abdomen, but he discovered not an accumulation of fluid as he had expected, but an accumulation of fat, revealed again when he opened the thorax. He had seen such fatty deposits in dogs at Mr Youatt's. For those animals, it was generally believed that frequent light meals were more conducive to health than larger, more distant ones. Now he wondered if the same might be true for larger carnivores. It made sense to him that it was, yet the leopards and tigers and lions were fed but once a day, with four pounds of beef.

Why? he had asked Fuller the next day. *Because that is the way it is done. That is what they do at the Tower. That is what Mr Cross does . . .*

Spooner was not satisfied with such logic. He decided that this was his opportunity for study. He would do an experiment, explore the issue of the carnivores' diet in detail. He mentioned his thoughts to Mr Youatt at a meeting of the Veterinary Medical Society; Youatt had often told him he should focus more on the academic side of his work and not be led by his knife. It was suggested that Spooner might attend the next meeting of the Committee for Science and Correspondence, of which Mr Youatt was a member, to propose an experiment. He was getting increasingly close to the Council and its members, Spooner had noticed. A good thing, he supposed, based on the man's new standing in the rarefied world of science: he was now writing a series of popular books on zoology for the Society for the Diffusion of Useful Knowledge (a Whiggish organization, seeking to educate the masses in a constructive way) and his post at the university had been confirmed. He hoped Mr Youatt's meteoric rise was progress for the profession as a whole, that it might make the Society take him, Charles Spooner, more seriously, too.

The Committee of Science and Correspondence convened twice a month at the Bruton Street offices of the Zoological Society, and Spooner was invited to join it on the evening of Tuesday, the 13th of December. He spent the day at the Gardens, and found himself stealing glances at the clock that had been lately placed in the turret of the Llama House. He liked the clock. In its shadow, the Gardens' daily schedule assumed a new formality. Today, the light had disappeared so early from the sky that the new lamps, placed around the Gardens to help the keepers working after dark, were already lit, though the clock had not yet shown half past four. Spooner left the rather bleak Gardens with the last of the visitors, and went home to prepare himself.

He arrived at Bruton Street in good time for the eight o'clock start. The night was dark. The porter ushered him from the cold into the dimly lit entrance hall, then the inner hall, where he directed Spooner to deposit his umbrella in the stand. He followed as the porter carved their way through the dark corridors with a lamp, the glow of which fleetingly illuminated a number of rather formidable creatures as they passed by. Large birds. Vultures, he thought. They passed a couple of closed doors on the ground floor before they turned towards the third. Was that parrots he heard further down the hall? He did not have time to dwell on the thought for the room he was now being led into was part of the Museum, an awesome sight. He was surrounded by cases and shelves loaded with jars of small animals, fishes, and preparations of organs and other body parts. Horns and skulls covered the walls. Any floor space not taken up by cabinets was filled with a free-standing creature. The first that the porter's lamp revealed – something large and furry – startled him. Was it a white bear? He must see some animals here that he had treated, he thought. An orang utan! Was it the one that had died before he had had a chance to see it? As the lamplight revealed a panda, tigers crowded together in lifelike poses, skeletons of foxes and weasels, he felt as if he had stumbled upon a strange supernatural gathering, its members frozen in time in the darkness.

He must come back for a more detailed look one day, he determined, as they mounted the stairs that led up to the first floor. He had seen other anatomical collections but this cornucopia of stuffed beasts was, he was sure, unique. He seemed to recall they even had a cameleopard somewhere. The porter led him to the floor above, and left him at the door to a well-lit large room that was obviously the main meeting room; numerous baize-covered benches and cane-bottomed chairs surrounded the two tables in the middle. Here, too, the glow from the fine gas lamps dotted around the room and the chandelier overhead illuminated some intriguing objects of natural history, not least a pair of glass-fronted cases filled with fish. A comforting fire burned in the grate, and he walked gladly into the room that was welcoming to him, filled with the murmur of quiet, serious conversation.

A number of gentlemen were already assembled. Mr Youatt was not present, so Spooner stood near a small group conversing by the fire, ostensibly to warm himself. In time, others arrived. He saw Mr Owen come in. He was more than six feet tall, with a large head and eyes – you couldn't miss him. He recognized Dr Grant, Professor of Zoology and Comparative Anatomy at the University of London no less! Spooner was in esteemed company. The talk in the group was largely of the recent case of the so-called 'London Burkers' – the Resurrection Men from the East End, the body snatchers who had been hanged just last week for the murder of a young boy. Many knew the man to whom they'd tried to sell the body, Mr Partridge, a demonstrator in anatomy at King's and the Windmill Street theatre. It was at the latter theatre that, ironically, the bodies of the murdered men had ended up: thousands of people had queued to see the remains. Someone quipped that at least it showed how great the interest in anatomy was now. More seriously, those assembled all agreed it was high time for a change in the absurd laws, which were causing such tragedies and frustrating the men of science who were trying to lighten the darkness of ignorance. And the mood was one of change, after all: the Whigs had just launched their third Bill proposing political reform, and the feeling was that this one might actually get through.

The gentlemen took their seats and, at eight o'clock sharp, according to the clock in the room, the Chair commenced the evening's business. He was not, Spooner was sorry to see, one of the great men of science he shared the room with, but one of the Society's aristocratic supporters. He presented some specimens he had brought for the occasion: two hybrid ducks he had bred. The preserved birds were passed around for inspection. Spooner had little time for what he saw as indulgence, for those whose aim was breeding and domesticating species for their estates and dinner tables.

He was far more interested in the young puma, which was exhibited next. It had been born dead in the Gardens. Preserved, it looked a sorry creature indeed. But there was no time to linger on it for there was much to get through. Mr Yarrell, the well-known naturalist and friend of Mr Youatt, read notes from his dissection of a large conger eel, and passed around preparations of the bladder and roe of the individual in question. But it was, of course, Mr Owen who commanded the room's attention. Recently returned from a trip to Paris, where he had spent time with the famous naturalist Georges Cuvier, he was the man of the moment. He exhibited the organs of generation of a female kangaroo. This was a creature Spooner had known in life, killed just the previous week, gored by the axis deer. He had been there the day it had happened, poor beast. Owen spoke

(somewhat gratuitously, Spooner thought) of the great anatomists he had been with in Paris. Even the radical thinker
Monsieur Geoffroy St-Hilaire, with his theories of the continuous chain of life and the possibility of the transmutation of
species, which the conventional Owen certainly did not share.

Finally, it was Spooner's turn. As a non-member, the Chairman introduced him to the Committee. The assembled were by
now growing restless, and he was a little nervous, so he tried to
keep it simple. He explained what he had found in the leopard:
the excessive depositions of fat in the thorax and abdomen. Mr
Owen commanded the discussion that followed, though
Spooner eventually succeeded in expressing his professional
opinion *that distant periods of feeding with full meals occasioned corpu-
lence and disease of skin, while frequent and more sparing meals led to the
recovery of health and activity.* He explained that this was corrobo-
rated by his observations on dogs. He enjoyed the reaction of the
assembled gentlemen: they listened to him. Mr Cox, a medical
man and one of the more radical of the Fellows (he had been
intrigued to learn of the leopard's immediate death upon its
exposure to the cold: he had an interest in the subject of the tem-
peratures at which exotic beasts could survive), said he thought
it worth undertaking a scientific experiment into the matter,
and put forward a motion. Mr Owen himself seconded it. The
motion was carried.

Spooner received the final approval of the Council a few days
before Christmas. The experiments in varying the frequency
and size of meals were to be tried on two leopards, two hyenas
and two ocelots. It was welcome news to the young man; an
exciting prospect for the coming year. Fuller did not seem so
pleased. It would fall to him to carry out the experiments, to
vary a routine to which man and beast had become accustomed.
Two hyenas were weighed on the 23rd of December, and the

experiment commenced: from that day on, one was to be given their daily three pounds of beef in two smaller meals, morning and night; the other was to be fed as normal, once a day, in the evening. They would still be fasted for one day a week, as all the carnivorous animals were. The inconvenience did not go unremarked upon by the keepers, who would now have to oversee an additional morning feed. The experiments on the leopards would commence in the new year.

It was a busy time for them all. The King had now donated to the Society the beasts from the remaining Royal Menagerie at the Tower of London, where exotic animals had been kept for the amusement of the court for at least six hundred years. It confirmed the Gardens of the Zoological Society of London as the appropriate home for the national zoological collection (though there might have been less noble motives for the donation: there had been a number of incidents of late, with animals attacking keepers and visitors). A leopard and a jackal arrived on Christmas Eve. Two lions, two leopards and a number of monkeys joined them in their new home a few days later, and the Tower's famous grizzly bear was also expected. Spooner's anxiety at this further increase of his workload was softened by the sense of achievement he felt at having secured the experiments: his first breakthrough in the two and a half years he had been at the Gardens. Nothing had happened regarding the hospital (the committee that had been established to investigate it had obviously not deemed it necessary). But he had this.

For months the newspapers had been listing cases of the Cholera morbus that had been spreading in the north of the country. In February it hit London. After the many painful weeks spent waiting for it, it was almost a bitter relief that it was come. Thankfully, it was confined to the East End for now. Spooner read with interest of the treatments suggested: immediate bleeding, purging, camphor and laudanum featured most frequently in the articles and pamphlets that flooded the capital. He was intrigued by discussions of the cause of the disease. For if the cholera was atmospheric, as widely supposed, he feared not only for himself: could deleterious miasmata, transmitted through the atmosphere, affect his animal charges? But he had more pressing concerns: his experiments.

Fuller claimed the leopard that was being fed less frequently was more ferocious than normal. He said the hyena was in low spirits. Spooner maintained that the only scientific way to assess the results was by weight. In mid-February, the reckoning took place. The leopard that had been fed twice daily had lost half a pound, the other had gained one. The hyena that was fed twice a day had also lost weight. Fuller was satisfied that this was sufficient evidence that normal feeding routines could and should be resumed. Spooner wondered if it might mean exactly the opposite. It was Fuller who wrote the report that was submitted to the Council.

Spooner was not yet ready to give up. More experiments could be performed. The Council agreed in late February to another: the two leopards and the two hyenas were to be fed once a day, but with differing quantities.

The experiments were a source of interest for Spooner in what were otherwise bleak times. The cholera did not abate. On the 21st of March, the King called for a day of fasting: the nation must humble itself before God, in the hope that He would lift the scourge that blighted it. Spooner did not believe the Lord was responsible. It was a matter for science: what caused its spread? But still no one knew, so the people prayed. The Gardens were opened but to Fellows and their companions only, while from pulpits across the metropolis words of repentance were spoken. Outside the churches, on the streets, other concerns were dominant. Thousands of protesters of the National Union of the Working Classes clashed with hundreds of men from the newly formed Metropolitan Police Force – established for precisely the purpose of maintaining order over the increasingly large and unruly citizenry. The Third Reform Bill was being debated by the House of Lords. Spooner hoped it would get through this time and that the welcome prospect of reform would not turn into the spectre of revolution. He found such disturbances of the masses terrifying, trapped as he was in the wild and dirty city.

Life at one of its most popular attractions, the Gardens of the Zoological Society, went on as ever. Discussions about the restrictive admissions policy began to appear in the newspapers – better enforcement had caused some consternation, it seemed – but that was as far as any talk of reform went. The public at large was not yet permitted access even to the park, which remained the preserve of the residents and the 'carriage set', who were allowed to pass through it.

A few days after the disturbances beyond the Gardens' leafy seclusion, the new President of the Society, Lord Stanley, took the head keeper's report on the feeding experiments to the Committee of Science and Correspondence. It contained Fuller's opinion that not only had it been proved it was not beneficial to alter the feeding regimes but that the alteration to the current practice of feeding carnivores twice a day was actually potentially dangerous, as it adversely affected their behaviour. For the time being, change would not come to the Regent's Park. Certainly not as a result of Charles Spooner's feeding experiments, anyway.

By the beginning of 1833 much *had* changed, both within the herbaceous borders of the Gardens of the Zoological Society of London and without. The cholera had been replaced by an influenza epidemic, which was far more egalitarian in its choice of victim. The Reform Bill had been passed in the summer of 1832, and the first general election under the reformed parliamentary system had slashed the Tory presence in the House of Commons.

Within the Gardens, change had been less radical, though the number of visitors had declined rather steeply over the previous year, no doubt thanks to the troubles in the capital. Overall, 40,000 fewer people had entered the grounds in 1832 than the year before. Despite that, the expansion of the establishment had continued, with more land taken in the South Garden, which had been filled with many new animals, in ever finer accommodation, all well heated, and now increasingly ventilated, too. Mr Cox had begun his own investigations into the atmospheric factors – humidity and temperature, as well as space for exercise and food provision – affecting the health of the animals, of which he was keeping the Council informed.

Despite his frustrations – the continued absence of a dedicated infirmary, the lack of time he had there (neither of which was likely to be remedied after the decline in the Society's income) – the medical attendant continued with relative satisfaction. He for one did not mind that fewer people were bothering him and the animals in his care. Besides, his school was doing rather well. He was charging students three pounds each for his course in demonstrative anatomy, and spent more time than ever doing what he loved: dissections. His two professional undertakings complemented each other nicely. Spooner could boast of his breadth of experience to his students, and continue to bring away the occasional choice specimen to dissect in front of them. In the middle of January, the Council allowed him the body of a rhesus monkey, which had come from the Tower Menagerie. The following week, when he attended the annual dinner of veterinary students from the college, he did so with his head held high. Mr Youatt was there too, as was surgeon-turned-zoologist Mr Bennett, the Secretary of the Society. Spooner noticed how friendly the two seemed.

On Monday, the 13th of May, London was shaken by a riot in Clerkenwell, when police clashed violently with working-class radicals, who were disappointed that the promised political reform had not gone far enough. Then, just a week later, Charles Spooner suffered a far greater shock. He was called into the Superintendent's office one morning to be informed that his services were no longer required. He would receive a month's salary and a gratuity of twenty pounds, in recognition of his four years of service. Spooner was much taken aback: *were they doing away with the post of medical attendant?*

Miller did not flinch. *In a sense, yes. They were taking on a Medical Superintendent instead.*

Spooner was quick to temper, and it showed now. His voice was raised. *What had he done wrong? What charge had been made against him?* Mr Miller insisted there was no criticism of his conduct. The Council had decided there was someone better suited to the needs of the establishment.

Mr Youatt was to start the following week.

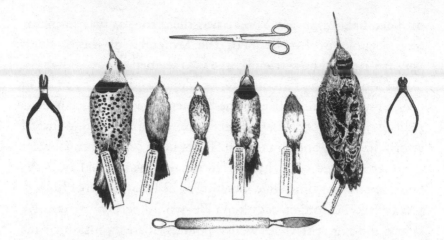

4. The Business of Bird Skins

Mr John Gould, Animal Preserver,
1830–33

When the new King acceded to the throne in the summer of 1830, he donated not only the living animals of his more extravagant predecessor's private collection to the Zoological Society of London, but many of the preserved ones too. Which was how it came to pass that in late August 1830, Mr John Gould was confronted with his most famous work of resurrection once again.

It was a Monday morning, one of the last days of a wet summer, and the chief animal preserver to the Zoological Society of London had walked to Bruton Street, as he always did, from Broad Street in Soho. Very recently (just this past week, in fact) his journey had been reduced by a few paces. A few very important paces: he and his wife had lately taken their own house at number 20, having lived for the first eighteen months of their marriage at number 12 with her relative, one Mr Coxen, an animal stuffer through whom they had met. As well as Gould's own salary of a hundred pounds a year, and the income from his private taxidermy business, his wife Elizabeth was now earning. He was contributing her careful drawings of his stuffed birds (done under his tutelage, of course) to the eminent ornithologist William Jardine's latest publication. They were moving up in the world. *He* was moving up in the world.

Mr Gould, a round-faced, soft-chinned man just approaching his twenty-sixth birthday, arrived at the door to 33 Bruton Street, having navigated his way between the rattling carriages, clunking carts and endless horses that choked Regent Street at this time of the morning. (It was a small mercy that the huge new omnibuses were not allowed so far into the city.) Gould let himself into the fine townhouse, his place of employment these three years past. He made his way through the entrance and inner halls to the office, just as he did every morning, to see what had been delivered from the Gardens of the Zoological Society along with the daily report from Mr Miller, the Superintendent.

Gould saw that Leigh, the clerk, was already at work before he had even entered the office, for his hat was hanging on the peg next to the framed map of the farm at Kingston Hill. The animals that lived (or, more exactly, died) at the farm were not generally his concern: he was called to deal only with those from the Gardens. And it was at this time of year, as the weather cooled, that the deliveries for his department started to pour in. The messenger had clearly just been to the park, as Leigh was pinning the weekend's reports to the boards behind his desk and the familiar grubby sacks lay on the table; two that morning. Sunlight crept in through the large windows, and the stove was not lit for it was mild. A good thing, Gould thought, as he turned to the sacks before him – he could smell the first sweet notes of decay: not too unpleasant, yet, but the animals must have been dead a few days now. On hearing Gould's footsteps, Leigh turned and bade him good day.

Gould mumbled a reply as he looked into the first sack: a

tortoise. They always came in at this time of year, and were not of much interest to him. He saw a white rat in there too. He opened the larger sack, and peeled back the cloth in which the body was wrapped, exposing a monkey. A baboon. He moved the beast – cold and firm to the touch – the better to observe its elongated face. It had a disproportionately large head, and on turning it, its striking blue and purple markings were revealed. Gould searched his mind to ascertain whether he'd seen this colourful species before. He could not remember having one here, but he recalled a similar creature at the Exeter 'Change. Jerry? Yes, Jerry the . . . He was on the brink of it when Leigh read to him from the Gardens Report: *It says here it's a ribbed-nose baboon.* Gould simply nodded, to imply that he already knew. Jerry the Mandrill – or ribbed-nose baboon, yes.

He was still not always confident at identifying species, or comfortable with the Latin lexis, and as for the varying systems of classification, well, they were still a little beyond him. It was frighteningly hard to keep up, especially now, when mankind's quest to uncover and identify each and every creature of God's world had sped up a thousand-fold in the wake of the new trade routes carved across it. Most of the fruits of those far-flung searches seemed to end up here. From Van Diemen's Land to the Cape of Good Hope, from Calcutta to Hudson Bay to the Tierra del Fuego they came to him: packing cases and crates filled with bird skins and beasts in brine and spirits destined for his workshop. There he resurrected them, turning the skins and pickled bodies back into semblances of the living wonders crafted by the Creator, preserved, describable, classifiable by the men of science whose activities revolved around the offices and Museum at 33 Bruton Street. Gould, too, was learning to describe them, to spot the minute differences that separated one species from another, an undiscovered species from those already known to man.

Many of the animals he worked on came from much nearer

home, of course. The menagerie at Regent's Park – though the more frivolous arm of the Society's activities, according to those who were more seriously engaged in making sense of the Animal Kingdom rather than just marvelling at it – had its uses. It was one of his biggest suppliers of animals. Like this *Cynocephalus* . . . Was that the designation for baboon? He liked to test himself. Gould looked down at it. It was quite unusual, and had not been cut up by Mr Spooner. Did that mean Mr Owen wanted to dissect it? The skin would need to be sent to the tanners pretty swiftly. He would ask Mr Vigors. A founder member of the Society and its current Secretary, Mr Vigors was temporarily overseeing the running of the Museum while they looked for a permanent superintendent. Gould liked to have an excuse to engage with him whenever he could: the Irishman was an excellent ornithologist, more or less in charge of the Society's scientific policy (he was working on a system of classification for the collections, according to the Quinary arrangement), and he had become a mentor of sorts to the animal preserver. Gould had clearly already impressed him with his dogged work and his dedication to detail, and he wanted to cement their relationship. He continued along the hallway, and looked into Vigors's office, but was disappointed to find the seat empty behind the desk. In fact, the room was devoid of life; unusual for this building. There was only the next best thing in it: four cases filled with his creations, modelled to *mimic* life. He preferred animals thus. Gould recalled the monkey that had once resided in here, terrorizing him – everyone. That creature was long gone now, but there were usually plenty of others, along with a dedicated keeper to look after all the living things that inhabited the building, especially in the winter months.

Gould walked on. The passage was lined with birds of prey that he had made up. The vultures: *Sarcoramphus californianus*, *Sarcoramphus papa* . . . He knew all their proper names now, after

years of mornings and evenings recalling them as he passed. He
continued past the Lower Museum Room, and the next closed
doorway, whose secrets leaked out in a series of squawks. They
knew it as the Parrot Room. Three extra cages and a macaw
stand had been delivered a few weeks ago. A young artist,
Edward Lear, had spent much time in there over the past summer, quietly observing and sketching the parrots. Gould could
not understand why he insisted on drawing them *in life*. He
could scarcely imagine a more preposterous way to waste one's
time! A man less confident than Gould might have felt it under-
mined his own craft . . . but he sincerely believed that the only
way to observe an animal was in the perfect state of a preserved
specimen, particularly ever-mobile birds. He and any naturalist
of repute. That said, he could not deny that the odd-looking
young man was good with a pen. Very good, in fact. So good
that Gould had made every effort to acquaint himself with Mr
Lear and his unconventional methods. He had gladly lent him
preserved specimens from his own collection of bird skins, from
which he was convinced he would produce more accurate repre-
sentations. But Gould was not being helpful out of generosity:
rather, he sensed Lear might be useful.

He made his way up the back staircase to the second floor. On
the first floor, the two large rooms at the front were occupied by
the meeting room and another Museum room, stuffed with
cases of different sizes. He manoeuvred his body around a case
of his birds for which there was space only in the hallway, and
now came to Mr Rees's room. The Assistant Secretary was
already at his desk and Gould nodded a greeting to him as he
went by. But Rees called to him: *We should be getting your giraffe
today, Mr Gould! Mr Vigors shall have to think where to put it!*

Gould replied cursorily, and continued to his Stuffing Room.
It was not exactly, as Rees had put it, *his* giraffe, though he liked
that Rees had called it so. Strictly speaking, it was the King's

giraffe. But he had indeed made it, just under a year ago. He had made the giraffe – and the giraffe had made him. It had been in the papers: Mr John Gould, chief animal preserver at the Zoological Society of London, entrusted by the King with the preservation of the most beloved beast in his menagerie. It had been the first giraffe ever seen on English soil, known by the masses as a cameleopard, for that was what they looked like, presented to George IV by the Pasha of Egypt. Gould had stuffed some birds and deer for the Royal Household – basic creatures in any taxidermist's repertoire – but a giraffe? The King's favourite pet? A creature that every man in the country knew about? That was clearly another matter, something special . . .

He had done a fine job of it. For John Gould was not a man to fear opportunities when they stared at him. He seized them calmly, held them just firmly enough, like a freshly expired bird he was about to start work on. Held them firmly and did what had to be done. So he had tackled the giraffe. Incidentally, it was not the biggest creature he had worked on (he had helped in the dissection of a whale that beached at Whitstable), though it was the most complex. A week it had taken him just to pare down the skin. He had worked hard, minutely, methodically, until he had made it his own, until he had given it new, more perfect life. And so John Gould had become famous, taxidermist to the King! He had made almost one hundred and fifty pounds from it, too, a year and a half's salary.

He had come a long way from the son of a humble gardener, hadn't he? His own taxidermy business at twenty years of age, then winning, three years later, the newly created post of animal preserver at the prestigious Zoological Society (by dint of the superiority of his stuffing over that of his competitors, when all were asked by Mr Vigors for an exhibition of their skill). And he alone knew how far he had to go yet. He had quiet, unshakeable ambitions, did John Gould. As well as a keen eye for the correct angle of a neck (however long), a strong stomach and a steady hand, traits that had served him so well, but which he secretly hoped he wouldn't need for much longer. He did not plan to continue as a taxidermist for ever, not even if the giraffe had made him the most famous animal stuffer in the land.

He would be glad to see it back here. It would remind him every day not only of where he had come from but of where he still wanted to go. John Gould was not a gentleman, not a trained naturalist, not a traveller. He could not afford the subscriptions into the eminent societies – the Geographical or Geological Society, not even the Zoological Society he served. (Though he had been made an associate, non-paying member of the Linnean Society a few months previously, thanks to the patronage of Vigors and other members of the Council.) John Gould was not even a man of much education: schooling had not been deemed necessary for the son of a gardener, trained to follow in his father's footsteps. But what he had not been given, Gould would take for himself. For here he was, in a rare place where there were possibilities for men like him. It was a place where *knowledge* meant power, not money or birth. Here, in the cluttered building on Bruton Street, where the order of the natural world was being slowly revealed, described and classified, skin by skin, creature by creature, piece by piece. Here, where he was becoming an expert in a time when experts were sorely needed. John Gould knew the secrets of the world would come to him in time. He had only to make sure he was ready to grab them. Before anyone else did.

Finding a space for a giraffe at 33 Bruton Street would be no easy matter. It was now more than four years since the Society had been established and this building taken for its purposes. Four years in which specimens had arrived at its door almost daily – and much attention had been focused on the Museum by the Council this past year. In the menagerie, the Society was limited by what could be kept alive, but here the ambition was to have a collection of creatures that illustrated God's wondrous Creation in as close to its glorious entirety as possible. Then it could be studied properly and therefore understood properly. The huge private collection of the late Sir Stamford Raffles, donated after his death by his widow, formed the basis of the Museum, along with much of Mr Vigors's personal collection. Additional donations from corresponding members (not to mention ambassadors, explorers, surveyors and tradesmen who were so inclined) and specimens from the Gardens were supplemented by purchases. Mr Vigors had recently bought a number of bird skins from Joshua Brookes, who was closing his Museum of Comparative Anatomy. (Unfortunately the hippopotamus specimen Brookes had offered the Society had proved too expensive to transport.) With Vigors at the helm, excellent progress was being made in the quest to accumulate an unparalleled collection.

The previous year a basic catalogue had been put together of some of the hundreds of specimens already in the Society's possession. More recently, many additional cases had been erected in the Museum to accommodate them and, in addition to John Gould and his assistant, John Gilbert, who were responsible for the setting up and display of the more interesting specimens, another assistant had been employed to look after the arrangement of shells, insects and other smaller subjects. But the Museum was packed to bursting, and many of the specimens on display were not even labelled. Then there were the cases in the storeroom, most of which had not been looked at more than once before they were put away. The jars of insects, bottles of fishes, crates of skins and skulls and bones, all had yet to be dealt with. Vigors was actively seeking a superintendent to take charge of it all, to arrange the collection in a way that it could be enjoyed and, more importantly, studied.

The most pressing need, however, recognized by the Council,

which met every second Wednesday, if not more frequently, was to find the collection a new home altogether. The limits of Bruton Street's architecture conspired against them: there was simply not enough space. In the meantime, John Gould's giraffe and its skeleton were placed in the Parrot Room.

In October 1830, after many months of searching, Mr Vigors appointed the Museum's first Curator, Mr Martin. Mr John Canton, the erstwhile assistant in the Museum, was dispensed with and a more suitable candidate, Mr Charles du Bois, employed in his place. Together, they set to work on the gargantuan task of finding order in the chaos. All the while their workload was added to by messengers, postmen and errand boys, knocking at the door with more cases to be opened, more specimens to be investigated. John Gould worked on upstairs, diligently, doggedly, as he always did – and made sure to impress Mr Martin.

It was not one of Gould's creations but a live animal that arrived at 33 Bruton Street and caused the greatest excitement that October. As summer paled to winter, many living, breathing, furred and feathered beasts were delivered there for safe keeping, in the annual exodus of the tender creatures from Regent's Park. But one arrived from much further afield: a young male orang utan, sent from Calcutta. George Swinton, Chief Secretary to the East India Company's Governor-General in India, was a zealous corresponding member of the Society and had sent the orang utan and a leopard. The leopard escaped on board the ship and was shot dead. The orang utan survived the passage but, upon its arrival in England, was too ill to be taken to the Gardens immediately so it was decided it should stay at Bruton Street, where it was warm and dry, to recover its health. Swinton had previously sent the Society a female orang utan, albeit preserved in spirits. When he first saw it, John Gould knew he would soon take possession of this one, too.

It was hard to believe the tales that the sailor who had cared for it brought with the half-dead creature: tales of him eating with silverware at the ship's table, taking himself to taverns to order his own breakfast. It could do nothing for itself now. It was put into a cage in the Parrot Room, where the stove was kept constantly stoked by Thomas Moore, the porter, who lived in the building. The Society's Fellows flocked to see it, though it was little more than a furry bag of bones, normally limp in the arms of a woman brought in to nurse it. A furry bag of bones . . . That was how John Gould saw it. He, too, called in to view the beast. To satisfy his own curiosity, yes, but also out of professional duty. It was always easier to stuff a creature one had seen alive. He wondered how useful his sketches of the sorry-looking creature might be when it came to mounting it in a lifelike pose. But he thought it best to do what he could. He did not rush his observations, though he did not relish being in the over-warm room with the dying beast, listening to its horribly laboured breathing. He would have preferred to be upstairs with those already deceased. His work, now as always, came above his own wants.

The animal preserver was actually far more interested in something else that came into the offices around that time: the first folios of Lear's *Illustrations of the Family of Psittacidae, or Parrots*, a work he was producing from the drawings he had made over many months observing the birds in the Society's collection. Lear had planned fourteen fascicules, priced at ten shillings each, and by the end of October the first two were ready to be sent out to the 175 subscribers he had engaged. Gould pored over them when Lear dropped them into Bruton Street; he had eagerly awaited them, though betrayed only a passing interest to their young author. His curiosity was justified. They were quite unlike anything he had seen before: life-sized plates of beautifully drawn and coloured birds that almost fluttered on the page before him. Lear had used the relatively new process of lithography – and exploited its true possibilities for the first time, it seemed. Never had birds looked like this on paper before: colourful, soft, alive.

Birds were John Gould's real passion. His only passion, perhaps, and where it had all begun. He had learned to stuff them when he was just a lad living at Windsor, where his father worked at the Royal Gardens. He should have been more interested in the living botanical specimens it was expected he would go on to tend, but he had set up his first little business, preserving and mounting the finest birds killed by the gardeners and gamekeepers to sell to the boys at nearby Eton College. He found he had a real knack for the careful, precise work of taxidermy. He would study the lifeless body of the bird intently, while it was whole, looking at the plumpness of the breast, the natural fall of the wing and splay of the tail feathers. He would commit it to the memory of his eyes and hands. Then and only then would he take it apart, slicing its belly and breast from throat to rump, and peeling off the skin to reveal the purple flesh beneath, the surface strangely, beautifully iridescent when first exposed. He was precise enough to keep intact both the skin and the membrane on the meat. It was neater that way, keeping the innards where they belonged. Then came the complicated parts: turning the legs and wings and tail inside out, cleaning the bones while preserving the integrity of the skin. He soon learned that the best way to proceed was to keep the feathers moistened and out of the way while he worked; to keep the skin damp so it didn't tear or break and could be manipulated inside out over the head once he'd cut off the skinned body and neck. He kept the mass of meat for reference when he came to reconstruct the bird later.

He learned how to wield each tool, how to keep his blades sharp, when to use a knife and when a flesher. He quickly and naturally absorbed the anatomy of the bird, learned how each bit bent and where everything sat in life; as he felt his way around a skull encased in the skin of the body stretched back over it, he was not blind for he could picture the shape and the layout all the while. He learned that a waterfowl was structurally different from a bird of prey and both were different from the smaller birds. He always looked for the clues that each little body gave him, always worked to the unique model of the bird he held in his hands at that moment. His natural seriousness meant he never grew complacent. He made mistakes, yes – a snapped beak, a lost clump of feathers, or he left too much flesh on the skin or a joint so the maggots came from inside out – but each he made only once. And then he had learned to transfer the art he had perfected from birds to other creatures. Even to a giraffe. But he always loved best the delicate puzzle of a bird.

And now, before him, he saw a means of capturing the wonderful, subtle beauty of the creatures he loved in a new way: on the page. Lear's talent was acknowledged by the scientific world, and he was made an associate of the Linnean Society the very day after publication. But Gould saw more than talent in Lear's beautiful work: he knew a business opportunity when he saw one. Natural history was fast becoming a most popular pursuit; beetle-, shell- and butterfly-collecting were fashionable hobbies, particularly for the idle middle classes. And these people – people with money to spare as well as time – wanted not only to see the beauty of God's natural world, they wanted to learn about it. The market for works of natural history was growing all the time, from those published for the masses by the Society for the Diffusion of Useful Knowledge to the expert works of ornithologists like John James Audubon or William Swainson. Gould saw before him, in Lear's beautiful, delicate, detailed works, a way of revolutionizing it. He knew about lithography and had discussed it with Lear: there was no need for an engraver to transfer the artist's drawings to a metal plate for the artist could draw directly on the lithographic stone. That made it accessible to the small producer. Lear – feeble and strange, no businessman – was not up to the task of exploiting its potential. But John Gould was. He had long known that, at the centre of a network of natural historians which spanned the globe, he was in the right place to do something remarkable. Now he saw the means to do it too.

He took a copy of Lear's work home with him to show Elizabeth. She was seven months pregnant with their second child. They had lost the first babe and she was anxious about the one in her belly. But Elizabeth worked on through it, turning out the drawings of her husband's birds as he instructed. She was a useful, practical woman, a former governess, educated and accustomed to work. That was why he had married her. Now John Gould told his wife that she must learn lithography. He would persuade Lear to teach her. They would create their own work of ornithology, just as beautiful as this one. In Lear's work he saw a future for himself, as bright and perfect as the lithographs themselves. He had found the method; he just needed to find the subject.

On its third day at Bruton Street, the orang utan became the concern of the Preserving Department, as Gould (and most of his colleagues) had predicted. A now well-practised process was begun where it would end, many months later.

The Stuffing Room was at the rear of the second floor. This was Gould's kingdom, his domain. It was a busy workroom, but there was order. It was lined with shelves holding the bottles and jars of his craft. Some were filled with chemicals and substances he used in the preserving process: camphor, ground arsenic, soap, potassium carbonate and chalk. Others contained small specimens in spirits, awaiting attention. Drawers hid the skins yet to be dealt with, to be dampened and softened to make them supple again. Tables around the edges of the room were crowded with the creatures they were already working on, wires and needles protruding from stuffed bodies as the skins and feathers stiffened in place. The inner room was lined with shelves, groaning under the weight of yet more animals at various stages of preservation. (The Society had just had a delivery of 171 Indian birds from the Asiatic Society in Calcutta, the results of a geological survey of the Ganges and the mountains of Upper Hindustan by Captain Franklin.) The smoke from the stove did not mask the room's unique smell – a mixture of the chemicals they used, the unusual odour of the skins drying out and the residue of the meat they had cut from them. It was so familiar that it had become comforting.

Gould's assistant, Gilbert, carried the dead orang utan, a most cumbersome load, upstairs from the Parrot Room, aided by the porter, Moore. The beast was thought to have been only four years old but it was already quite sizeable so negotiating the crowded corridors, its long limbs swinging as they went, was no easy matter. Gould awaited them, standing before one of the large tables, the one with the great vice, his notes to hand. When they came through the doorway, with the body of the orang utan between them, he stepped back to allow them to place it on the table. Moore scuttled off; Gould and Gilbert got to work. Time was always of the essence for the taxidermist, but it was especially the case for large mammals as their decay was very rapid, and the orang utan had died some hours ago. The stiffening of its muscles was already easing off – Gould could see that as he watched Gilbert arrange the beast on its back, limbs wide. They then stood before it in silence. Its fur was a bright orange-red, surprisingly long and spraying out from its body, like the unkempt hair of a child. At the end of the long arms (so much longer than its legs), the hands were closed in loose fists, and the feet were remarkably similar. Its head – with a light, furless muzzle, almost the colour of human skin – dropped to one side, the eyes open as if they were looking into the corner of the room. It was now obvious how emaciated the creature was. Beneath the prominent ribs the torso fell away in a sharp concavity to protruding hipbones. They stood and looked the beast over, the silence broken only by the whisper of the stove in the corner.

They had prepared and sharpened their large skinning knives, which were laid in readiness on the table next to them. But Gould did not reach for his, not yet: the measuring and observations must come first. He was a meticulous worker and he knew that it was at this stage that a taxidermist did his most important work. He checked the notes he had made of the creature a few days previously and took extra measurements around the neck area – it was there that distortion and stretching were most likely to occur. Satisfied, he moved aside to let Gilbert stuff the creature's mouth with cotton, to prevent any moisture leaking out, and prepare the powdered chalk to absorb any blood. Only then did Gould reach for his knife. He brushed the hair carefully out of the way on the midline of the body to reveal the pale skin beneath, and made a single characteristically neat incision from chin to genitals. Yes, it was a good first cut: perfectly skin-deep. The aim was to make as few incisions as possible to preserve the integrity of the skin and what lay beneath. Not only because Gould did not want any intestines or blood to soil the fur, but also because the body was destined for the Dissecting Room above.

Letters had already been sent out to those Fellows who might like to watch Mr Owen perform the post-mortem. Once Gould and Gilbert had removed the skin, the naked carcass would be carried up the flight of stairs and laid upon the dissecting table. Many pairs of living eyes would answer the call to crowd around the body of such an interesting creature, straining to see as Mr

Owen's knife cut and pulled it apart. The Preserving Department downstairs, meanwhile, would continue, carefully paring down the huge skin. It was slow work. Only when every last bit of meat was removed and the skin was thin and supple could it be sent to the tanners. Once Owen's examination was complete, the choice organs and muscles – anything deemed of special interest – would be preserved in jars of spirits for the purposes of future examination. The plundered carcass would be taken to the Macerating Room in the stables at Camden Town, where the skeletonizing process would commence. Nothing would be wasted that could be of scientific value. Skin and skeleton would eventually be returned to Bruton Street, both to be displayed in the Museum – if they could find a space for it – after John Gould had worked his magic, of course.

On the evening of the 9th of November, 1830, Mr Owen presented the results of his investigations upon the orang utan at the first ever meeting of the Committee of Science and Correspondence. On the day of the meeting, the Museum staff were in a state of some excitement. The Committee was intended to unite those who could attend its meetings in person (the Council members, Vigors, Sabine, Youatt and other such experts) and corresponding members working in the field, and act as a means to coordinate the acquisition of live donations. Furthermore, it recognized the serious scientific contribution of which the Society was capable, and presented a new forum in which to develop it. As such it was a victory, of sorts, for those who worked on this side of the Society's affairs in the Museum.

These were exciting times indeed – both within the walls of 33 Bruton Street and beyond. A week after the gentlemen had filed into the meeting room on the first floor to listen to the fascinating remarks of Mr Owen on the late orang utan, the Tory government was toppled. John Gould took no interest in the political struggles that were rumbling throughout the country, however, and did not add his voice to those calling for reform. He was finding ways to make himself heard in his own way. He believed that, in time, he would take his own seat at the table in the first-floor meeting room, among the elite men of science who were deciphering the natural world together. He hoped he would not have to wait too long. He was on his way now. He had found a special collection of birds, a special collection indeed. This, he had decided, was to be the subject of his first work of ornithology.

Perhaps he had already come across it when he first held Lear's plates in his hands. Perhaps he knew then what he would do. Gould himself liked to perpetuate the mystery of where and when he came across the collection that would make him famous (at least in the circles he cared about). Perhaps he had it from Mr Leadbeater, trader in bird skins, or one of his other contacts. (He had made it his business to know all the bird dealers, collectors and ornithologists in London and beyond, and at Bruton Street, he was superbly placed to do so.) Whatever its provenance, by the middle of November, a remarkable collection of more than a hundred bird skins from the largely unexplored region of the Himalaya Mountains had found their way into the personal possession of Mr John Gould.

It was obvious when he first laid eyes upon the collection that the birds he saw before him were not only beautiful but also largely undescribed. He was known for his sharp eye for detail. Even Mr Vigors had sung praises of his observational skills at a meeting of the Zoological Club of the Linnean Society, when Gould had pointed out that a bird mislabelled as a redstart was in fact a new species of warbler. But if John Gould knew the extent of his own talent, he also knew its limits. He was no ornithologist, not yet. In fact, he had no great love for the systematic, time-consuming work of identification and classification. Nor could he commit the details of a bird to paper as he could to a dried-out skin stuffed with wire and wood wool. He was no draughtsman. Yet John Gould knew his own talents – and one of his greatest was how to spot others who could help where he was deficient. His wife could draw. And take his instructions. He would ask Mr Vigors to identify the birds and provide the text (with a welcome dose of prestige) to the work he had planned. He, John Gould, would oversee it all. Vigors agreed to help – how could an ornithologist (and an acquaintance besides) refuse such an enticing, such an enthusiastic invitation? And so *A Century of Birds from the Himalaya Mountains* was born.

He and Elizabeth began work straight away at Broad Street. Despite the demands of his job at the Society, Gould sketched every bird himself, then supervised Elizabeth as she drew them more properly. That was how they always worked, and that was how he filled the dark hours when he wasn't at Bruton Street in the last months of the year. He knew exactly how things should look – the size and angle of the beak, feet, wings, neck – but he could not make his pen replicate it. So she became his hands. She worked tirelessly, day after day, as her belly swelled. Mr Vigors got to work too. His task was not an easy one, either; these were uncharted ornithological waters he had been asked to navigate. The natural world and its order – God's order, as he saw it – was still in many ways a mystery, even to experts like Nicholas Aylward Vigors. The Swedish botanist Carl Linnaeus's system of taxonomy, now almost three-quarters of a century old, had at least introduced a standard means of nomenclature, with names based on genus and species. Prior to that, many species had been named a number of times over. Vigors studied Gould's birds, trying to work out if they had been identified before, giving the correct Linnaean names to those that had and new ones to those that had not. He declared that there were at least twenty undescribed species of bird in Gould's collection. A pretty little bird Vigors identified as belonging to the genus *Cinnyris* he named after Elizabeth, *Cinnyris gouldiae* – in recognition of her talent. Or, perhaps, her diligence.

Out of sight at their home turned studio, she first drew the birds, then transferred the drawings to lithographic stones. Lear had taught her the process, willingly sharing what he himself had learned, for he considered himself a friend of the older, more confident Mr Gould. Tall and gangling, with an awkwardness not quite disguised in his friendly manner, Lear spent many hours hunched down to her level, showing the heavily pregnant Elizabeth how to draw directly on the chalky limestone blocks with a special crayon. He showed her the freedom it gave the artist that engraving denied, the way he could move the crayon just as he did a pen on paper, with elegant, flowing strokes. Elizabeth was a good student; she spent many days in the low light of the new winter practising what he had shown her. Each day, as her husband went out to work at Bruton Street, she would heave her heavy frame to her desk where, with her husband's drawings and his scribbled instructions before her, alongside the large, shiny stones, she would set herself to her task.

Gould had looked for a publisher for their first ever work, but none was forthcoming. The weight lent to their endeavour by Vigors was not enough to offset the fact that John and Elizabeth Gould were virtual unknowns in the field. Unperturbed, Gould decided to publish it himself, just as Lear had done. He knew he had the contacts, thanks to his position at the Zoological Society, to attract enough subscribers to make it financially worthwhile. On the 23rd of November, Mr Vigors presented the previously undescribed specimens of Gould's birds to the second meeting of the Committee of Science and Correspondence, along with a selection of Elizabeth's drawings. Gould was proud – what progress he had made already! But, more importantly, he recognized how *useful* such publicity was. The Proceedings were published and sent to eminent institutions, as well as to every Fellow of the Society. The list of subscribers grew and grew.

By the middle of December, Gould had fifty subscribers, and the first five plates — all of previously undescribed birds — had been transferred to stones ready for printing. One was of a beautiful pheasant, *Tragopan hastingsii*, and Elizabeth had captured quite perfectly the elegant line of the neck her husband had insisted upon. Vigors, however, had not kept up. He was overwhelmed by donations coming into the Society's office. But Gould could wait: he would publish the letterpress descriptions after the plates. The stones were taken to Hullmandel's lithographic establishment at 49 Great Marlborough Street, just a few minutes' walk from Broad Street. There, Gould watched anxiously as they were laid on Hullmandel's press. Hullmandel worked carefully, wetting the stones before applying the oily ink, then laying the paper on top, finally turning the star-like wheel of the press. Gould watched the first folio removed: the pheasant his wife had drawn looked back at him, in perfect form.

On the 20th of December, 1830, the first fascicule of *A Century of Birds from the Himalaya Mountains* was sent out to the fifty subscribers. In large, imperial folio size, the beautifully coloured birds were set against black and white backgrounds. Each bore the signature 'printed on stone by J. and E. Gould'. The very next day, Elizabeth Gould gave birth to her second child, a son: John Henry. Four days later, London was covered with snow. John Henry's first Christmas was a white one; and the year that loomed for his father sparkled with promise.

On the 1st of January, 1831, a review of the first part of *A Century of Birds from the Himalaya Mountains* appeared in the *Athenaeum*. John Gould, ALS (Associate of the Linnean Society) was announced as an ornithologist to literate society. That was indeed the case, but he remained, six days a week, the animal preserver for the Zoological Society. He did not forget that it was through his position there that he had been able to start his climb into the elite world of natural history. He asked the Council, in early January, for permission to let their name stand in the list of subscribers to his great work. They, of course, agreed. *Wasn't the fellow becoming an asset to them?* But they would have to wait for the next fascicule. It would not be published until February – in the first month of the new year, Elizabeth was allowed a few weeks of respite to recover from the birth of their baby. The studio at 20 Broad Street was quiet.

Quite the opposite was true of John Gould's workplace, not far away in Bruton Street. There, despite the best efforts of the new Curator, Mr Martin, to impose some kind of order, the situation grew ever more chaotic. The Lower Museum Room was already overflowing into the Parrot Room, which already housed numerous live animals, sheltering from the winter at Regent's Park. (Two large cages had been purchased to contain them all.) Things were being lost. At the end of January, Martin noticed that a number of shells were missing from a cabinet in the lower room. The case had been improperly opened. They must have been stolen, he reported to the Council, the culprit clearly a visitor, though of course he could not be sure.

The Museum was open to Fellows of the Society and their invited guests, just as the Gardens were, though they came in much smaller numbers. The previous year almost two hundred thousand visitors had walked through the menagerie gates. Only fifteen thousand had come through the door at 33 Bruton Street. It was a constant disappointment to Vigors, and others on the Council who saw the Museum as the scientific heart of the Society, that there seemed to be less interest in visiting the preserved collection. The only explanation was that it was inadequately displayed. Finally, in late January, real plans were put

into motion to remedy this unsatisfactory situation: a committee was appointed to investigate the erection in Regent's Park of
a Museum building better capable of accommodating everything. It was hoped that the wonders of the collection would
soon receive the acclaim they deserved.

In the meantime, space had to be found at Bruton Street for
all of the new specimens. The orang utan was soon to be among
them: the skin had been returned from the tanners, and the skeleton had been fetched from the Macerating Room, cleaned of
all flesh after many weeks in water. (It took longer for the water
to do its work at this time of year, when the weather cooled
it.) Gould and Gilbert were now working on mounting the
beast. They grappled with the large skin, which was heavy still,
despite the many hours they had spent thinning it, paring it
down by countless strokes of their blades, removing the last rel-
ics of flesh. They worked to Gould's earlier measurements and
sketches, as well as looking to the shape of the skull they had
before them. They did not mimic the pathetic form in which
Gould had seen the creature alive. Stuffing it with wire, sawdust
and cotton moulded around a wooden frame, finished with clay
and glass eyes, they gave it a rather more animated pose. When
they were satisfied (and John Gould was only ever satisfied when
it was perfect), they called Moor, the porter, and the Assistant
Curator, Charles du Bois, to carry it downstairs to the Museum
and place it where Martin directed.

Gould would leave it to the Curator to find a space for it; that
was not his concern. He left the ordering of the collection alone,
though he had doggedly learned the Linnaean classifications
used to place the items in their rightful groupings. The orang
utan would be displayed alongside the numerous other specimens of Mammalia in the Lower Museum Room. The orang
belonged in the second order of Mammalia, Primates, with
the other Quadrumana. These included the mounted orangs,

donated by Sir Stamford Raffles, and a few more (including a young one) preserved in spirits. The first order of Mammalia was the Ferae (according to Linnaeus, though French naturalist Cuvier had more recently termed them the Carnassiers), and the Museum had mounted specimens of Arctic bears, polar bears, black bears, in varyingly aggressive poses, along with a famous sun bear, former resident of the Tower Menagerie. All of these vied for space with dugongs, snarling tigers, wolves and weasels. Tortoises and snakes, skulls and horns covered the walls, and shells occupied the tables in the room's centre. Besides the birds, which were all kept upstairs, it seemed that almost the entire Animal Kingdom was resident here. Appreciating it, though, was not easy: many of the specimens were unlabelled.

In this era of discovery, putting a name to every creature was work enough. Yet naturalists like Vigors wanted to do more than name them: they wanted to put them in their rightful place. The straightforward, comprehensible concept of a Great Chain of Being, a hierarchy ordained by God with man at the top of an ascending series of life forms, had been revealed to be over-simplistic, not least by the knives of comparative anatomists. Similarities and differences discovered in anatomical structures hinted at more complex relationships. It was for men like Vigors, and the other naturalists who came and went through the Museum's rooms, to unravel them. Linnaeus's taxonomies were seen, even by himself, as merely provisional. Cuvier had come up with his modern version, but he was *French*.

Vigors (and the Zoological Society of London) was a supporter of a relatively new *British* system of classification: the Quinary System. Devised by entomologist William Sharp Macleay, it organized the natural world according to a system of intermeshing circles of life, each containing five 'types'. Macleay identified five animal kingdoms, which each contained five classes, which contained five orders, which contained five genera, which contained five species of living organism. Presented as a divine geometric ordering, the system saw only *graduated* shifts in nature, the forms within each circle arranged according to similarity of structure to the next form. Though elegant, it was not an easy way to classify the natural world, and it was not a popular system beyond the walls of Bruton Street. Vigors had devised a Quinarian System of classification for birds a few years previously, but it had come in for a great deal of criticism from his fellow ornithologists. Even John Gray, the Keeper of the Zoological Collection at the British Museum, contradicted it.

John Gould tried not to trouble himself with such business (apart from a diplomatic adherence to Vigors's classifications when called upon for such). He left that to the others. Over the spring of 1831, he busied himself with his publishing project. He ignored, too, the political turmoil that often spilled on to the streets of the capital. He stuck absolutely to his strict and ambitious plan. From February, when Elizabeth was able to work again, the remaining parts of *A Century* came out thick and fast. Gould promised his subscribers, whose numbers were growing all the time, one each month; the second in February, the third in March. They were not disappointed. Neither was its author. It was opening doors for him, precisely as he had planned.

On the last day of May, John Gould bade goodnight to his assistant as they both packed up and left the Stuffing Room at the customary hour. But Gould returned to their place of work later on that light summer evening. Just before eight p.m., he let himself into the building for the second time that day. He wore a different suit of clothes, one that did not betray the nature of his work: smart evening dress, with cloak and hat. He had a small case with him, which contained a number of specimens he was to exhibit to the assembled company. He was not entering the offices of the Zoological Society of London in his capacity as animal preserver: Mr Vigors, who would take the chair, had invited John Gould ALS, the published ornithologist, to present to the Committee of Science and Correspondence. The day had come that he had long dreamed of: he was taking his place alongside the leading natural historians of the day.

By the time a new Whig government had settled into its seats in Parliament in July, John Gould had published seven parts of his work as scheduled. He was becoming a valuable asset to the Zoological Society. When he requested a four-week leave of absence from his employers, it was granted without hesitation. It was hardly a holiday: Gould planned a tour of the north of England and Scotland, visiting his naturalist acquaintances. Lord Stanley, an avid collector of birds, had recently acceded to the presidency of the Society. He looked favourably on the budding ornithologist's endeavours. How could he not approve of his quest to accrue more specialist knowledge and expand his professional networks? The plans for a new Museum were advancing; the committee assembled earlier in the year had reported on possible sites for a building in the Regent's Park, adjoining the existing Gardens. The Council was now poised to apply for permission from His Majesty's Commission of Woods and Forests to build it. With the increased visitor numbers and higher profile the Museum was sure to attract, the Society would need experts like John Gould on hand.

Before he set off on his own business, Gould was dispatched in mid August to Portsmouth, on behalf of the Society, to assist in the selection of shells and fishes from a collection that had been offered to the Council. At the end of the month, his own trip commenced. He visited Manchester and Newcastle, and stayed on the estates of esteemed gentlemen naturalists Sir William Jardine in Dumfriesshire and Prideaux John Selby in

Northumberland. He talked birds, and engaged in his only hobby: a spot of fishing – or, rather, observing the fish and smoking cigars. At the end of September, he travelled to York to speak at the inaugural meeting of the British Association for the Advancement of Science. Styled a 'Parliament of Science', it had been set up by a close-knit group of gentleman specialists and Oxford and Cambridge experts, esteemed genteel men of science: just the type with whom John Gould wanted to be associated. The ninth folio of his ever more popular *A Century of Birds from the Himalaya Mountains* had been published, and he presented some of the specimens of the creatures described therein, along with examples of the plates. His drawings were displayed alongside those of the great ornithological illustrator Audubon, who was American. His superiors at the Zoological Society must have been pleased that Gould, their own man, was standing alongside such a master. He was an asset to his employers and, in matching up to the renowned foreigner, an asset to his country. The Association's stated aim was, after all, to promote science *within* Britain and *for* Britain.

Gould returned to London, covered with glory. But his triumphant homecoming was tainted by the bad news he met at Bruton Street. He might have been on the rise, but the Museum he worked for was not. His Majesty's Commissioner of Woods and Forests had turned down the Society's application to build a new one in the Regent's Park. The grander building that would operate alongside the menagerie and must surely bring in more people to admire the collection – to admire *his* work – was not to be.

That autumn, it was not visitors but an endless stream of donations that occupied the animal preserver. His department was exceptionally busy. The Lords of the Admiralty had recently deposited the greater portion of the Zoological Collection of the late Captain Foster, who had led a scientific expedition to the South Atlantic and Pacific in the *Chanticleer*, and the whole of that formed by Captain King of the *Adventure* during his three-year survey of the southern coast of Patagonia. Individual members had been just as generous: one Mr Ellis presented a splendid collection of 253 preserved bird skins, many of them new species from the interior of Africa; a Mr Lindsay donated 56 bird skins from the Philippine Islands, three-quarters of which were new to science. And Mr John Gould himself – in recognition of the encouragement afforded him in the publication of his work on the birds of the Himalaya Mountains – presented to the Society all of the 120 specimens from which the drawings were taken. Surely it couldn't go on – one London townhouse could simply not contain all the spoils of British exploration. The preserved collection now amounted to around 30,000 insects, 4,000 birds, 1,000 reptiles and fish, and 600 mammals.

Other collections were growing too, the main rival being Gray's Zoological Department at the British Museum. Yet the Zoological Society of London, though unable to attract visitors to the Museum, seemed only to be increasing in reputation among active naturalists. Many were just faceless names at the bottom of letters accompanying packing cases; others called in personally to Bruton Street with their spoils. Some even visited before they set off, to seek advice on the best means of preserving and packing specimens, and even to be furnished with equipment and allowances to aid their endeavour. In the autumn of 1831, one young gentleman naturalist and geologist from Shrewsbury did just that. A recent Cambridge graduate, he was to join the second South American survey to be conducted by the Admiralty, this time on board the *Beagle*. His name was Charles Darwin. He was the grandson of Dr Erasmus Darwin, the natural philosopher who had some rather radical views on the generation of species, as far as Gould recalled.

Mr Darwin wanted to make sure he was prepared for the

round-the-world voyage, which would last at least two years, and looked to the Society's naturalists for help. He called at Bruton Street on a number of occasions while in London in advance of his departure. He spent time with Mr William Yarrell, one of the founding members of the Society and a naturalist of some repute. They ventured out together to buy the pistols he would need to procure his specimens. Mr Darwin then wanted to ensure the specimens would endure the passage home. He already knew how to skin and stuff an animal, as every naturalist ought. He had been taught the principles of taxidermy by a freed slave while at Edinburgh University, but that on its own would not be enough when working in the inhospitable remote places to which the *Beagle* would take him. Yarrell taught him how to preserve specimens in jars, using bladders, lead or tin foil, and varnish. He also met with the natural-history dealer Mr Leadbeater, who showed him how to pack skins with tobacco, camphor and turpentine. Darwin learned that Captain King – whose specimens he saw being sorted by Vigors and Gould in the crowded rooms of Bruton Street – used arsenical soap and preserving powder; and that the brine used for meals on the ship would do for preparations, if nothing else was available.

The young man bustled somewhat clumsily about the Museum, brimming with excitement, preoccupied with all the questions he had to ask, all the information he wanted to glean. He was clearly restless, eager to leave London behind on one such visit. Gould looked on as Darwin glanced at his specimens as he made a quick tour. Among the aquatic birds displayed in the front drawing room, Gould made sure he introduced himself. He also made sure he delivered his own useful advice (for was he not the very best in the preservation business?). As they spoke, Gould looked over the tall, enthusiastic young man before him, with his piercing blue eyes. He would remember him. Charles Darwin, he sensed, might be of future use – if he survived the travails of such a voyage. Plenty didn't.

Gould envied him, a little, about to embark on his adventure. He was self-funded, of course – these fellows often were – and that was a luxury he could not afford. But he was realizing that there was a limit to what he could achieve as a 'museum naturalist', a limit to what he could do with other people's finds, even if he had tapped into the best networks of traders and travellers. He began to think of a life outside the privileged confines of the Zoological Society at Bruton Street – of a life in the field, where he could make some truly remarkable (and marketable) discoveries of his own. He was not afraid of taking risks if the rewards were high. He did not get ahead of himself, though: he knew he still had progress to make there, opportunities to exploit.

Despite all the help he received from the Zoological Society, and the obvious quality of the specimens turned out by its Preserving Department, Darwin remained undecided about where he would ultimately deposit his yet-to-be-assembled collection. Although he had initially planned to leave it with the Zoological or Geological Society, by the time he left London for Plymouth whence he would sail, he was veering towards the British Museum. Perhaps it had been obvious that the Museum at Bruton Street was about to burst. All the same, Mr Darwin was made a corresponding member of the Zoological Society.

On the 27th of December, the day that the *Beagle* finally set sail from Plymouth, Mr Vigors presented the last group of the birds from Gould's Himalayan collection at the year's final meeting of the Committee of Science and Correspondence. Gould was almost done with his *Birds from the Himalaya Mountains*. The last fascicules were published in the first months of the new year, as cholera, which had reached northern Britain the previous autumn, now swept through the capital. Vigors's letterpress descriptions, however, were still far from complete. Gould had learned a lesson: he would not make the mistake of partnering with another man again, not even an eminent ornithologist like Vigors.

By the spring he had decided on his next work, one of much greater magnitude than the first, which he alone would write and oversee. This time he would not trouble himself with undescribed foreign birds. He would turn to a more popular subject matter: *The Birds of Europe*. Elizabeth would do the lithographs, and he recruited Edward Lear to help. Elizabeth was pregnant again, and Lear was suddenly at a loose end. He had struggled to keep up with the production of his own series on parrots, and when Gould had offered to buy the copyright and finish the series, Lear, naive and poor, had agreed. Gould had not done as promised. He told Lear that the parrots series could wait. Their efforts were concentrated instead on his own work. It was a masterstroke: he had reduced the competition and secured one of the great ornithological illustrators for himself.

On the 6th of June they had finished the first part of this work, and Gould presented it to the Council. It was dedicated to them and to Lord Stanley. In July the *Magazine of Natural History* waxed lyrical about it: 'admirably executed . . . equal, if not superior, to any other ornithological production in Europe'. The good reviews continued as he brought out two subsequent parts over the remainder of the year. Elizabeth gave birth to another son in October, Charles, and took just a few weeks off. The third part of the series was sent out to subscribers in December. John Gould was pleased with its success, of course. That did not mean he was satisfied. He never became complacent. For a start, another general election was taking place, and this one *did* interest him. Mr Vigors was standing as MP for Carlow in Ireland. Gould had to plan for the eventuality that his biggest ally at the Society might soon become rather distracted.

*

The new year began with much activity at the Museum of the Zoological Society of London. Dr Grant, the professor of Comparative Anatomy at the new London University, had agreed to host a series of talks at the Museum for any members who wanted to learn about the classification and structure of animals. On the first day of 1833, Grant arrived at Bruton Street. In his mid-thirties, he was immaculately attired, and armed with a quick wit and a long list of instructions. He was a somewhat retiring man, but his reputation preceded him. He was a proponent of the Continental theories of anatomy, as advanced by Monsieur Geoffroy St-Hilaire, believing in a unity of plan in the whole Animal Kingdom, as well as Lamarck's theory that a species could transform into another. He was a celebrity in the world of zoology and comparative anatomy, and a growing presence within the Society. John Gould was wary of his radical hue.

He and Gilbert were working on a m'horr antelope, a loris, a bandicoot and a wild boar that day and tried to stay out of the commotion that accompanied Dr Grant's visit. In the Dissecting Room above them, a large black tortoise was currently opened up upon the table. When Grant saw it he requested that all the anatomical preparations be finished as soon as possible. He explained to the Curator, Mr Martin, as they walked around the building, that in his lecture series the animal classes were to be examined in zoological order, commencing with those that approached nearest to man, and terminating with the simplest known forms. Mounted specimens and anatomical preparations to illustrate the zootomical details, from across the entire collection, would need to be made ready.

The first lecture was just two weeks away, and over the following days the cases of the Museum were opened and the skins in the stores were pulled out. Everything was checked for insect and moth damage, to see if the spirits needed topping up and which specimens needed mounting as a priority. Gould could have done without the ensuing disorder. He could not walk anywhere without encountering Martin or the new assistant, Pearson, scurrying somewhere behind an antelope skin or an armful of bottles. Gould remained calm, focused on his own work. By the day of Dr Grant's first lecture, he had finished his work on the antelope, loris, bandicoot and boar. He had also preserved the skins of a porcupine, a common fowl and a harnessed antelope, skinned an axis deer, set up and put on appropriate stands a number of bird specimens and a boa for display, purchased a pigeon and a cuckoo and watched his giraffe (stuffed skin and skeleton) moved to its proper place in the Lower Museum Room alongside the other Mammalia.

Gould's diligence was paying off. On the day of the first lecture, as the final preparations were being made, wayward specimens located and moved into the meeting room under Grant's directions, John Gould received word that he had been elected a Fellow of the Linnean Society. It was an honour for any man. It was an honour indeed for an animal preserver. He joined the members who had assembled in the meeting room for the lecture as John Gould FLS.

Animal preserver: it was a title that didn't express the gamut of responsibilities that John Gould now had within the Zoological Society of London. On top of his heavy workload in the Stuffing Room, he was also entrusted to make any acquisitions he deemed necessary for the collection, to fill any gaps in the animal series. The Society's ambition of possessing a zoological collection that approached as complete a picture of the Animal Kingdom as possible was, of course, a quest rather at odds with the realities of its situation. Where would they put it? When the medical attendant, Charles Spooner, asked to be allowed the body of the rhesus monkey that had arrived on the day of Grant's lecture, the Council was only too happy to agree, and Gould was glad to see it sent off. He had bigger beasts to concern him for the time being, not least the skin of a lynx from the Gardens, now deposited in a vat of alum water to await his attention. Over the next few weeks, a box arrived from a corresponding member in Mauritius containing three bird skins, the skeleton of a large monkey, various bones, several at least supposed to be those of a dodo – in other words, a typical delivery, which required sorting. Gould also purchased a number of skins, which needed attention, and a donation of sixty-nine bird skins was made by the Royal College of Surgeons. They were Australian and Gould, enthralled, lost many hours to them.

On top of all this, outside his working hours at the Society, he was still overseeing *The Birds of Europe*, and looking beyond it to his next venture. Elizabeth and Lear (who was beginning to spend much time at Knowsley Hall in Lancashire, home of Lord Stanley, the Society's President, which Gould thought could only be a good thing) were working well together, and the reviews for their plates were still glowing, so it seemed sensible to be considering the next publication. The only problem was time, or lack thereof. Even with his unstinting diligence he was finding it increasingly hard to fit everything in. But John Gould, as ever, had a plan.

One morning in February, on his way upstairs to the Preserving Department, he paused at Mr Vigors's office. He greeted Vigors, as he always did when he found him there. That day he lingered longer than usual, and asked if he might have a moment of the Secretary's time. Since he had been elected a Member of Parliament, Mr Vigors seldom came in and was about to step down from his post at the Society. But John Gould had something he hoped they might discuss before he left. He had a proposition for him.

On the last day of February, the newly appointed Superintendent of the Ornithological Department of the Zoological

Society of London arrived for work. The morning before, he had been a mere animal preserver. John Gould had been promoted. At the Council meeting the previous day, Mr Vigors had proposed it and his fellow members had not hesitated to second it. Gould's salary was to remain the same but the terms of his engagement were to be altered. He would still oversee the Preserving Department, but he would also take full responsibility for managing the Ornithological Collection (which was, in reality, merely recognition of a *fait accompli*). It was, surely, only in the Society's interest to agree.

It was appropriate that today – his first day in his new, more senior role – John Gould had important business to attend to. He had been told to expect a delivery from the Saffron Walden Museum. He had arranged an exchange of duplicate specimens of natural history with them and was anticipating the arrival of fifty birds and one quadruped; an axis deer. It was planned that he would be present to oversee the delivery, to check everything was included and undamaged: under the terms of his new position, he was not obliged to come into the offices daily but was in charge of his own schedule. It was precisely what he wanted and precisely what he needed to manage his ever-expanding portfolio of interests: bird dealer and collector, expert ornithologist, publisher and animal preserver. He did not plan to do much of the latter, any more, except for his beloved birds. He was excellent at delegating, and he had trained John Gilbert well.

In April, Edward Turner Bennett took over as Secretary of the Society. The staff of the Museum Establishment had been busy trying to get the place in order in advance of his arrival. The assistant, Pearson, had been cleaning the bottles and topping up the preserving spirits. Gilbert had been examining the condition of all of the birds in the Museum. It seemed an appropriate moment for a spring-clean. Mr Bennett, of course, realized that the Museum needed a great deal more than that. Upon his appointment, he inherited the job of overseeing the continued discussions about finding new premises for the ever-expanding collection – discussions that were becoming a little heated. There was a growing feeling among the Museum Establishment, echoed by some of the Society's membership, that this branch of it was lost in the shadow of the more glamorous sister institution two miles to the north. There seemed to be no end of resources for the Gardens, for the purchase of new beasts to be admired rather than studied, yet here – where the real science happened – they were reduced to this state of chaos.

Bennett was an avid naturalist and collector. He helped alleviate a little of the pressure on the storerooms at Bruton Street by relieving the Society of some surplus specimens: first, two bottles containing a fish and a quadruped in spirits, then the body of a chinchilla, which had arrived from the Gardens one Saturday in May. John Gould was in that day, overseeing the packing of duplicate specimens for Ipswich Museum as well as keeping an eye on Gilbert, whom he had left in charge of stuffing a lion and a young zebra that had come from the Gardens, aided only by Pearson. Gould made sure to seek out the new Secretary whenever he himself was in, which was no more than a few times a week in the spring and early summer of 1833. He was contracted to stuff 400 bird skins a year for the Society, but he did those at his studio at home, where he could keep a better eye on Elizabeth as she worked, and make arrangements with his newly employed secretary, Mr Prince, about the various publishing projects he was working on. (He was thinking he might do a series on toucans next, wonderfully visual birds, which was sure to sell.) He came in for the meetings of the Committee of Science and Correspondence, at which he presented with increasing frequency. He also came in to supervise the exchanges and purchases he made on behalf of the Society. In the middle of May, while the Museum staff was in the midst of a general inspection of the collection and an attempt to clean, reorder and appropriately label it, Gould brought in an additional ninety-seven bird skins for them to deal with. He had sold them to the Society himself.

Yes, he came in as little as possible – and planned not to visit at all over the summer. In June he requested, and was granted, a six-week leave of absence. He was to tour the museums of Europe, primarily to find new material for his series on *The Birds of Europe* – but, of course, it would also be of benefit to the Society if he expanded his own knowledge and formed connections with experts on the Continent. At least, that was how he presented it to his employers.

On the 5th of July, he made his way to Bruton Street, and entered through the door he had passed through six days a week for six years. Today he did not stop to see what had come in from the Gardens. He went upstairs to bid good day to Gilbert, who was busy labelling the birds in the Museum rooms. A mammoth task and one Gould was not sorry he had been relieved of. He did no more than take a cursory look at the panda skin and (almost complete) skeleton of the same that had been donated a few days previously. He listened, inattentively, to Gilbert's account of the theft of the hummingbirds, and of Pearson's dismissal for negligence. He did not concern himself with the Pearson affair. He was sorry to hear of the hummingbirds' departure: he loved the beautiful little creatures.

He was there to see Mr Bennett and, as soon as he could, he left Gilbert at his work and went downstairs. He knocked on the door of the Secretary's office on the ground floor, and was pleased to find him at his desk. *He wondered if Mr Bennett might write him a letter of introduction to some of the museums he planned to visit?* Bennett was more than happy to oblige. Gould watched his pen move across the page, leaving a most pleasing trail in its wake: 'I shall feel obliged by your giving him any facilities which your regulations admit to forward his views . . . A kindly intercourse of mutual assistance is at all times gratifying to us individually, while it advances most materially the interests of science.' Yes, that would do very well.

His task accomplished, John Gould walked out of 33 Bruton Street and into the July sunshine, the letter of introduction neatly folded and secure in his breast pocket. He turned left, and went back to Broad Street. He was looking forward to his trip. It was not exactly 'field work', not exactly an expedition, like those he had rather enviously helped numerous naturalists prepare for (though he had not abandoned the idea of making such an expedition himself, one day). But if John Gould was going to be a museum naturalist, for the time being at least, he was determined to be the best. Determined to be an international expert, the chosen representative of the prestigious Zoological Society of London.

Another man might have allowed himself a moment of quiet celebration, as he walked home, reflecting on the Continental adventure he (the son of a gardener!) was about to embark upon.

But John Gould was not like other men.

5. Gifts from Afar

Devereux Fuller, Head Keeper,
1833–6

It was not the first time Devereux Fuller had made the journey south, from the Zoological Gardens in the Regent's Park to Mr Cross's Zoological Gardens in Newington. It was a wet afternoon in early September and he watched the familiar shop-fronts of Regent Street pass by the clammy windows of the omnibus. On the horses dragged it, to Charing Cross and the Strand, now much changed, with Mr Burton's hospital almost finished. On across the granite bridge straddling the Thames, a tangled mass of coaches, omnibuses and pedestrians above, grey waters choked with boats below. The Palace of Westminster in the distance, next to the arched bridge, glimpsed in snatches through heads and hats. St Paul's, seen clearly from his own window. On to the other side of the mighty river, past the smoke-blackened bricks of the Shot Tower rising menacingly from the south bank. And on, the view changing to brothels and gin shops as the reeking river disappeared, unseen, behind.

He jumped down at the busy junction of the Elephant and Castle. Dodging endless coaches and their passengers, the steaming piles of dung and resisting the temptation of the tavern's swinging sign, he walked south. Past the almshouses, to Newington, where the houses and streets thinned out, fields and greenhouses appearing in the gaps between, where a man dared breathe, long and deep. A pleasant corner, chosen by Mr Cross for the latest incarnation of his menagerie. So different from the 'Change on the Strand, or even the King's Mews where his animals had last resided. So much like the setting for Fuller's own Gardens on the opposite side of the city. Supposedly, the two societies were not rivals. The Council of the Zoological Society of London had given Cross their approval to set up his Gardens beyond the great divide of the Thames. Supposedly, the two were to cooperate in the name of zoology. Supposedly. But Devereux Fuller, head keeper of the menagerie in the Regent's Park, did not see it so. Neither did Edward Cross. He was sure of that.

Fuller had had dealings with Cross a number of times in the six years he had been in the service of the Society. He knew him as well as he cared to. He approached the entrance to the Surrey Zoological Gardens. It must be nigh on a year since he had last been called here – and it was changed. He could see so already. He announced himself to the money-taker and passed into the extensive grounds. Now at the end of its third summer season, it was impressive. He was sorry to see it. Parts of the establishment were rather like his own: the rustic lodges he passed at the entrance, the raised bear pit. Not the huge conservatory. That he had seen even from beyond the gates. So much glass: even on a dull day like today it seemed to sparkle; the largest continuous glass surface in Europe, so it was said. Fuller skirted the lake. He remembered the posters he had seen over the summer for Cross's 'Fancy Fete', promising an acrobat ascending a rope across the water to the tallest tree on the island. Balloons too. The Council had not even permitted a military band in his own Gardens, though it had been suggested this past season. He knew what they thought: such things weren't 'scientific'. Fuller was not one to correct them. He just did as he was told. (And did it well. He would not have been there for almost six years otherwise, would not have been asked to take over from Cops as head keeper a mere six months after he had started if he was not good at his job.)

Fuller had come today, on the Council's orders, to look over a Sing-sing antelope that Cross had offered for sale. They were keen to have a living specimen for themselves. A lad showed him to the creature's enclosure. He could see straight away that it was a sorry-looking beast, ragged and thin. The boy caught it with a lasso and held it, head down, as Fuller walked around it cautiously. One of his men, James Goss, had been injured by a deer this past season, and just a matter of weeks ago one of Cross's men had been killed by a gnu. Apparently he had been beating the animal when it turned on him. Fuller despised Cross for having let that pass. Cross should have taught his men better, disciplined them. It caused Fuller grief that he had lost Graves to the bear (was it three summers previous?), but he had learned from it, of that he was sure. He liked to think he never underestimated an animal now. He didn't have much to fear from this one, though, he could see that. The Sing-sing had pretty striped horns, but was very weak. Probably wouldn't survive the winter. He made up his mind: he'd come back for it in the spring if it was still alive. Save himself the trouble of trying to get it through the cold. He bade the lad goodbye and made his way towards the exit.

He did not need to take on any more risk himself. He had enough to worry about as it was. This year, winter had come upon them already, a few days past. Unannounced; like a highwayman. The heavens had parted like they had been ripped asunder, the rains rushing out like blood from a gash. When it was only August and they were unprepared for it. He and his men had dashed around the grounds like madmen, covering the exposed cages and aviaries with sailcloth and sacking to try to protect the tender creatures from the unrelenting downpour. Even so, they'd lost a number of birds within hours of the first cool drops, which he had felt on the back of his neck as he leaned over the lioness with the Medical Superintendent. She had not been right since she had aborted her cub a few weeks earlier. (That had been no surprise: they never had any luck with the pregnancies of the big cats.) They hadn't been able to move her out of the rain. She had followed the birds and died the next morning. They'd lost the chittah since, too.

He sighed, audibly. It had been a bad few days. And there had been the zebra a week ago. Cholera, Mr Youatt had said. The word did not frighten him. Troubled him, mind. He'd be a fool if it didn't. He had attended the post-mortem, in the new Dissecting Room made over to the Medical Superintendent, alongside the surgery. The Council now expected the head keeper to attend post-mortems whenever he could; they thought he might learn from them and be better able to care for the beasts. Of late, they were all for educating the keepers. They had placed books at the Gardens too – as if they had time to read about the animals when they had to care for them from six in the morning until night! He preferred to go on what his gut told him. Trust in his experience. He usually didn't mind the dissections too much. But the zebra! He could still taste the stench that had forced its way into his mouth and nose as Mr Youatt had cut the beast open. Good God, he had never smelt anything as foul as its rotten insides. He had held on as long as he could, standing tall before the assembled company – Gilbert and Alexander from the Museum were there, as well as some medical men – but he had not been able to endure it. He had ducked outside and vomited by the wall. Kicked some dirt over it, ashamed.

Thinking about it now made him thirsty. He passed the

refreshment stall on his way out of the Gardens. He inspected the delicacies they were offering. Ices, lemonade, custard (baked and boiled), jelly, ham sandwiches, sausage rolls, sheep's tongue . . . He looked at the men and women queuing for them. More ordinary-looking than those allowed into his Gardens, he thought. (At least, more ordinary than the Fellows and their families; other people who weren't so smart still managed to get hold of the necessary orders of admission – he'd seen them being sold at the York and Albany Tavern.) A woman brushed past him, sipping a cool glass of lemonade. Visitors to his Gardens couldn't even get a cup of tea inside. Why the Council permitted only the sale of refreshments for the animals, he did not know. Beer-sellers sprang up outside the entrance on busy summer Sundays. Some of his men, the married ones who lived at their homes, were thinking of setting up beer shops themselves. Make a bit of lucre on the side. The Council would not encourage that. Better for them to offer a drop of liquid within the Gardens? That was his thinking.

He would resist Cross's offerings, he decided. Take a quick ale at the Elephant and Castle before he headed north, if there was time. It was getting late and he wanted to be back for the feeding hour. It must be past three already. He walked on, trying not to look at anything as he passed. Not wanting to be impressed by what Cross had done, he supposed.

The first weeks of September rolled by as normal. Normal, as far as life in the north-eastern corner of the Regent's Park ever was. Jack the elephant swallowed a woman's reticule, complete with keys and . . . all the things a lady kept in there. Fuller remembered the journey he had made from the docks with Jack. He had thought the beast a wonder then, as it had plucked hats from the crowd with its great trunk and delivered them to its mouth. He had been proud it was he who led him. More than two years ago, that was, but Fuller was as attached to him as

ever. But he had his concerns that Jack would do more than just
eat hats and reticules, one day. He worried the elephant was
'going bad'. He remembered Chuny.

Wren, Jack's keeper, had not reported the latest incident to
Miller. Wren would probably get into trouble for that. But what
could he do if the men didn't respect the Superintendent? So
long as they respected *him*, Fuller did not intervene. He understood their impatience with all the regulations, the systems. Told
them so, too, after a drink. More and more of his own day he
spent doing paperwork: his joint monthly report with Mr
Youatt, the return of provisions, any other thing the Council
demanded of him. He did not enjoy the writing. He could have
become a clerk if he had wanted to do paperwork indoors! And
yet, now the weather was turning cold, he found he did not
mind sitting at his desk in the warmth of his rooms behind the
aviary. Not now Sophie and little Eliza were there. So long as
the babe was quiet. He was still surprised by how much his wife
had brightened up his apartment at the Gardens. He even looked
forward to leaving his men and his beasts and getting back there
now. She had made his den into a home.

The usual routine of work went on, day in and day out, for
Fuller and his men. At their stations as close to six in the morning as they could make it. Cleaning the filth out of the dens.
Getting the Gardens ready for the day. Dirty work done and
work dress on, for those who were able, by the time the visitors
came through the gates. Doing as bade by them until dinner-
time. Men ate before the beasts; feeding time for the animals
was in the late afternoon. Then came the sunset bell and the visitors cleared away, the Gardens shut up half an hour later with
the second ringing of the bell. The men prepared their charges
for the night, then most disappeared themselves for food and
warmth and drink. The watchman came at eight to keep the
fires burning and notify the head keeper if anything was wrong.

So, too, came the rats. They ruled by night. Whatever was done to try to keep them away from the beasts, the rats got in. Day in and day out, so it went.

No two days ever the same. That September, one of the monkeys had had tumours. Fuller and Youatt had tried and failed to catch him. Hunt, one of the keepers, had been detailed to the kangaroos, to keep a close watch on them. They had been unwell over the summer, throwing themselves about the paddock again. Youatt said he had discovered the cause. Apoplexy. That was what was making them act so strangely. Hunt gave them salts once a week. The deer were fed on corn, preparatory to the breeding season. The Medical Superintendent himself was taken ill next, Fuller left to tend the sick animals alone. He knew how to administer the basic drugs. Knew how to draw blood, and did so. He felt more confident about caring for the sick ones now, since he and Youatt had been at their twice-weekly rounds together. So it went. Where no man could predict what would happen next, just work on. And Fuller oversaw their labours all.

In the third week of September, Mr Miller called Fuller into his office. He delivered some remarkable news: a giraffe was on its way. Already on a boat from the Cape, it would be here any day. The Superintendent told Fuller that he was to inspect it upon arrival at the docks and make sure it was healthy. The Society hadn't agreed to the purchase yet, but all the same, Fuller was to make all necessary preparations for its reception. He was stunned. A cameleopard was a prize indeed. No one had even known what they looked like, until the old King George IV was given one a few years back. Few had seen the King's giraffe, kept for his own amusement at Windsor, but Fuller had. He had seen it, stuffed, in the offices at Bruton Street.

To think, now they were going to have one alive. In his Gardens! Preparations for its reception were made immediately. Mr

Burton drew up plans for its accommodation, consulting the firm that was shipping the beast about its unique needs. The Council was planning on making it a special exhibit and wanted suitably grand accommodation. Fuller could hardly believe it was happening. London would go wild whatever they housed it in. A live giraffe. In his Gardens! Now what would Cross make of that?

The creature arrived in England in November. Fuller was not called to inspect it. The message that came for him from the Superintendent was unwelcome: the giraffe had not survived the passage. The Society bought its skin and skull for the Museum, for twenty pounds. Perhaps Fuller might see it there, then. That month there was discussion of moving the Museum to the north bank of the canal and the men joked that *they would have a giraffe in the Gardens, after all!* Fuller could only laugh along. The disappointment was a hard beginning to the winter season. Much dreaded this year, every year.

What Fuller and his men did not know was that far, far distant from the dripping trees and freezing mud of the Regent's Park, and the puddled pathways they trod among the cages and dens, the search for a giraffe was not over. Word was out that the Zoological Society of London wanted one and would pay for it. It reached Malta, made a British Crown Colony after the war with the French, where a customs collector, one Mr Bouchier, was stationed. Mr Bouchier, at the heart of a vast network of traders and diplomats, wrote to London: he would spread the word. He would get them a giraffe. His letter arrived in the last days of the year. All hope was not lost.

Fuller did not long mourn the giraffe. His mind and energies were occupied in trying to keep alive the stock already in the Society's possession. It was more important than ever to hang on to as many animals as they could. The Society's funds were in a poor state, so he'd been told: visitor numbers had dropped again this summer. Now the farm was to be sold off. His brother, Joe, was head keeper there and would be out of a job. Fuller did not want the same to happen to him, especially not now that he had a family to support. He worked hard over the winter, a wet one. Rain drenched the Gardens and its inhabitants; rain that trickled from the cages and fences that contained the few creatures that had not been shut away; rain that soaked Fuller and his men.

Youatt was recovered from the illnesses of the summer and they resumed their twice-weekly general inspection of the menagerie, as ordered by the Council. Fuller had not welcomed this incursion on his time when Youatt had begun in his post back in May. Not at first. But he had grown to accept it, to see it, even, as a chance to make sure he himself hadn't missed anything. Youatt listened to him, respected all he knew of the animals and their habits. Not like Spooner, so proud and quick to temper, younger, with more to prove. Fuller had viewed Spooner much as he did the bigger carnivores: with cold caution. (Youatt had told him that Spooner had set up a school now, doing rather well. Good luck to him, he supposed.)

Youatt was not satisfied that it was simply the winter's work, the mortalities they always suffered at this time of year. He thought they could save more, if only it could be established what was doing them harm. Then they could make changes in their care. Fuller was wary of change. Unnecessary tinkering was dangerous for the beasts. For their keepers, too. Yet he felt under pressure about the mortalities, more now than ever. So he did what was required over the months of their first winter together. He answered Youatt's questions and shared his knowledge with him. When the tortoises had died, one after another in December, Fuller had agreed they could try a more 'natural' approach. They would give them a little garden with sun and shade, a nook in which they could make a winter retreat. When the parrots died in alarming numbers, drooping suddenly and strangely, at first they moved their cage closer to the fire in their winter quarters, as they usually did. But the parrots continued to droop, so Youatt suggested they try the opposite: fresh air. The first roseate parakeet they took out into a rare breath of winter sunshine died almost immediately. Youatt was undeterred. In their joint report to the Council in January, Medical Superintendent and head keeper suggested a new type of cage in which they were exposed to the air. The two men did not always agree: when the old lion fell ill, Youatt said it was jealousy that had done it; jealousy of the young lion that shared the cage below him with the lioness. Jealousy! Once you started giving vicious beasts like that human emotions, well, that was when it became dangerous to care for them.

The lion died anyway. In the post-mortem Fuller observed, he saw the rotten liver that Youatt plucked from its carcass. A horrible mess of greenish black. (*Was that what jealousy did to you?* he laughed with Sophie afterwards. *Then he'd better not allow himself to be jealous of the way his men looked at her sometimes.*) In the new year the kangaroos became strange and ill again, and this time Youatt's ministrations did not help. A mother neglected her young. They took the tiny little thing into the surgery, tried to warm it by the fire. It was no good. He remembered when he and Joe had first found a tiny baby in the pouch of a kangaroo at the farm, no more than an inch long, covered with blood. No one had ever seen a baby kangaroo like that before. Mr Owen had put that in a paper, even.

Their best efforts did little. The deaths went on, and would continue as long as the winter did. Fuller knew how it worked. Youatt had not seen six winters as he had done. He watched his birds and beasts slung into sacks, destined for the Macerating Room or the Museum. Same as always. Soon the carcasses would not have to go far, if they were to be preserved. That February, the architect Burton was about, drawing up plans for a museum building on the north bank of the canal.

Once the worst of the winter was behind them, Fuller repeated the journey to the Surrey Zoological Gardens. The Sing-sing had survived the cold thus far, and the Council was still keen to have it, so he purchased it from Mr Cross and had his keepers pack it into a crate, to be driven across the city to its new home. That was the easy part of his day. He had also agreed to the purchase of an Arctic bear; that would need some seeing to, to get it to the Gardens and housed without incident.

Fuller was away from the Gardens a great deal that spring. He travelled often to the farm at Kingston Hill. The animals kept there had to be found new homes before it was sold: deer, cattle, fowl and rabbits of more and less exotic breeds, some zebra and quaggas. The kangaroos had been moved to the Gardens a few years back so Mr Owen could study them, though the farm was where most of the experiments in breeding and the like took place. The President and the other gentleman naturalists were keen to produce the finest creatures for their own estates. A luxury the Society could ill afford now, he supposed. Some of the beasts Fuller would find space for, along with their sheds and enclosures, at the Gardens. Most were to be sold at an auction. It was a big job.

He could get to Kingston and back in a day if he had to, if he left before dawn. It was only twelve miles away. Or thereabouts. But he enjoyed the times his work demanded he pass the night there (the eight shillings he could claim in travel allowances, too). He could spend time with his brother, Joe. They were fond of one another. Devereux had got Joe his first post with the Society. His brother had joined him at the Gardens not long after he had started there himself, then moved out to Kingston when that land was taken. The farm wasn't unlike the place where they had grown up together, in Hertfordshire. Where they'd run wild in the fresh air and open fields. Fuller liked being there. And when he had cause to stay the night, the brothers could have a drink together. After the day's work was done. Fuller had only a couple, mind, had reined in the habit after Windsor. He knew the Council would not let him get away twice with drunkenness while on Society business. He knew his place.

In late March, after one such overnight trip, he was returning with the latest batch of animals. Eight deer – three wapiti, two sambur, two Corsican, and one red – had been loaded onto the wagon behind him, which was slowly and carefully making its way north. Fuller was going to fit them in at the Gardens. Old carpenters' sheds from the farm had already been moved there to house them. For now, the beasts were packed into small transport crates, limiting their movement. Deer could be skittish. Fuller hoped they would have an uneventful journey. Only a few months past, a menagerie caravan had overturned in Ireland and a tiger had escaped. No one hurt, but the animal had begun to work his way through his travelling companions: a monkey, a raccoon . . . Fuller never took any chances. Hunt had come to help him this morning. He was a safe pair of hands. The other animals he would go back for next week. There weren't many left at the farm now the auction had been and gone. He'd watched the auctioneers rattle through their business in the Gardens before the assembled gentlemen – animal traders and breeders, mainly – seated in the chairs they had set out. Thirty-two pounds or thereabouts had been made. They had expected more.

The wagon clattered along the road. So much quieter there than in London. They had seen only a few farmers' carts and mules since they had quit Kingston Hill. Only his and Hunt's conversation disturbed the peace. They spoke not of the deer they carried behind them, which they could hear, occasionally, moving in their crates, but of a creature more exotic. More worrying. They spoke of a rhinoceros. One had come to London; it had been landed, alive, at St Katherine's Docks, imported by an agent of the East India Company. It was to be auctioned next week at Tattersall's. The Society would bid for it. Neither man had ever seen one in the flesh. But they knew how big and strong they were. Jack was difficult enough, at times. *Wasn't the rhinoceros fiercer? With his horn?* Scared, excited, they spoke of it for most of the twelve-mile journey. As the spring afternoon turned cold and the men could see their own breath and that of the animals, seeping through the gaps between the wooden slats in the crates, they spoke of the rhinoceros.

Cross bought it. Bennett had gone to Tattersall's for the auction on behalf of the Society, but he had not outbid the proprietor of the Surrey Zoological Gardens. Apparently the creature was as small as a pig and terribly lame, and the Society did not have money to spare if it was to be wasted.

Edward Cross was not one to let reality get in the way of a spectacle. He was a showman, and he made his money back out of the creature, imperfect as it was. In early April, as Fuller was occupied in packing up the last animals from the farm, Cross was advertising his latest exotic acquisition to the world. One could not open a newspaper without some extravagant claim about the beast, or pass through a coach or omnibus station without seeing a poster proclaiming his prize. So it seemed, anyway. Then, to add insult to injury, in early May – on a fine afternoon when the Duchess of Kent, no less, was visiting the Gardens – the Sing-sing Fuller had bought from Cross keeled over and died. Fuller was furious. He felt it almost as a personal slight from the man.

But he had forgotten how quickly things changed in this

game. He would not have to wait long before the Wheel of Fortune turned again.

Hundreds of miles away from the paddock where the Sing-sing's stiff body is being dragged out of sight of the visitors, in the great expanse of the Atlantic Ocean, the *Lord Hungerford* is cutting its way northwards. On the last leg of a four-month voyage from Calcutta, it is approaching European waters. The seven-hundred-ton ship, once in the East India Company's service, now a free trader, rolls from one side, then to the other, then back again. With every motion, salt spray splashes onto the stinking deck, the cold ocean mixing with the shit, piss and food slops daily spilled from chamber and kitchen pots onto the wooden slats. Thus has she fought her way here, via the Cape and St Helena, and now the last miles of the African coast pass, unseen, to the east.

It is a familiar route for the experienced captain at its helm. Farquharson has sailed Indiamen from London to Bengal and back more times than he can count. But he has not always had such interesting cargo on board. He has never shared his ship with a fully grown rhinoceros before. The huge beast seems well enough, after all these months, down below in the dark, swaying hold. Not that he is any expert, but the passage, rough as always, has not troubled it. It eats and sleeps down there as it always did. Neither has it troubled him, shut up in a crate not much bigger than its ten feet length. Like the sailors, who scurry about their captain now, the beast is used to confinement. It is all it has ever known, so Farquharson was told when he purchased it in Calcutta in the last weeks of 1833 before he lifted anchor and set sail down the Hooghly and out into the Bay of Bengal.

From their last stop at St Helena, word was sent on ahead, that the *Lord Hungerford* bears unusual cargo. Valuable cargo, the captain is sure of it. His letter will reach England any day now.

He hopes that the news it contains – that he is bringing an enormous, healthy rhinoceros with him, to be sold at auction to the highest bidder – will cause quite a stir.

Fuller could always hear the noises of the birds and beasts – even when he was in his rooms with the windows firmly closed, and in the middle of winter when the heavy curtains were drawn against the cold. He could definitely hear them now. It was an early summer's day and Sophie had opened a window to let some air into the sitting room. The noise didn't bother her any more: the constant chirping from the aviary just behind their lodgings and the occasional, almost pig-like grunt of the pelicans in their enclosure beyond. He remembered when he had first moved there how strange it had been to think of sharing that little corner of the park with so many wild animals. Dangerous animals. He had soon grown used to it, but when Sophie had arrived three years ago he had felt the tug of anxiety again. He had kept a closer watch on everything thereafter. Last year, when two wolves had escaped one night, he had made sure the keepers were punished. The men must understand the consequences a broken lock on the gate to a den could have. Especially now that they had beasts as big as the rhinoceros. The Zoological Society of London had not been outbid this time: for £1,005 paid to Captain Farquharson, the beast had been theirs. It was double what Cross had given for his rhinoceros. But this one – Fuller's – was enormous. His was the real thing.

Sophie was clearing away the dinner. The head keeper picked up his cap and set off for the afternoon's work, stepping into the living orchestra of sound on the other side of their front door. He walked to the front of the building that housed his home and turned into the passage between the aviary and the pelican enclosure. Now his expert ear could identify the sounds of the individual birds coming from the aviary, and further away he

could hear the high-pitched cry of the emus that had been let
out into their yard that morning. He thought he even heard the
deep, almost strangled cry of an elephant, on the other side of
the public drive behind him. He hoped no one was teasing Jack.
The elephant was getting more difficult. Fuller had been speaking to Mr Burton about how best to accommodate him safely.
He'd had him moved to the Wapiti House recently, adjacent to
the paddock and pond where the female elephant was kept.
(They'd had her a year or so. She was no trouble.) They had discussed concreting the floors and strengthening the walls
there. Now that they had the rhinoceros to house, too, they were
planning a new building secure enough for them both.

Louder than any of the animals, to his ears at least, was the
noise coming from the humans. The shrill laughter of the ladies
and the lower tones of their male companions reached him from
the lawns ahead. The Broad Walk through the park had been
opened to the public for the first time that summer, and added to
the general noise of the place on a sunny day like today. It was
June and the Gardens were busy – more so than usual, thanks to
the newest arrival. News of the rhinoceros had travelled far. It
was gratifying that its colossal dimensions were much celebrated.
Fuller wondered what Mr Cross made of that. Sundays were particularly chaotic and police officers were required to help maintain
order at the gates, where carriages clustered, like flies around
dung. Fuller had once been a special constable, with the task of
protecting the peace; he had not minded passing on the duty to
the newly formed police force. This past Sunday – the day after
the rhinoceros's arrival – more than two thousand people had
come through the gates. A higher number than usual, these days.

Fuller's job was not to concern himself with the visitors,
among whose voluminous skirts and walking sticks he now
found himself. He had reached the path around the lawns.
Groups of frock-coated men walked the landscaped green

sloping to the pond. He saw some children quietly watching the ducks and geese. At least that was something – most thought nothing of terrorizing them. He passed a group that had set up camp around a tree near the path and were moving some of the chairs into its shade. The visitors paid him scant attention even in his keeper's dress.

It suited him to be ignored. Today and always. The tigers were dying; Mr Sabine was reviewing the keepers' occupations and wanted some information from him for a report for the Council (Fuller was worried he was trying to get rid of some of his men; he'd have to prove that none could be spared); and he wanted to discuss changes to the carnivores' den with Mr Burton. But all that would have to wait until a little later. He was on his way to supervise the rhinoceros's bath-time. They were going to let him into the elephant pond.

Fuller had been relieved to learn that the rhinoceros coming into his care had a history of confinement. That made an animal more manageable, less fearful of its human keepers, although that could prove dangerous in itself, of course. The beast was not yet mature – perhaps four or five years of age, it was reckoned – but it was big. Big and solid as an ox. Ten feet and six inches long from the root of the tail to the tip of the snout, and four feet ten and a half inches tall at the loins. He'd had it measured when it had first arrived, a few weeks ago now. He had inspected the beast carefully then, cautiously, though it seemed unperturbed by its recent adventures, happily eating the oranges proffered to it. He had expected it to be like a squat elephant. It was much stranger, grotesque even, in the flesh, with its ill-fitting suit of skin, hanging from it in great folds. Like plates of armour too large for it. Wart-like bumps on the rear and very little hair on its body. A dark stumpy horn. It looked like it came from another world. It did, he supposed. India was a place beyond his own imaginings.

Fuller watched as the beast was led from its temporary home in an apartment of the Wapiti House to the elephant paddock adjoining, waddling on its tiny legs. A crowd had assembled to watch the spectacle, and formed a second layer around the elegant iron railings that surrounded the large paddock, with its pond at the centre. The people pointed and called to it and each other. The noise concerned Fuller a little, but the creature seemed happy enough as he was guided along by a collar its keepers had placed around its neck. They had decided it would be safe to move him in the daytime, for that was when it was warm and they thought the rhino would be glad of the water. Henry Wright had accompanied the beast on its long journey, and had agreed to stay in the Gardens for a couple of weeks to settle him in, and to teach his new keepers what he knew of its quirks and habits. Fuller had decided that Hacker would take over from him. He was there now, holding the second rope that was slung around the creature's middle. It hung loose, for the animal followed Wright obediently, through the gate from the yard he currently occupied and into the paddock. Once he was in, Fuller closed and locked the gate behind them. Gave it a firm shake, just to make sure.

Jack was shut up in his quarters, out of sight. He had been worse than usual of late – probably because he was not getting the attention he was accustomed to. The cakes and treats sold by Mrs Fidd were now bought to give to his new neighbour. That wouldn't last long: Fuller knew all too well how quickly the sheen of novelty wears off. He was glad the rhinoceros was proving such a success. It took the pressure off him for a bit – perhaps Mr Sabine and the Council would not be looking to make 'savings' everywhere now that takings at the entrance were up. The crowds cooed in unison as the rhinoceros made his way into the water at the shallow end, where Wright and Hacker had led him. He moved his head slowly from side to side as he trudged in, until the water reached the top of his stunted legs. Then he ducked his snout under the surface. The crowd cheered. A slow and clumsy creature, he did little in the pond beyond submerging himself, his surprisingly hairy ears and snout protruding above the surface. So unlike Jack and the female elephant, which played in the water, like children. Fuller was pleased that the creature was proving so manageable, despite its size, yet he wondered if they should strengthen the railings here. Just in case. He would talk to Mr Miller about it.

Everything seemed to be in order, so he bade Hacker and Wright farewell. He wanted to check the tigers. So many of the carnivores had been ill in recent months. The summer months in which they should have been enjoying more favourable health. The male and the female tiger had been suffering from a violent cough for weeks. It rattled through their emaciated bodies. He and Youatt had tried everything they could think of. They had given them calomel in the blood of a lamb he had had slaughtered. The tigers had purged so violently that the spasmodic movement of the muscles was visible beneath their skin. It had had no positive effect. Now the keepers had been instructed to give them milk and warm blood, but they were certain to lose them. Fuller started making his way through the spectators, towards the entrance to the tunnel to the South Garden. He paused, then turned around. He'd say hello to old Jack first.

It was a dry Thursday afternoon in the middle of July. Fuller had just finished the bi-weekly inspection of the animals, alongside Mr Youatt. The Gardens were busy. There must have been well over a thousand people through today, he reckoned, and it would be closer to two thousand by the time the closing bell rang. He and Youatt had been occupied with the lioness. They had lost both tigers now. The dissections revealed their lungs to be a mass of disease. Youatt had wondered, many times, if the corner of the grounds where the carnivores resided was the real killer. Something was not right. Fuller hoped the new den he was planning with Mr Burton might help, that more would not follow the others to the Museum, destined to survive here only once they were stuffed. Talk of moving the Museum to the Gardens had ceased again. Apparently it had been decided it was better to have it more centrally located, more 'conveniently' positioned for the gentlemen of science it was supposed to attract. At least he wouldn't be faced daily with all the beasts he had lost.

He tried to focus now on saving the lioness. He did not want her going to the Museum, wherever it might be. They had been feeding her live food every now and again. That seemed to help. Fuller was on his way to see about a lamb for her evening feed. But he was stopped by one of the keepers' helpers running at him at full speed across the courtyard. Breathless. Panicked. The news that spilled from his mouth between his gasps for air caused the head keeper's stomach to clench with perfect fear: the rhinoceros had escaped. Fuller did not wait to hear the details. He ran. He ran as fast as he'd run since he was a boy.

By the time he reached the rhino's temporary home in the North Garden, breathless himself, the danger had passed. The animal was within its enclosure. Innocent as a babe as it munched its hay. By the time Fuller had refilled his lungs with air, fury had set in. He turned to the keepers who stood by the entrance, dishevelled after the chase. Hacker looked a sorry state indeed. His hat was missing, his hair wild. Fuller put his own cap back on, then found himself shouting. *Would someone tell him what on God's earth was going on?* But he could see the answer for himself. Hacker was drunk.

Four days later, Hacker was still suspended from duty. First thing in the morning, Fuller was summoned by the keeper who had taken over the rhinoceros's care. He had been having his breakfast with Sophie, but abandoned it half eaten. The night watchman had observed the rhinoceros seeming uneasy in the night. Now the animal was rolling around on the floor of his enclosure. Fuller thought it looked like colic. He and the keeper roused the beast and let him into the paddock, hoping that exercise would help. It normally did. It was clearly his abdomen that was troubling him. It was a Monday, thankfully. Youatt would be in soon.

Over the course of the day the rhinoceros got worse. When Mr Youatt arrived, they managed to get him back inside his den. Fuller had already had the beast's enormous belly rubbed. The men had had to apply considerable pressure, which concerned him. But the beast had submitted to their hands without a struggle. Now Youatt ordered it repeated with hot water. The Medical Superintendent prescribed castor oil and laudanum, and had the keeper pour it down the beast's throat when he rolled onto his back. It got worse as the day aged. The hot water embrocation was changed to turpentine. That seemed to soothe him somewhat. Twenty-six grains of calomel were hidden in a carrot, which he ate. At four o'clock the rhinoceros began to roll on the floor, like a ship in a storm. Fuller called all available men to the den. They put a collar over the beast's neck, ropes around his limbs. Fuller was wary of putting himself in danger. Sophie had chided him when he dashed home for dinner: *he must take care of himself, he was a father now.* But he could not expect his men to do what he did not dare. They held the enormous, writhing rhinoceros still enough to get three pints of castor oil down his throat, the struggle being traumatic for man and beast alike. The rhinoceros finally lay still on the floor, strangely pathetic. His limbs twitched.

The sunset bell rang. Still there had been no relieving evacuation. Who knew if the animal would last the night? The men quit the stifling hot, smelly den and breathed in the warm air of the summer evening. Youatt and Fuller both gave instructions to the keeper to rouse them if the rhinoceros deteriorated. Both knew that if he died – the most expensive creature the Society had ever purchased – it would be a serious matter. Youatt seemed almost excited by the challenge, determined to save it. Fuller was exhausted already – and he knew he would not get much sleep that night.

The rhinoceros survived the night but had not improved when Fuller saw him first thing the next morning. By the evening he had been force-fed seven pints of castor oil and forty grains of calomel. Still no evacuation. The third day of the beast's struggle found Fuller in a bleak humour, weighted by burdens besides the worry over the rhinoceros. The newspapers (and consequently the Gardens' chatter) were full of news of Cross's latest acquisitions at the Surrey Zoological Gardens: two elephants shipped from Calcutta. In typically flamboyant fashion, Cross styled the pair as 'high caste'. Just to outshine his rivals. That was not all. The Council's ruling on the Hacker incident reached Fuller and his men that day. A Committee of Discipline had been established. The Superintendent read to each man in turn the new rule imposed upon them: *that if hereafter any servant of the Society be found to be intoxicated while on duty, such servant was to be immediately dismissed.* Fuller, too, had to hear it spoken aloud to him. Silently, he listened to Miller. Humiliated, both men conscious of his own transgressions in the past.

Hacker was allowed to return to work. The rhinoceros knew him, it might help. Something must help! That evening, the head keeper mustered the full strength of the Gardens. He had the men rope the creature, hold him still enough to force three pints of castor oil into him. Youatt was not there. But Fuller was desperate. He could not just leave the beast to his fate. He would not lose him! The rhinoceros had just been released from the men's ropes when a small quantity of faeces slipped from its rear. A small, hard lump. Fuller prayed silently that it was the beginning of the end of the ordeal.

Four days later, a week after he had been taken ill, the rhinoceros called for his food at feeding time.

The English summer slipped into autumn, September into October, and the last warmth in the air faded away. A strange fog descended on London, blinding the city for an entire week. A week after it had lifted, smoke filled the sky above the Thames for some days: the Palace of Westminster was aflame. It had been the site of so much strife these past years, with the Whigs and their reforms, and by the end there was nothing left of it. Fuller was reminded of the danger of leaving anything to Fate. The rhinoceros had recovered fully; the Society's investment was safe. But what of the men tending him? He had been anxious since the animal had escaped. And now he well knew how many men it took to still him. He had already secured leg chains for him. For Jack too. Jack was continuing to exhibit signs of aggression. By early November, Fuller had developed a method of securing both animals in the event of them becoming violent. He proposed it to the Committee that now oversaw the running of the Gardens.

There seemed to be committees for everything. A 'modernizing' spirit was at work within the Society in the last months of 1834, as it had been at work beyond it; the desire to make everything more efficient reached everywhere. A new automated system of admission was introduced, with turnstile gates. A well was dug. A steam engine was built to power it. A refreshment stand was introduced — and that was a development Fuller understood and heartily agreed with. The men wondered aloud, *Would they get automated keepers next?* Some things did not change: the rats still terrorized the beasts; the beasts still stank; the men still cleared the animals' mess each morning as the darkness lifted, and stuffed the rat holes with broken glass although it never helped. Another year in the Gardens of the Zoological Society of London limped to a close. Another cold winter was under way. A winter, Fuller knew, that would carry away more of his charges.

But in the midst of it, at the very beginning of January, some good news reached the Gardens that brightened the short, cold days a little. The Council had had word from a contact in Malta. A customs officer there had written to them that a Sudanese trader, one Monsieur Thibaut, had embarked on a mission on the Society's behalf. He had set out from Cairo the previous April and was hunting for giraffes in the Nubian Desert.

More than three thousand miles distant from the Regent's Park, it is also cold and inhospitable. On the first day of 1835, as the letter from Malta is read to the Council in the offices of the Society (which remain at Bruton Street, though the search for new premises for the Museum has begun), Monsieur Thibaut is leaving the Kordofan Desert. He has spent many weeks in its forbidding sands, he and the party of local hunters that make up his caravan; he has tempted them along with promises of the fortune that will be theirs if they succeed in their unusual mission. They are approaching Dongola.

Monsieur Thibaut is weary and disappointed. It is at least five months since the hunting party captured their first live giraffe, a young one, left alone and vulnerable after they had chased its mother and killed her with their sabres. They have caught four more since, alive and young enough to tame (they have killed and eaten many more, cooked on fires blazing in dark desert nights). But in the recent cold of December, as the five creatures were pulled along by the men riding camels, four have perished. Monsieur Thibaut's plan – to reach Dongola, whence he would travel up the Nile to Wadi Halfa, from Wadi Halfa to Cairo, from Cairo to Alexandria, from Alexandria to Malta and from Malta to London, there to deposit his prizes – will no longer do. One small giraffe is not enough to show for eight months' hard work. He has more than twelve years of experience in these lands and he knows he can do better. He decides that he will leave this giraffe in Dongola, turn around and set out again, back into the inhospitable sands of Nubia, in search of more. And that is exactly what he does.

Another summer season had come round, the eighth that this corner of Regent's Park had been opened to visitors, with Fuller as head keeper for each one. And what had they learned? Too little, it seemed. Mortalities were worse than ever, especially severe among the carnivores. During April and May of 1835, a lioness, a lynx, a jaguar, a leopard and a tiger were lost. Fuller wondered if they could ever learn how to care for them better. These were wild beasts, after all. The Council thought differently. Infused with the spirit of modernity and efficiency, it did not accept that the animals' longevity was beyond their control. A committee had been established the previous summer to investigate the condition and mode of treatment of the animals. Now they were ordered to make searching enquiries. All Fuller could do was submit to it and instruct his men to do the same.

He focused on what he *could* control: the danger to his men. He procured spears to manage the elephant in the event of it becoming violent. Four posts were put into the enclosure it was currently occupying, which its legs could be fastened to. Additional iron and strong wooden bars were installed. These were temporary measures: in May, Decimus Burton began the new building, warmed, ventilated and strong, that both Jack and his new rival would occupy. It made Fuller's mind a bit easier. His wife's, too. Sophie was expecting their second child.

The Society hoped other exotic species would arrive that year: money had been sent to Malta for the giraffes they had been promised. Fuller tried not to think about them until the arrangement was more definite, though he knew how much they were needed. The rhinoceros had not reversed the overall decline in the number of visitors to the Gardens. There had been more than two hundred thousand in 1834. But that was a few thousand less than the year before, which was a few thousand less than the year before that . . .

The Surrey Zoological Gardens had disposed of its rhinoceros to an American. Cross knew his specimen had been well and truly outshone by the colossal beast at the Regent's Park, but he also knew the value of novelty. It turned out he had another card hidden up his sleeve, revealed to the world at the end of May: he had purchased an orang utan. It arrived in London from Calcutta on the 26th of May, aboard the *Orontes*. On that day he held a Grand Fete in honour of the Princess Victoria's birthday. The posters were plastered all over London. Fuller spotted one, just a few moments from his Gardens, at the York and Albany Tavern where he had come for a drink at the end of another long day. He read the proclamation of the delights Cross was peddling: 'In addition to the usual attractions of the Gardens, Mr Green, the veteran aeronaut, will ascend in his Grand Coronation Balloon! One hundred feet in circumference, from a raft on the lake, being his 198th and 199th ascents, accompanied by the Celebrated Monkey Jacopo, who will descend in a parachute!' Tainted his beer, it did.

The summer season of 1835 was a tense, uncertain time. There had been more political instability and another general election earlier in the year – though that did not much concern Fuller or men like him, who had no real hope of acquiring the property that entitled a man to a vote. Neither protests nor Reform Bills had changed that. Fuller was more concerned about the politics closer to home. There had been, by all accounts, much conflict within the Council between the reformers (men like Dr Grant and Mr Cox) and the more old-fashioned members, which had meant that little could be decided upon. It didn't help that the Commission of Woods and Forests was being obstructive again. The eastern side of the park had been opened to the public that Easter, after many years of outcry over its exclusivity; new gravel walks had been built to accommodate them. And yet – or perhaps because of it – the Society had been denied permission to build cattle sheds on pastureland they had newly acquired. Sheds were not a luxury. They were desperately needed to protect the animals from the inclement weather, now so close Fuller could smell it in the early-evening air, a hint of winter's more brutal chill. Mr Sabine was looking into ventilation of various animal quarters, as well as warming the dens, hoping that one or the other might help preserve lives. Sometimes, in his darker moments, Fuller felt that it was all futile, that he was as ignorant as ever of his charges' needs.

One small, rather bitter consolation was that Cross's orang utan did not long survive. It lasted less than two months. So it was not just himself who could not keep his animals alive. No one really knew how to care for the poor creatures, thrust into the middle of the stinking, busy, disease-ridden city. Especially not the monkeys, of all sizes. Their lungs always seemed to be eaten up by it. Lungs he had to see all too often, diseased and bloody, cut up on Youatt's dissecting table.

Far away, in the cold, grey waters of the Atlantic, the *John Cabot* is making its way to England. The crew is busy while the seas are gentle. Things change so quickly in that stretch of water. Two of the younger seamen – boys, really – kneel side by side in the sharp sea air, hard at their daily task of scrubbing the deck. It is never clean, never even close, but they scrub on. Scattered around them, more men are at work, and above, in the rigging, two men are checking the ropes. They hold on with their legs as they deftly work their hands, seemingly oblivious to the rolling of the ship taking them through a great arc in the grey sky.

Suddenly a loud noise tears through the quiet. An animal's bark. A dark shape right at the top of the rigging begins to move, to descend: a compact, furry creature with four long limbs, with which it nimbly swings itself from the top of the mast down to where the men work in the rigging. They barely look up. The creature – a chimpanzee, it is now clearly seen – grabs for the rope one of the sailors is moving through his fingers. The sailor pushes the beast's hand away – *Bugger off, Tommy, and bother the cap'n!* He jerks his head downwards.

The chimpanzee does as bade, continuing down the rigging. At the bottom he drops onto the wooden deck, gets up on his two legs – he is as tall as a child of three or four when he stands – and hoots, once, twice, turning his head to take in the scene around him. But the seamen aren't playing, not today. He drops onto his knuckles and scampers off towards the hatch, which leads into the dark bowels of the ship – down to the mess, then to the hold crammed to bursting with barrels of sticky palm oil, brought from the forests of Gambia. Whence he himself came. Perhaps he remembers the feeling of wet warmth beneath the forest canopy and the rough, living wood beneath his feet, so different from the long-dead wood of his new home. Perhaps he remembers how he was ripped from his mother's long arms as she died, killed by hunters. Or perhaps he does not.

The animal swings down the ladder and disappears out of sight. The men work. The *John Cabot* rolls on, bound for England. They aren't far now.

Fuller was ill in August. Then, at the end of September, Hacker fell ill. Inflammation of the lungs. Humans were not immune to the creeping cold of the Gardens' damp clay soil either, it seemed. Hacker was not, fortunately, so ill that he was unable to continue his work with the rhinoceros. A relief to Fuller, who did not trust the beast yet, and did not want to disrupt its routine. His anxieties were proved justified. One afternoon, at a moment when Hacker had his back turned, the creature surprised him. Hacker did not know what had happened, but the shock of the attack took its toll on him. Now he was unable to work at all. Mr Woods, the medical attendant who looked after the servants of the Gardens and their families, recommended that Hacker spend some time in the country to recover his health. At a meeting of the Council at the beginning of October, it was agreed to allow him a gratuity of five pounds to cover his travelling expenses so he could have the respite he needed. Fuller would have to do without him for the foreseeable future.

At the same meeting, the Council made another decision, which would determine the coming months for the head keeper to a far greater degree. They considered the news of a chimpanzee for sale, which had just arrived in Bristol, brought over by a trading ship's captain with the intention of making a little money for himself on the side. It was a not uncommon practice, these days: with so many animal dealers and menageries, the two Zoological Gardens in London, others in Bristol, Liverpool and Dublin, another talked of for Manchester, there would always be a buyer for an interesting creature. This time, the Society was offered it. Fuller was ordered to go and inspect it. If he saw fit, he was to purchase it for a sum not exceeding fifty pounds.

Fuller had forgotten quite how much he hated travelling long distances. Now he remembered, with every sinew of his exhausted body. He had left Sophie and the two little ones in the darkness long before dawn (he had a son now, too, baby

William) and had set off for Lad Lane in time for the first stage-coach of the day; he managed an ale in the Swan and Two Necks when he got there, hoping it might still his nerves and prepare him for the long road ahead. He had drained his glass and watched the coming and going of horses and carriages, mailbags and newspaper-sellers, busy in the first light of dawn beyond the window. He had brought one of the keepers' helpers with him. He was sorry to take more manpower away from the Gardens – the animals in the temporary dens were being moved to their winter accommodation today – but he thought he might need an extra pair of hands.

Now, the other side of a fourteen-hour journey of great discomfort – though he recognized it was far worse for the poor beasts pulling them along, thrashed and sweating all the way – he was a broken man. He had almost fallen as he stepped down from the carriage at Broad Street. He hoped the blasted railways everyone had been talking about for so many years would come here. They were building one in London – he had seen the tracks near the new London Bridge but they only went as far as Greenwich. Could they really make longer journeys? Would they be comfortable? Fuller looked over to the boy, who had sat in the cheap outside seats for all those miles. God knew how he hadn't perished. He didn't look far off it. His lips were purple. He said nothing, unable even to move out of the way of the stable hands, who shouted to one another as they detached the steaming, panting horses from the carriage and led them away. The coachman followed with the lantern. The evening was cold and very dark.

Fuller took the bag and the pair headed for the White Hart just a little further along Broad Street. He did not know Bristol but the gentleman he had sat next to, into whose extensive thighs he had been thrown every time the coach hit a bump on the road, had said it was the best of the inns on the street. Fuller did not want to be kept up all night by drunken sailors. He hurried along. Anxious, he could feel the weight of the leather purse in his pocket, stuffed with the Society's money. Fifty pounds! More money than he felt comfortable carrying in the dark in a place like this. He did not yet know how much the ship's Captain Wood wanted for the beast, but he would not leave Bristol without the chimpanzee. Of that he was determined. He could only hope he might find a creature in good health, though experience suggested it would be otherwise.

The buildings alongside them were tall, four-storeyed terraces, candlelight spilling out of the lower windows, with men's voices. Fuller was in such a rush to get to a hot meal, a drink and a bed that he carelessly stepped in puddles and piles of muck. Filth splashed over his shoes and soaked his ankles. He strode over the threshold of the inn, out of the darkness into the comforting glow of light and the clatter of voices and glasses. The lad stumbled in behind.

It was raining quite hard when, the next morning, the two men approached King's Wharf. The new harbour was an impressive sight, even half hidden as it was behind the wet grey mist. The pair had stopped for a moment on Bristol Bridge, despite the rain, to take in the scene. Masts filled the horizon, like stripped winter trees rising up from the river; wherries loaded with passengers – faceless beneath caps and coat collars – criss-crossed its pocked surface. Must be on their way to work, though it seemed a little late for the factories. It was already almost nine. A drop of water slid from Fuller's peaked cap and they carried on.

King's Wharf was beneath the grand parade of houses on top of the rock cliff that ran alongside the river on its eastern side. *Redcliffe Parade, you can't miss it*, the innkeeper had told them that morning. He was right. The fine three-storeyed townhouses peered down at them through the rain, and set against the dark wall of rock stretching beneath, the words 'Richard and William King' were unmistakable, painted in tall white letters on the side of a squat wooden building. Moored outside was a great merchant ship, its masts bare and its decks busy. The *John Cabot*. Wooden barrels were amassed on the quayside, and still more were being pulled noisily from the hold as they approached. A sledge was loaded with one, two, three of the barrels as the horse it was attached to stood stock still in the rain. Patient and bored. The men worked in silence too, wet clothes sticking to their skin. Fuller asked one where he could find Captain Wood, and was gruffly directed to the wooden warehouse. He went inside.

Some hours later, he was spat back out into the grey day. The rain had eased off. So had the activity, the barrels nowhere to be seen. All were now safely ensconced in the caves behind the offices. A couple of soggy workers remained on the quayside next to the ship, a wisp of smoke curling from the pipe they passed between them. They watched with obvious interest as Fuller approached. He and the lad had a third figure between them, the purpose of their visit accomplished: Tommy the chimpanzee was now the property of the Zoological Society of London. Fuller's face did not hide the triumph he felt. The beast was healthy. The beast was his. For only thirty-five pounds! They had paid thirty times as much for the rhinoceros and already the novelty had worn off. Tommy would be a hit. He was sure of it. A curious, and rather wonderful little creature, this one. That much was already clear.

Tommy was just two feet tall from head to toe. Even walking upright as he did now, holding his new keeper's hand, he did not reach Fuller's waist. He was about eighteen months old. That was what Wood had guessed, from the story passed on by the Gambian hunters from whom he had bought the beast. Fuller had agreed as he looked Tommy over, although he had no real idea – he had never seen a chimpanzee before. He had not even seen the orang utan the Society had had so briefly some years ago, or Cross's. Neither had lasted long enough. Fuller did not like to think of that now. He held Tommy's hand firmly and proceeded along the quayside. Captain Wood had told him Tommy was easily managed and much accustomed to people, and that it would be better to walk him than to force him into a crate. Fuller hoped he was right. Wood had told him more than once how much the crew had grown to love the animal, which had entertained them all on the passage, climbing up the rigging whenever he could. The captain had been visibly pained to see them go. Tommy, too, had been distressed when he had been removed from his makeshift cage in the warehouse. As though he had known what was happening.

Now he was quiet, perhaps a little scared, but compliant – thank God! Fuller had neither the manpower nor a plan, beyond a length of rope, to deal with the beast in the event of it being unwilling but Tommy seemed not to want to cause any trouble, just stepped awkwardly along. He was really quite a sight, dressed in an old white shirt, the tatty ends of which came down almost to his pink, hairless feet. It did not quite cover his arms, and thick hair, a shocking black, protruded from beneath the cuffs; a dark fringe over his very human hands. He reminded Fuller of his daughter, Eliza, when she had recently been learning to walk: Tommy's free hand dropped every now and then to seek out the wet, bumpy stone. The fine mist of rain had left silver droplets on the dark hair that surrounded his pink face and the fairer whiskers around his mouth. His big brown eyes gave nothing away, directed downwards at his feet as he walked in this manner. Upright, not natural to him. He did not look back at the ship, or the last of its men, who watched the strange trio depart.

Back on Broad Street, Fuller was pleased to see a coach waiting outside the White Lion. The horses had not yet been tethered to it, but the coachman stood guard and a couple of passengers, two young men, scruffily dressed, waited with their bags. Inside, on the other side of the window glass, the face of an elderly gentleman was visible. He had taken the best seat, away from the ever-juddering wheels. All their eyes were fixed on the trio as they approached. *Were they really going to get on?* Fuller could see no better way of getting them all back, and sent the lad into the office to buy three tickets: *two inside and one out.*

After a not inconsiderable amount of trouble and delay, they had managed to persuade both proprietor and coachmen of the Night Regulator to let them on. It had pulled away just as it was getting dark. Tommy and Fuller sat inside, the lad with the other poor wretches outside at the rear. The three were back in London by seven the following morning. Tommy had been a surprisingly good traveller, despite the bumpy ride, though none of them had slept much.

Now, man and chimpanzee were in the kitchen of the keepers' lodgings in the North Garden. The helper, exhausted after his ordeal, had gone to his bed in the room above the Wapiti House. Fuller was in no hurry. He nursed the cup of tea the cook, Mrs Williams, had made him. His eyes followed Tommy's every move. Mr Miller had called in to see the creature too. They both watched him now, tugging at Mrs Williams's skirts as she tried to finish washing the dishes from the keepers' breakfast. Mrs Williams seemed unperturbed, turning to chide him and laugh, conscious that in front of the Superintendent she could not be seen to avoid her work. Tommy made a noise, a soft hooting sound, through protruding lips in response. He stood upright, one hand holding onto her skirt. *Tommy.* The chimpanzee looked at Fuller with large eyes when he called his name. Any fear he had had initially of the man had long gone. Fuller offered him another apple – he had had one, with some warm milk, when they had first arrived. Tommy knew he liked them now. He bounded across to where the head keeper was seated at the table to snatch it with his long fingers. He was still wearing the old shirt, and could almost have been mistaken for a slum child, sitting on his haunches, eating the apple with big, greedy bites.

Tommy was strong and healthy. It was marvellous to watch him. And another thing: he seemed happy here. Miller agreed. He should stay in the keepers' lodgings for the winter. It was a bad time of year for an ape to arrive with them, just as winter was drawing in. Exactly the same time of year as the orang utan back in 1830. They should not take any unnecessary risks. Put a cage in here for him, in the kitchen where it was warm. Fuller was finishing his tea, ready to go and give instructions accordingly, when one of the keepers, John Foot, suddenly appeared in the doorway: *Jack has been on the rampage, broken his tusk smashing up his den.* Fuller told Foot to keep an eye on Tommy, bade the Superintendent good day and put on his cap. He had hoped to see Sophie, Eliza and the new baby, get some sleep, but that would have to wait.

Jack had torn off a full twelve inches of one of his tusks, trying to prise a wooden board from a wall in his den. It was a matter of grave concern. Not the tusk, that wouldn't hurt him, the behaviour. After the incident with Hacker, the rhinoceros had caused no further worry, but Jack . . . Fuller hoped he would not get worse. The new house for the elephant and rhino, with all its added durability – a brick floor, oak railings – was not yet ready to take them.

Fuller did not get his rest. The following day, a leopard, an ostrich and an ichneumon died; on the next, a tiger and a tortoise were lost. And so it went on. The Council appointed yet another committee to work with the head keeper, the Medical Superintendent and the existing committees responsible for animal health to investigate the health of the large carnivores, among which the mortality was so very alarming.

But then there was Tommy, who was never left alone. Even Fuller, who had so much to do, would find himself calling into the keepers' lodgings to spend a few welcome minutes in the warmth of the kitchen. Sometimes he caught the morning ritual, when Tommy's face and hands were washed and his hair was combed. Tommy would happily undress himself, though he never could manage to get his clothes back on. He had agreed to part with his old shirt now, in exchange for a Guernsey frock, which he wore accompanied by a little sailor hat. He had a cage in the corner, though he was rarely inside, unless it was to swing from the branch when he was asked to do so by his admirers. He would rattle the door incessantly if he was shut away in it, but thoroughly enjoyed climbing on top of it, especially to find something new to prod or try out with his teeth. The keepers just made sure the windows and doors were closed and let him roam free, more often than not. Foot had formed an instant rapport with the animal and Fuller had appointed him principal keeper. Tommy would throw his arms around him and bury his head in his bosom. Foot was mad on the animal. Mrs Williams remained the chimpanzee's dearest ally, though: Tommy's favourite spot was the old woman's lap as she rested by the fire. When she had to go about her cleaning duties elsewhere, he pined for her. But he never wanted for attention. *Everyone* loved Tommy.

Endless people came to visit him – politicians and society ladies and gentlemen – and Fellows came to the keepers' kitchen with more serious ends in mind: scientific study. One afternoon, not long after his arrival, Mr William Broderip, a naturalist and member of the Council (and a lawyer by profession), wanted to do some experiments and asked for Fuller's help. Fuller had done as requested. He had placed one of the pythons in a hamper and a small tortoise in another basket and carried them up to the keepers' lodgings, where Mr Broderip was testing Tommy's reactions. Fuller caught the end of a rather amusing scene: Tommy gazing in wonder at his own reflection in a looking glass, pressing his face to it, turning it over to see what was behind. *Just like a savage might!* Mr Broderip exclaimed. Fuller waited patiently, standing by the door. Tommy was presented with various other things (sugared almonds, a glass of sherry, a cocoa-nut) before the hamper was requested. Fuller brought it in from the corridor and laid it on a chair near to the dresser, opened the lid and removed the blanket in which he had wrapped the live serpent. Tommy noticed the hamper and sprang his way towards it, but recoiled in horror when he saw what was inside. Genuine horror. He hooted in fear as he ran to Foot for protection. *He must remember them from his infancy in Africa! Or is it instinct?* Mr Broderip made notes with his pencil, before instructing an apple be placed by the hamper, to see if Tommy could be tempted towards it. Fuller almost felt sorry for the poor creature, cowering behind him. Though the fear was short-lived: Tommy was soon gambolling about the kitchen once again.

Mr Broderip presented his findings to the Committee of Science and Correspondence at the end of October. They were duly published in the Proceedings, which were then quoted by the more popular press. Tommy was growing famous. Mr Scharf, who had done a set of lithographs of the Gardens, hurriedly added an extra one of the chimpanzee. Copies sold in vast quantities. The new 'star attraction', the newspapers called him! There was even a ditty that went around London about Tommy. Sophie had repeated it to him:

> The folks in town are nearly wild,
> To go and see the monkey-child,
> In Gardens of Zoology,
> Whose proper name is Chimpanzee.
> To keep this baby free from hurt,
> He's dressed in a cap and a Guernsey shirt;
> They've got him a nurse,
> And he sits on her knee,
> And she calls him her Tommy Chimpanzee.

Fuller revelled in it. His Tommy, so famous! He thought of Cross. He must be choked with jealousy.

It did not stop him feeling under pressure as winter drew in, given the recent high rate of mortality and the increasing attentions of the various committees upon it. In his darkest moments Fuller worried, even, that he might lose his job. (Then what would happen to them all? Would Sophie and the children end up in one of the new workhouses?) He requested permission to attend a meeting of the Council in early November, to explain a discrepancy between his own returns of the deaths in the menagerie and those of the keepers. He did not want it to look as if he was trying to cover anything up. Not that it looked good, either way.

But the Council was easily reassured. The animals they had lost were not on their minds, not nearly as much as Fuller had feared. No, they asked about Tommy. Fuller was praised for how he had handled the purchase of the chimpanzee.

In early December, the Council held a meeting at the Gardens. Its members greeted the head keeper warmly when they met him at his work. A few days earlier, Tommy had suffered a strange twenty-four-hour seizure of sorts, to everyone's dismay –

he had quite lost the use of his legs – but was fully recovered, Fuller was pleased to report. Hacker was also over his illness, back from his respite in the country. The current phase of works on the Elephant House had been finished that morning. A good day already, it got better still. Along with news of a potential new site for the Museum, at Leicester Square, the Council reported the contents of a letter from Mr Bouchier in Malta: Monsieur Thibaut had arrived there, in late November, with four living giraffes. The boat was now in quarantine, accommodation being readied for the animals for the coming winter. The Zoological Society of London could expect to meet the most exotic creatures they had ever received in the spring.

Word got out quickly. *The Times* ran an article in the first days of the new year announcing the giraffes' imminent arrival. Other papers too. As soon as Mr Cross found out the Society's giraffes were on the way, he was in touch to ask if he might purchase one. *On any terms,* he said. Fuller had been satisfied with the Council's answer: no. They would have four; Cross would not have a single one. But Fuller dared not be excited, not yet. Not with so much to do before the animals arrived. A committee had been formed to oversee the details of their transport. The President, the Earl of Derby, had contacted the Admiralty to ask for their help. (Fuller had long known him as Lord Stanley, but his father had died so he had inherited the title. Fuller knew him well: he was constantly requesting loans and exchanges of animals.) Mr Burton drew up plans for the giraffes' accommodation: an ornate barn in the North Garden. This time it was hoped that his efforts would not be wasted. If the animals had survived as far as Malta, surely they could make it to London?

The usual worries were taxing Fuller's mind. The new den for the elephant and rhinoceros had not eased his concerns about the beasts and safety. One morning Jack had smashed into his neighbour's enclosure. The keeper had found the rhino at the elephant's side, his horn beneath Jack's belly, Jack trembling like a pup. Fuller ordered all the doors strengthened with oak and sheet iron. What if either of them got out? Jack was never to be left unattended in daylight hours. That meant more work for them all, of course. His men were already fearful of the rhino, even reluctant to clean out his den. A committee was set up to look into it. Fuller hoped they would find a solution before anything bad happened.

With Tommy it was different. He was not a concern, he was a delight. And as sprightly as ever, despite the cold! Fuller was proud that he had managed to keep him alive. He was fond of him, too, if he was honest, perhaps more fond of him than he had ever been of any of his charges. He saw him only as another beast, and Mr Youatt agreed, but others said he was more like a child than any other intelligent animal. (Someone had even mistaken the chimpanzee for a plasterer, when they had found him, back turned, pressing his hands against the wall in the kitchen!) At night when Fuller was doing his final rounds, he would often call into the keepers' lodgings to check on Tommy. He would sit there and watch him sleep, as he sometimes did with his own babes. Tommy had a curious way of sleeping: in a seated position, eyes closed, leaning forward with his arms folded. Sometimes even with his head in his hands. He did that when he was awake too: he would hold his head as he watched the men eat their meals, following each morsel from plate to fork to mouth, hooting and stamping if they would not let him sip from their glasses of porter, perfectly emulating his human friends' manner if he was permitted to drink too. Tommy was becoming part of all of their lives.

As Fuller sat and watched the dying embers of the fire (where was the watchman? He was supposed to keep the fires alight), Tommy slept in his cage. Fuller thought back to the early days of his work at the Gardens, when they had far fewer creatures to care for and he could spend time with the animals. Now his work was as much about looking after his men as the beasts, his daily routine filled by management of assignments and provisions as much as anything else. Except in those quiet moments after dark, moments he cherished: Tommy sleeping next to him as Fuller sat by the fire, watching the red coals slowly fading to black. Fuller thought of the future too, the year ahead. He allowed himself to think of the summer of 1836, when they would have a chimpanzee *and* four giraffes in the Gardens! He pictured the fine den they would build for Tommy, where everyone could see him, the giraffes towering above even the trees, looking down on the crowds below. It was a waking dream that he enjoyed. He smiled to himself. What would Mr Cross make of it?

In February, Fuller heard alarming news. Cross had instructed his agent John Warwick to procure some giraffes and bring them to London as quickly as possible. If the Society would not share with him, he would beat them to it. Warwick had already proceeded from England. Treachery indeed, this was. Warwick had worked alongside Fuller at the Gardens back in the early days, then had transferred to the Museum and left in a row over wages. Now it seemed that he and Cross were conspiring to rob the Society of its big moment. Rob *him* of his big moment. Fuller was spitting mad.

The Society wouldn't just let him win, though. The race was on. The giraffes had cost them an extraordinary amount already, and if they were not the first on display in this country it would be money ill-spent. Fuller knew the advantage was theirs. They had the creatures, which were waiting to be transported as soon as the weather was kind. The 'Giraffe Committee' began to explore other ways of getting the animals back to London. It looked into steamers. If these modern ships could beat the winds with their engines, the Society could beat Cross. It would cost them dear but it was the only way to guarantee they would win the race. And the Society was determined that they should, no one more so than Fuller.

They needed the weather to improve before the creatures could be brought to London. It showed no sign of doing so. March was a wet month. A very wet month. Tommy sickened at the start of it. Mrs Williams noticed that he was not quite himself, and he was off his food. Fuller went to see him straight away. He did not like what he saw. Tommy would not even touch his favourite delicacy: ripe apples. And there was something about his demeanour that Fuller recognized. It scared him. Tommy had been his personal triumph, he felt. Now he did not like where it might end. Fuller was feeling under pressure again as it was. A letter had been published in *The Times*, from an anonymous correspondent, criticizing the treatment of the animals: the undrained, soggy ground they lived on, their lack of protection against the elements. It had obviously been written by someone with something to prove – one of the men voted off the Council, perhaps. All the same, he did not need Tommy to fall ill now.

But it happened. Tommy had a fever, which grew worse, despite the calomel and buckthorn Mr Youatt administered, and the bleeding he attempted – for which Tommy did not forgive him: he showed Youatt the marks left by the lancet when he came again. His capering around the kitchen diminished. He still did not take his food. Youatt called in his surgeon friends to help. On the rounds Fuller had to do with the Medical Superintendent, he hated to watch as Youatt prodded and poked Tommy and inspected his faeces, which came in stinking gushes prompted by the medicine, with blood and mucus. Tommy soon stopped taking even the milk in which Youatt administered the drugs – magnesia and antimonials now – so that he had to be force-fed. The chimpanzee seemed not to trust any of them after that. Fuller called in to see him less and less frequently as the month went on, coming reluctantly when the panicked keepers called for him. He could not bear to see him like that, sickening and scared; he did not want to give up on his dream of Tommy the Chimpanzee, the star attraction of the Gardens over the sunlit days of summer. He did not want to imagine what the Council would think if he lost Tommy now, when winter was almost over.

He distracted himself with the preparations for the giraffes. The Giraffe Committee had done a deal with the Peninsular Steam Navigation Company, which had recently started a steamer service between England, Spain and Portugal. They had paid a thousand pounds to charter the *Manchester*, a six-hundred-ton steam vessel. Once it had carried the precious cargo to London, the giraffes would need temporary accommodation while the grand home Mr Burton envisaged for them was being realized. The huge costs already incurred made further outlay rather difficult for now. There had been some controversy about the expenditure. Fuller ignored it. He had enough to worry about without the squabbling of the Council and the Fellows. He allowed himself to feel excited about the giraffes instead, as the rest of London was. He often saw progress reports in the newspaper and stories about the animals' behaviour. Apparently one had been seen to cry when its companions were out of sight. Fuller doubted that, but he would soon see for himself. He hoped. He prayed.

Less widely rumoured was that Warwick, now in Alexandria, had succeeded in obtaining some giraffes of his own. Fuller made sure he was in the know, though. He turned it over in his mind as he worked. He remembered Warwick well. He thought on it, as he tried not to think about Tommy. Tommy, who – despite a seeming improvement in the middle of March, when he would take a little milk again – grew thinner, duller. Tommy, whose dark eyes did not follow his keepers around the room any more and scarcely registered Fuller when he had to confront him, twice a week on his rounds with Youatt, and all the various other medical men he brought with him in those difficult days. Now Tommy just sat by the fire in his little Guernsey shirt. Right up close to it for its warmth. He would lean his cheek on his palm and look into the flames. When Mrs Williams had a moment to spare she would help him up to sit on her lap. Just sit: he did not play with his toes or try to grab anyone and anything that passed now. His hairy hands were still as he looked into the fire with wide, dark eyes.

In the third week of March, Tommy started to cough and was breathing with obvious difficulty. Still the visitors traipsed in and out of the lodgings; even the Princess Victoria and her mother were shown up to see him on his little deathbed, for that was obviously what it was. Mr Youatt was at a loss as to what to do now that he had tried everything: cutting his gums in case teething was the cause of it all, warm baths, ginger tea. Nothing had worked. Tommy's face blanched; his eyes sank further into it. Fuller ordered a fire kept going in the kitchen day and night. *Perhaps if Tommy could hang on until the spring he would pull through*, some of the men said. Fuller waited for the inevitable.

The end came five days after the royal visit. The chimpanzee, which had spent his first years in the forests of West Africa, which had been snatched from his mother by hunters, which had crossed the Atlantic with commercial sailors, which had travelled by coach from Bristol to London, which had lived for six months in a small lodging in the middle of the biggest city in the world, died before the embers of a kitchen fire on the 25th of March. He had screamed with anxiety the evening before, but the end, when it came, was calm: he took off the blanket he lay under and put his arms around his beloved keeper's neck, held his face close to his and died without a struggle. His body was bundled up and taken to the offices at Bruton Street, where Richard Owen cut it up before a crowd of Fellows. The details of the abscesses and ulcers in his gut were presented to the Committee of Science and Correspondence. His death was reported in newspapers in towns and cities all over the country.

The little kitchen fell quiet. The cage was removed but its presence, its late occupant's presence, lingered, like the unwelcome smell of a consumed meal. Life at the Gardens went on, a little less jubilantly than before. At least as far as the humans were concerned. At least for a little while.

Fuller threw his energies into finding a temporary space for the giraffes. There had been discussion of accommodating them away from the Gardens as a separate exhibition, but nowhere suitable appeared. So Fuller was ordered to find somewhere. It would have to be the Elephant House, he reluctantly admitted. No other building could accommodate them until Burton's dedicated Giraffe House was complete. Yet he dreaded to think what Jack would make of another move: he was only just settling down now. He had read of a visitor attacked by one of the tigers when Mr Wombwell's famous travelling menagerie was at Carlisle; the victim had later died. He dreaded such an occurrence on his own watch. But he had no choice except to move Jack back into the Rhinoceros House. He would find space for the rhinoceros elsewhere.

News reached the Society that the *Manchester* had quit Valletta harbour on the 3rd of May and was now *en route* to them, with two gazelles, a lioness, a lynx and the four healthy giraffes on board. Just days afterwards, they learned that Warwick had left Alexandria with three giraffes. The race was on. If the *Manchester*'s voyage was uneventful, they must, surely, win. But Fuller

had not forgotten the last giraffe that had made its way to
them, the creature so keenly awaited, which had arrived as a
carcass. The *Manchester* was reported as landing safely in Gibral
tar on the 10th of May; Cadiz the next; then Lisbon on the
sixteenth, where thousands of people boarded the steamship to
see the creatures for themselves. All were yet alive. On the 20th
of May, it reached England and docked at Falmouth just long
enough to get word to London to expect their arrival in two
days' time.

On Tuesday, the 24th of May, Fuller made his way to the East
India Docks to await the *Manchester*. She was due to arrive that
evening. He wanted to be there early to make sure he was on the
spot as soon as she docked to see the animals and speak to the
men who had cared for them before he made any arrangements
for onward transport. He wasn't concerned about the lynx, the
lion or the gazelles. But the giraffes, who knew what they would
need? The Regent's Canal Company had offered to transport
them by barge. He wondered if they might be better walking.
He would wait and see. Hunt, now assistant head keeper, was
back at the Gardens, waiting to receive his instructions.

Thus Fuller found himself at Blackwall, alone. He had jour-
neyed by omnibus, packed in among drab men who had the
look of clerks, and come in through the main gatehouse, just
one vehicle in the endless stream of carts, carriages, horses and
people passing in both directions through and around the archways under the clock tower. He jumped down from the bus into
the chaos of people and barrows. He would walk the last bit, he
decided. Fuller had been within the walls of the East India
Docks many times before. He thought of the day when he had
picked up Jack and wondered if what he was about to do would
eclipse that triumphal procession. He did not stop to ruminate
on it. He strode on into the noise, hearing the drum-like boom

of barrels rolled across the stones, the splash of ropes in water, the hammering of tools on iron, the cries of men and the screech of gulls. The coarse songs of sailors unseen.

Five or six huge wooden vessels were tied to the quayside, masts crowding a sky streaked with smoke. There was much industry in this part of London now. One East Indiaman was unloading as he passed and Fuller found himself among the dockers. A ragged bunch of men, they were. Casual day labourers, poor souls, one slip away from the workhouse, these days. He felt proud in his fine uniform, a man of importance. He passed the merchants, counting their spoils in makeshift quayside offices. None of this was novel to him, but thrilling, somehow, all the same. He breathed in the smells of the world, of the tea, spices and wines that had travelled so far to this spot. If he had been a philosophical man he might have felt that in this moment, on that quayside, all the wide world was come to him. But Devereux Fuller had only one matter on his mind that day: four giraffes from Egypt.

He headed beyond the import and export docks and the yard to the riverside beyond, the newest part of the docks: Brunswick Wharf. It had been built only in the last few years for the new steamships, the river wall clad entirely in iron sheet piling. Quite a sight in the sunshine. Things were happening in this part of London, no doubt. Work was under way again, after the floods and financial problems that had stopped it, on the Thames Tunnel nearby at Rotherhithe. Part of the new railway, which would in time run as far as London Bridge, had opened at Greenwich. Fuller had read in the paper that thousands had taken the train to Mr Cross's most recent fete in honour of the Princess Victoria's birthday. He had put on a show with a hot-air balloon. It was going up again today, Fuller remembered, and half wondered if he would see it from there. The day was clear, but Surrey Zoological Gardens must be five miles away.

Fuller looked away from the sky and scanned the quayside instead. One steamship pulled up alongside, not the *Manchester*. There were few people about. He would go and get a drink somewhere comfortable, wait for his ship to come in. There was a fine hotel directly on the quayside, a grand building with big windows overlooking the river. He would not belong there. There was a tavern at the rear, next to the stables, the Brunswick Tap: that was where he would go. To still his nerves. He always carried an element of caution, always more so when victory was close.

They disembark the giraffes just before dawn the next morning. Monsieur Thibaut walks them out, their spindly limbs stretching for the hard quayside in the first light of a new summer day. Thibaut, then the Arabs in their native dress, the Maltese attendant too. Led by ropes, the creatures come willingly. Tame and trusting. The lion, lynx and gazelle are gone already: they were removed on the previous day. The barge had been dispatched but Thibaut and Fuller had agreed that walking the giraffes would be best. And thus the strange caravan sets off on the final leg of its long, long journey. Strange creatures in a strange land. Through the dockyard. On to the streets of London.

There are challenges along the way, for Thibaut and his men. In the neighbourhood of the Commercial Road, the giraffes are terrified by a cow in a nearby field, and will move on only when it has been driven to the remotest corner. A show bill on a tavern on the City Road scares them as much. Monsieur Thibaut, who knows his charges well after all these months in their company, feeds them lumps of loaf sugar and urges them on.

The animals arrive at their new home by way of Gloucester Gate, reaching it as the light warms the sky and the earth beneath. Police await, in case of crowds. Yet the giraffes and their guides share the early-morning streets with a few market carts only, and a handful of onlookers, those up at dawn to greet the newest residents of the Regent's Park. Fuller is here, of course. Here to watch these graceful, mysterious creatures as they are led into the park, to see them stop to eat the leaves of the trees, new to them. To share in this moment: a quiet triumph.

The crowds came later. So many people were desperate to see the giraffes that the Society had to put an advert in the newspapers about overcrowding on the drive, and a sign by the gates to try to maintain order. Fuller understood the attraction, for he loved to watch them himself: those creatures moving so gracefully, on legs that looked as if they might break. Creatures that had been brought across the world so that he might observe them, or so it felt.

The Giraffe House would be built in time but for now they were kept in the Elephant House. So, too, were their Nubian attendants, who inhabited it alongside the animals. The dark-skinned men in their exotic dress, with their exotic language, were as much a part of the attraction as the giraffes, for Fuller as for everyone else. He had learned the names the Arabs had given their charges: Selim, the Fortunate, the one with a talisman around his neck; Mabrouk, the Favourite; Guib-allah, God's Gift; Zaida, Happy. And the four creatures indeed seemed happy, if you could call it that. Healthy, anyway. As he watched them, he tried to imagine the desert they had all come from. Monsieur Thibaut had told him a little of it. He could almost feel the hot African sun on his face. Africa. So far away yet now they owned a piece of it. Four pieces of it. Four giraffes!

A triumph, made sweeter by the fact that Cross had been beaten. On the 27th of June, Warwick and his giraffes reached the Thames. A month too late. Half of London had seen such creatures in the flesh by then. Even the Princess Victoria, the much-promoted patron of the Surrey Zoological Society, had

been to see the four already residing at Regent's Park. The triumph belonged to the Zoological Society of London this time.
It belonged to Fuller. The only thing missing was Tommy,
although he was not missed by the visitors as much as Fuller had
feared. The giraffes were loved now. Mr Scharf was in the enclosure in those first weeks, drawing them for his next lithograph,
a souvenir for the crowds who poured in in their thousands to
catch a glimpse of the newest arrivals. That summer there were
more people in the Gardens than Fuller had ever seen. He was
busier than ever. He, too, had almost forgotten Tommy.

Almost, but not quite.

**Extract from the *Waterford Chronicle*, Saturday, 9th
April, 1836**

THE CHIMPANZEE died on Saturday morning, the 26th,
at his residence in The Zoological Gardens. *Troglodytes Niger*,
Esq., more commonly known as Mr T. Chimpanzee.

We understand that he suffered very little in his latter
moments. He seemed perfectly aware of the approach of
death, and what is more extraordinary, resigned to the event
in the midst of this most surprising consciousness.

The results of the dissection add to all other wonders of the
case, for we are told by some eminent anatomists who were
present at the operation, that unless they had been fore-
warned, all that they saw of the conformation of the animal
would have led them to pronounce it human.

6. From Mockingbirds to Man

Charles Darwin Esq., Corresponding Member,
1836–42

Among the countless ships that are being blown across the vast, glittering Atlantic Ocean that June afternoon – the northbound trading ships loaded with fragrant tea and spices; the slavers heading westwards with their illicit cargos of misery; a ship blazing south, loaded, perhaps, with the unwilling or optimistic migrants destined for the colonies of Australia – there is a British naval ship, returning home. A ten-gun brig, ninety feet long and twenty-four feet wide, it has circumnavigated the globe. Now it cuts its way northwards through the choppy waters, bathed in the golden light of the late afternoon. This ship's hard-earned cargo is not men or goods, but measurements and charts; the results of a survey of the South American coast that has lasted four and a half years.

Packed away on it, there are some more unusual treasures, too. Beneath the sailors busying themselves on deck in the last warmth of the day, in the tiny poop cabin behind the wheel, a man sits among papers and cases. A man who does not wear the clothes of the seasoned sailor but who now wears their same grizzled look. Thin, bronzed, he is leaning over the chart table that almost fills the cabin. He has become accustomed to this place over the long months they have spent at sea, but he yearns for more space; space to investigate his haul properly. Laid out before him are just a few of the many fruits of his private labours on this voyage, not charts but notebooks filled with his own musings. And some bird skins, hastily but not inexpertly prepared.

Around him, hidden in boxes and drawers, are the other creatures he has assembled. Bird skins and fossils and mammal skins and plants, and spirit bottles filled with fish and insects and small beings of all kinds. They are the physical mementos of four and a half years in the jungles and cliffs of Bahia, the earthquake-ruined city of Concepción, the savage lands of Tierra del Fuego, the contested rocks of the Falkland Islands, the wilds of Uruguay, the wonders of Tahiti, the new world of Australia. He feels as if he has preserved and packed half of the world into turpentine, camphor, tobacco and, above all, in spirits. Many of the spoils are already back in England, sent from harbours dotted around the globe. He wonders what secrets these specimens hold. He fervently hopes they hold something at least of interest to the experts at home. He has had news from England that some of his writings have already been published, to great acclaim. He is desperate to prove himself to his peers. To his family, too. They had hoped he would lead a quiet life in a country parish. He does not know what his future holds.

Now, while the ship is in the great expanse of the Atlantic, he finally has a moment to take stock of his researches, to work on cataloguing his haul. Time to go through his notes, so many notes! And to look again at his more recent finds, which have not been sent on but are coming home with him. Before him on the chart table are the little bodies of some birds he shot on the strange, burned islands of the Galapagos. Little brown mockingbirds. He is looking intently at the one in his hand, then to the others on the table, from them to his notes. As the cabin rolls gently from side to side (he barely notices it now, though it once made him so ill), he is seeing that the birds from different islands are not quite the same. He is recalling that the locals had told him each island had its own unique creatures. Is this true? If it is true . . . if the original species has adapted itself to each island, to make new ones . . .

Oh, he has so many questions. Questions: the most precious cargo that he is bringing back with him, and one that will not fit into crates and cases, barely even on to the pages of his notebooks. He silently urges the *Beagle* to make haste, for now he longs for answers. And he is sick of the ocean. The sun is setting on its great expanse now, the light falling from the endless sky, but still he leans over the chart table, looking at the birds. Willing the ship to make haste. For England and for answers.

Seeing his collection again now, in the cold light of a London autumn day, he could not help but think he had been somewhat overzealous. It was late October, and he had come to Greenwich to be reunited with his possessions and his servant, having left both on board for the last leg of the voyage from Cornwall. He had disembarked at the first opportunity, at Falmouth: four years and nine months away from home had been quite long enough for him. Tired, ragged and homesick, he headed directly from Cornwall to Shrewsbury to be reunited with his family.

Coming aboard the *Beagle* again, he felt the bite of nostalgia when he saw his nameplate on the poop cabin door: *Charles Darwin*. Nostalgia not just for the many, many months he had spent in here, for all those nights rocking in the hammock slung above the table, looking at the foreign stars and dreaming of home, but for the enthusiastic man who had left this cabin just a matter of weeks previously. The dark and stormy English night he had stepped into at Falmouth had seemed so full of promise, then. *He* had felt so full of promise, so eager to share his tales of gauchos and savages and giant tortoises and volcanoes with his family. Eager to show off his findings to those who could help him to decipher them. Now, less than a month later, he looked at the collection he had amassed and it felt more like a burden. He wondered what on earth he would do with all of the bones and bodies and bottles and rocks he had so conscientiously, so blindly assembled.

It was a damp grey afternoon. In place of the sound of the men singing on deck above and the creak of the boat around him, he now heard the constant clatter of wheels on stone on the quay outside. You could not escape the noise anywhere in this odious city. He had had enough of London already and he had only been there a few days. After seeing his family at Shrewsbury, he had headed straight for Cambridge to see the Reverend Professor John Stevens Henslow, Professor of Botany and his mentor. It was Henslow who had inspired him as a student and who had put him up for this expedition all those years ago. It was Henslow whose advice he now sought. *What on earth was he to do with all of this stuff?* Henslow had directed him to London.

Darwin had done as advised, and spent the past days pounding the dirty streets, calling upon the capital's finest geologists and zoologists. The excited reception he had long anticipated was not what he met. The reality was that no one seemed to want to take such a load off his hands, not even the specimens he was sure were as yet unnamed. The Zoological Society Museum and the British Museum were sinking under the weight of donations from people just like him. Collectors were in abundance; real naturalists were few. It had been a deflating few days. Now, as he trawled through the remaining contents of the cabinets and chests in his cabin, he knew that his voyage was far from over. It seemed increasingly likely that he would have to wait some years before he would make any sense of it.

Darwin instructed his man, Covington, to pack up the plants he had collected on the Galapagos. They seemed to be in a reasonable state of preservation. At least that was something – everything had survived. Even the little pet tortoise he had taken on James Island was still crawling about the cabin's floor. He would take the plants with him today to send on to Henslow. The rest could wait. The *Beagle* was making only for Woolwich now. He and Covington could do their work there, offloading the bulk of it. Besides, with nowhere to send stuff on to there was really no rush, other than his own yearning to be done with it all and back in the peace and comfort of Cambridge. London was exhausting, with its politics (so much had happened since he had been away) and its oppressive, unhealthy atmosphere. He was starting to think that a clergyman's life might be for him after all.

Tonight, at least, he had something to look forward to. He had been invited to a tea party at Mr Lyell's house. The great Lyell, the most famous geologist of all, wanted to meet him! Yes, that was something. He looked over to his copy of *Principles of Geology* on the bookshelves that constituted the ship's 'library'. He had devoured it when they had first set out. He had been lying in his hammock under the skylight when he had first read Lyell's theory that it was gradual processes that shaped the earth, not the cataclysms, like the Biblical flood, that most geologists described and most people believed in. Henslow had told him not to take it too literally, but Darwin had seen evidence of its veracity in all of his subsequent explorations. The theory explained so much: the seashells he had found way above sea level, the rising of the water line by a few feet after the earthquake in Chile . . . On his return he had been gratified to find that these ideas of gradual processes in nature were now becoming more widely accepted. It opened a whole new intellectual territory! In geology, anyway. Such ideas were still considered rather dangerous in more animate parts of the natural world. He was impatient to discuss his thoughts with Lyell. He had new evidence to add to the theory – like the upheaval of mountains he had witnessed after the Chilean earthquake – which he was eager to discuss with the great man.

Yes, he was excited by the geology, making progress with it. It was the zoology that was the worry. Perhaps he might make some headway with that tonight too, he thought. Mr Owen would be there and had already said he would dissect some of the animals preserved in spirits. His was the only offer of help Darwin had received on that front so far, save that from his old Edinburgh tutor, Dr Grant, to whom he had been close when he had been a student there. Now in London, Grant had offered to look at the corallines. Darwin sensed that allying himself to a 'transmutationist' would probably do him few favours. Perhaps he could sound out the party guests on that tonight too. Mr Broderip of the Zoological Society would also be there. He must make sure he was impressive on his debut into the upper echelons of London's scientific elite.

He should get off the cramped ship. He needed time to prepare himself. He took the plants Covington had assembled for him, said goodbye, and disembarked from the *Beagle* once again. The river that greeted him stank. His neck was stiff from stooping in the five-foot-high cabin. How had he managed all those months? More pressing, though, was how he would manage in this foul city. He steeled himself for his journey back into it, to his brother's house in Great Marlborough Street, where he was staying. He wondered, again, whether he had made the wrong decision, whether he ought to have listened to his family, eschewed this life and chosen the peace of a country parish. He tried to concentrate on the evening that lay ahead. He had already worried too much about what lay beyond it.

The induction into Lyell and Owen's intellectual circle gave Darwin's quest a useful boost. By the time he and Covington had unloaded all the crates of specimens from the *Beagle* at Woolwich, there were takers for many of them.

The men he had met at Lyell's party had confirmed that Darwin's instincts had been correct: he should be wary of Grant. The man might be teaching in a university now, but his ideas of an entirely self-sufficient nature were not accepted by the scientific elite that Darwin was interested in joining. The idea of life being governed by nature's laws alone was considered most dangerous in this politically charged climate. At a time when the God-given right of Church and state to rule the masses was being challenged, it would not do to suggest that in the natural world power came from below, as Grant did. It was a shame. Darwin well remembered the intellectual sparring he and his tutor had enjoyed in his time at Edinburgh. His old mentor had always been a progressive, and had long rejected the accepted idea that the fossil record supported the idea of successive geological cataclysm and creation, only now becoming more widely discussed. He recalled Grant's effusive praise of his grandfather Erasmus Darwin's work *Zoonomia*, with its risqué idea that all warm-blooded living beings were so similar in structure they must share origins. Though he had been proud as a student when he had spoken of it with Grant, Darwin had his future to think of now: he had to be practical and could not risk an unwise association. Association with his grandfather was beyond his control. But the friendships he fostered now were not. Darwin politely declined Grant's offer of help.

He had four additional boxes sent to Henslow in Cambridge: two of geological specimens, one of spirit cases, the last of bird skins and insects. He had distributed others among London experts: Mr Broderip had agreed to look over the shells; Mr Bell, with whom he had become acquainted at a dinner of the Linnean Society, had said he'd take the crustacea and reptiles. The fossils in particular had caused much excitement already. Darwin had delivered them to Mr Owen at Hunter's Museum in the Royal College of Surgeons. As they unpacked them together it was immediately obvious that they included some wonders. Within a matter of weeks, the ever-diligent Owen had named two new ones: the first was the head of a form of gnawing animal the size of a hippopotamus, *Toxodon*; the other a giant sloth-like creature, a *Megatherium*. So important were they that the college even had casts made of them to be sent to the British Museum.

Finally, things were starting to happen for Darwin. He focused on the side of his researches that seemed to be going somewhere, quitting London for the comfort and seclusion of Cambridge to write a paper on the geology of the Chilean coast.

On the 4th of January, 1837, Charles Darwin was scheduled to present his debut paper to the evening meeting of the Geological Society. While he was in the capital, he thought he might as well take the opportunity to offload the bulk of his zoological specimens. He had delayed so long because it had not been clear *where* he should offload them. He had revisited the Zoological Society's Museum when he had first arrived back in London and formed a poor impression of it. Now, having also witnessed the sniping at one of their scientific meetings, he had an equally poor impression of their zoologists. (Dr Grant had been voted off the Council last year, and there was still much division between the 'reformers' and the rest of the Society, it seemed.) Yet Owen seemed to think highly of the Society, especially now the radical Grant was less involved. Besides, at the British Museum the situation had seemed yet worse: collections were left for years without being so much as looked at. Darwin had decided he might as well deposit his with the Zoological Society as anywhere else. He did not want to keep them: he had enough to do. As well as his geological work, Captain Robert Fitzroy, who had headed the expedition, had proposed a multi-volume history of the *Beagle*'s voyage, and he had begun preparing his journal for publication.

Which was how it came to pass that, on the first Wednesday in January, Darwin found himself arriving at Leicester Square. He was accompanied by Covington, who in turn was accompanied by 80 mammals and 450 birds, skinned, in spirits and packed into boxes. It was a fine-looking city square, though the gardens in the middle required attention, Darwin noticed, as they pulled up. Once the preserve of artists and aristocrats, it was in an area that was now becoming known for its entertainments. The Savile Palace Exhibition Rooms and Theatre were on the northern side and Mr Barker's famous panorama was just around the corner. The Zoological Society of London had been located there since the previous spring. After much fussing over whether to build their Museum in the Regent's Park or take a building elsewhere, the Society had rented Hunter's former Museum House.

As Darwin stepped from the carriage into the freezing morning air, it seemed that every single hearth in the city must have a fire blazing in it. He hated the smoke, longed to be back in Cambridge. He was nervous about the forthcoming evening and his presentation, and hoped the business would be resolved quickly. He left Covington unpacking the carriage and hurried to the door, on the eastern side of the square, a few doors down from Jaunay's hotel. Number 28 was a large, old-fashioned townhouse, modernized with twin columns flanking a portico and fine iron gates to the street. It was here that Charles Darwin now presented himself, longing to be out of the cold. He was relieved to be ushered inside by the doorkeeper. She showed him into the stone-flagged entrance hall. He paused a moment to look at the cases displaying natural-history specimens, then stepped into the office in the front room to inform the clerk inside of the purpose of his visit and that Covington would need help with the boxes.

The main museum space was on the first floor, and Darwin had asked if he might there await Mr Waterhouse, the Curator. It was an impressive sight, at least fifty feet long, he guessed, stepping into it, and double height, with skylights in the ceiling far above him. An elegance, but perhaps not the best means of lighting a collection one wished to study in detail. He struggled to see the dried reptiles in a well-filled cabinet he had approached. Poor lighting aside, the space was a marked improvement on the small rooms of Bruton Street. The renovations that had still been under way on his last visit were now almost complete, he noticed. The galleries that lined the room, and the staircases leading up to them, were finished, and put to use. He gazed up at a crowd of skeletons on the northern gallery above him.

Some elements were clearly not yet perfected. It was almost as cold inside as it was out. He noticed a couple of smoking braziers among the exhibits, which threw out too little heat to keep humans warm yet perhaps enough to damage the preserved creatures. Darwin was glad that he had kept his coat and hat on as he wandered around among the free-standing Mammalia that filled the great floor space. He stopped before a very lifelike orang utan. He read the label. It was from the menagerie: 'Wurmb's Orang (young)', written in red ink. '*Pithecus wurmbii*. Died in the Menagerie. Presented by George Swinton, Esq.', written in black beneath. He had heard about it: it must be the orang utan Owen had dissected. Such a shame he had missed it:

he had never seen one in life. Adjacent was a larger female, donated by Sir Stamford Raffles, a number of gibbons, too. Several big cats – lions, pumas, tigers, panthers – were crowded in as well, all labelled 'Died in the Menagerie'.

The Museum's collection was huge. *In the region of four thousand birds and nine hundred mammals in all,* so Mr Waterhouse informed him with raised eyebrows and a smile, when he found Darwin among the Catarrhini, the Old World monkeys. *He was busy preparing a catalogue of them all.* Waterhouse had been appointed Curator upon the Museum's move to its new premises. A former beetle enthusiast like himself, Darwin thought him a decent fellow. Not least because – despite the five thousand specimens he already had here – he was prepared to take on the 530 more that had just arrived on his doorstep. By now, Covington had probably brought them into the building. Not only was Waterhouse prepared to take them, he also seemed genuinely interested in them.

Waterhouse apologized for the cold, and the braziers, explaining that the installation of hot-water heating pipes was now almost complete. They passed a couple of workmen as he led Darwin to his own rooms on the second floor, where they sat to discuss the collection. Waterhouse said he and his Assistant Curator, Mr Martin, who had previously looked after the collection at Bruton Street, would take care of the Mammalia. He'd pass on the bird specimens to the Superintendent of the Ornithological Department. Darwin was pleased: Gould, from what he knew of him, was a very competent naturalist. His correspondents had kept him up to date with the goings-on in natural history while he was away and he had heard much of his fine publications. Waterhouse explained that Gould had now given up his stuffing work for the Society, but he still had charge of all things ornithological. A shame, thought Darwin, and one that prompted him to specify that he wanted all specimens properly mounted, as well as the entire collection catalogued. Water-house agreed.

As he left the building, Darwin felt lighter – 530 specimens lighter. He wondered how long he would have to wait before he learned anything of them. For now, anyway, his work was done. They were off his hands. He fetched Covington, who was waiting in the hall, and they departed. He would have plenty of time to prepare for his more important engagement of the day, the real reason behind his trip to the capital: his debut at the Geological Society that evening. Lyell was the President, and he wanted desperately to impress him. This was his chance to shine in front of the geological elite. To shine, or to stumble.

He shone. The new face on the geological scene, and his paper, were much applauded. Charles Darwin was stepping into the spotlight. Just a week later, his ornithological collection was presented at a meeting of the Zoological Society. Gould had started work on Darwin's birds immediately he received them. At the Committee of Science and Correspondence on the 10th of January, where a number of Darwin's specimens were displayed, Gould reported his findings on the Galapagos birds. He presented eleven new species, which he had identified as a series of ground finches, so peculiar in form that he suggested they were an entirely new group, confined to the Galapagos. Darwin had assumed, because of the diversity of their bills, that they were wrens and blackbirds as well as finches and had paid them little attention. The discovery of exotic species was always exciting news, and these got into the London papers. Darwin's sister Emily wrote to him from Shrewsbury that she had read of it in the *Morning Herald*. The family was proud of him.

Darwin's lack of faith in the Zoological Society had clearly been misplaced. Over the coming weeks Gould continued to work through each avian group in turn, while Waterhouse and

Martin busied themselves with the Mammalia. All presented their findings at subsequent meetings of the Committee of Science and Correspondence. Unfortunately, Darwin did not have the capacity to pay these much attention. He was back in Cambridge, a helpless victim of the influenza epidemic sweeping the country in the early months of 1837.

It was not until Darwin returned to London at the beginning of March that he was able to follow up on his zoological specimens. Since recovering from influenza, he had been much taken up with the geological side of his collection, working on his book on South American geology. He had become quite a celebrity in geological circles. Lyell had used his Presidential address to the Society's annual meeting in February to celebrate Darwin's fossil discoveries, highlighting the fact that his hammer had unearthed specifically South American species, that the extinct quadrupeds were closely related to their present-day successors. Proof, as far as Lyell was concerned, that there was a 'law of succession', which had caused the earlier mammals to be replaced by others of their own kind. It had given Darwin much to think about. Why did past and present species seem so similar in each place? He was pleased his fossils were attracting so much notice.

Back in London, for the foreseeable future now, he turned his attention to the hundreds of recent mammals and bird specimens he had carried halfway across the globe. Mr Gould's work in particular seemed to be progressing well. At least in so far as Gould had many questions for himself, the collector. Darwin was not surprised. He knew the birds had been rather casually labelled, especially the Galapagos ones. He had been tired by that late point in the voyage, and those baking hot, dismal heaps of lava had hardly inspired him. The exception had been the mockingbirds. He had been curious about them from the start,

and had carefully labelled them with details of exactly where he
had shot each one.

Just a few days after his arrival back in the city he disliked so
much, Darwin walked the short distance from his brother's
house to the porticoed entrance of 28 Leicester Square. He was
pleased to find it was warmer when he was shown into the hallway by the attendant, who took him to the receiving room at
the back of the house this time, there to await Mr Gould. He and
Gould did not know each other, though they had been introduced when he had visited the museum before he departed on
the *Beagle*. That seemed a lifetime ago.

When Gould appeared he looked different, and Darwin was
aware that he probably did too. He had lost so much weight on
the voyage and was yet to gain it back. Gould, on the contrary,
was fatter than before, his round face rounder still, and his suit
much better cut. Evidence of his recent successes, no doubt.
Gould greeted him politely rather than warmly. Darwin
thanked him for the work he had been doing. Gould said little,
only suggesting they proceed upstairs where he had some of the
specimens at hand.

They sat in one of the rooms on the Curator's floor. Gould
had a selection of Darwin's bird skins laid out on a table. *The
Galapagos specimens were the most remarkable*, Gould began, gesturing to those before him now. *Nearly all were previously unknown to
science, seemingly unique to that archipelago.* He caught his audience's
attention and, without niceties, proceeded to lecture Darwin on
what exactly he had found, and question him on what he yet
needed to know. As Gould started to tell him about his Galapagos hawk, Darwin realized he hadn't even brought a notepad
with him to write anything down. Gould passed his visitor a
piece of paper from the desk, without ceasing his delivery of
information. He was clearly a busy man. Darwin scribbled. He
put a question mark next to the first word he wrote, *Buteo*, which

was Gould's verdict on the hawk he was now holding and talking about. Darwin had grouped it with other South American Caracaras, based on its cry and its mode of flight. *Was it not of the genus* Polyborus? he interrupted Gould, who said he would re-examine it, and moved on.

It was with Gould's analysis of the finches that the conversation grew interesting. He told Darwin that he had now identified thirteen new species of Galapagos finch. Darwin could barely scribble fast enough to keep up with Gould as he spoke his way around the little stuffed finches on the table before them, telling Darwin the name he had given to each bird. What he had thought was a mixed bag of different species was actually a single closely related group. But they had looked so different with their different-shaped beaks! Gould moved on to the mockingbirds. He explained that three of the four were different species, each closely related to the others and the parent South American species, yet each entirely distinct. They were not just varieties, as Darwin had presumed. Darwin pressed him on this, but Gould insisted. Darwin had carefully labelled these birds, with their islands of origin. Each different species had a different island home, he noticed, with no little degree of excitement. He turned to Gould. *What did this mean?*

Gould was not to be drawn on the meaning of anything. He was there to deliver his findings, his observations and classifications, and that was what he continued to do. The two men spoke about the birds' affinities to the mainland South American species, and about how the birds' individual characteristics varied according to the different islands. The notion of species that were perfectly adapted to their habitat was an old one – the idea of a wise Creator and his perfect designs – and one Darwin himself had believed in. Yet now the evidence looked different. To Darwin, at least. Species that were each unique to their own island, yet all closely related to a mainland species . . . He felt he was moving into exciting new territory. John Gould did not seem to go there with him. He simply packed away the specimens, neatly stacked his notes and made to show him out. Darwin stopped him; said he would like to have a look at some of the exhibits before he left. He wanted a moment to himself.

Darwin looked in on the Museum on his way past. The fish at the east end of the exhibition room were being attended to by an assistant, who was taking them out of their cabinets and topping up the bottles with spirits. Elsewhere in the room a skeleton was being set up – that of a large ape. He went to view it more closely. It was a chimpanzee. *Died at the Gardens last year*, the man who was working on it explained, when he approached. Normally Darwin would have been fascinated, but now he could scarcely reply: his mind was otherwise occupied. He needed to think about what he had just been told, and made his way to the front door.

When he reached it, he realized he was still clutching the piece of paper. He paused and looked at its many small scribblings. He had written 'Galapagos' in large letters at the top, across both sides. He slipped it into his case before he retrieved his hat and scarf. He needed to keep it safe. He had a feeling that it would be significant. He recalled his thoughts when he had looked at the mockingbirds on the *Beagle*, that if the original species had adapted itself better to suit each island's conditions, adapted from the parent species to make new ones, it would undermine the stability of species. That would support the argument for transmutation, the idea that one species could change into another. Was that not what Gould's identifications had just shown? This possible conclusion now pressed itself, unarticulated, upon him. As he stepped into the brisk March air, he was grateful for its sobering chill.

On the 14th of March, Darwin moved out of his brother Eras's house and into rooms he had taken just a few doors down on

Great Marlborough Street. He had realized he would need to be in London for the foreseeable future. Rather than answering the questions he had accrued on the voyage, he seemed to be forming new ones. Bigger ones. Ideas that threatened to undermine everything that respectable men of science – men who had invited him into their fold – stood by. Unwelcome suggestions that had nudged at the periphery of his mind for some time now stood at its centre, demanding his full attention. He was a man led by facts and, as unpalatable as it might seem, he could not pretend he did not see what he now believed had been revealed to him: that species were not immutable, placed on the earth, already perfect, by the hand of the Creator.

Not long after his meeting with Gould, Darwin took himself into his room and opened the little red leather notebook that lay on his desk, one he had started on the *Beagle*. Beneath his notes on the fossils he had been discussing with Owen, he wrote, 'One species does change into another.' There. It was done. He was a self-confessed 'transmutationist'. Now came the real challenge: he needed to be able to explain it, to justify it, to come up with a proper theory. He was surprised by how excited he felt.

He could only hope that his specimens and notes held more clues to such an explanation. He mentally raked over them all, looking at them from a different angle now. After the revelation with the mockingbirds, Darwin recalled the Galapagos islanders telling him that each island had its own distinct creatures, not just birds but tortoises too. He wanted to look into this further. He chastised himself for not having labelled the other Galapagos specimens by island. Fitzroy and Covington had some. He could compare his own with theirs, to see if he could glean more information about exactly where each had come from. He asked Henslow to make the Galapagos specimens his priority when studying the plants, and to ask his brother-in-law,

Leonard Jenyns, who had agreed to look at the fish, to do the same. Geographic isolation was clearly a factor in the creation of new species.

He thought about the bird species he had collected on the South American mainland too. How did they compare to the island ones? He thought about an ostrich specimen he had in his collection and that Gould had described. The crew of the *Beagle* had half eaten it before Darwin had realized it was a rare bird of which the Patagonian gauchos had spoken. From the head, neck, legs and one wing Darwin had saved from the table, Gould had proved it to be a new species. It was much smaller than the typical South American ostrich Darwin had studied on his travels, the *Rhea americana*, and the plumage and beak were different. This was a case quite apart from the Galapagos island species; here were two examples of mainland South American birds, whose territorial ranges overlapped. He supposed that they were descended from a common parent. They had not been isolated from each other geographically, yet the differences between them were significant and there was no intermediate species. Had change, therefore, happened at one blow? The rheas suggested as much. That went against earlier theories of transmutation that had species gradually changing over time because of degeneration. But if in one blow, then how? Such questions had his blood racing as he sat at his desk, scribbling his illicit thoughts in his notebook. There was so much work to do.

On the evening of the day he had moved into his own rooms, Darwin once again made his way to 28 Leicester Square, leaving Covington at the work of unpacking. He was to join Gould as he presented at the Committee of Science and Correspondence. They were to talk about the new species of rhea. Owen was in the chair. Gould began by presenting the specimen, announcing that he had named it in Darwin's honour: *Rhea darwinii*. As

Darwin looked around at the assembled gentlemen, nodding their approval at Gould's diplomatic gesture, he wondered how they would react if he declared himself a 'transmutationist'. Such ideas were considered revolutionary, quite literally. Through the treatment of Grant, the Fellows of the Society had made it crystal-clear what they thought of anyone who espoused them.

Darwin, however, was wiser than Grant – or perhaps he simply cared more for his standing among the gentlemen he now stood to address. Darwin had absolutely no intention of sharing his thoughts with them, or not until he had had the chance properly to interrogate them himself. On that March evening, Charles Darwin's speech was confined to details of the rheas' habits. The gentlemen nodded in their happy ignorance, praising the fine observational work of the young man in their midst.

By the time spring had turned to summer, Darwin's notions on transmutation dominated his thoughts. He had never felt so stimulated or so . . . important. It made him rather anxious. He might no longer crave the country parish but he did like the security and status that came with his newfound position within the scientific community. He wanted to retain it. He was hoping to acquire a government grant to publish a series on the zoology of the *Beagle* now, and the Earl of Derby, President of the Zoological Society, who was currently in Town, had put a positive word in the ears of the powerful for him. He had finished his journal of the *Beagle*'s voyage and was awaiting the completion of the other volumes so that they could be published together. He had carved a role for himself as a respected man of science and did not want to compromise it, yet the direction in which his thoughts were moving was threatening to mark him out as a radical thinker.

It was a bind indeed, but not one Darwin thought need prevent him pursuing *all* his ambitions. His solution was simple: he started a private notebook, in which he would pose the questions he dared not voice in public. Pose the questions, and hopefully answer some. He had already committed his first musings on his personal theories of transmutation to his old notebook. Cogitating in writing on such conundrums as the role of geographic isolation – present in the case of the finches and mockingbirds, yet not in the rheas – which he could not do in spoken words. Now he set about his illicit task with a sense of real purpose. In the middle of July, as the capital was welcoming in the new era that had come upon it in the shape of the young Queen, and was sent once more to the polls as a result, Charles Darwin sat in his study in Great Marlborough Street. Before him on his desk was a small notebook. He opened the brass clasp of the brown leather cover to reveal the virgin beige page before him. He dipped his pen into the inkwell and wrote decisively 'C. Darwin', and beneath it, *Zoonomia*. Yes, the title of his grandfather's book. Here, at least, he need not hide from the association. Here, he might as well embrace it. It was liberating.

He allowed his thoughts to run wild and free as his nib struggled to keep up, its jottings filling page after page after crisp new page. All the things he had observed on his voyage and stored in the recesses of his mind were summoned, pulled into mental view and investigated in the burning bright light switched on by the analysis of his specimens by experts, like Gould and Owen. He considered reproduction and sexual mixing, how offspring might become permanently changed, how a race alters itself to the changing world. He thought of the savages he had encountered. He thought of the island species of the Galapagos. How genera were specific to the same country. How geographic isolation speeded change. He recalled the distinctness of the Australian Mammalia. He thought of the two ostriches, how a species had changed over space. Must they also change through time? He thought of his *Megatherium* fossil, similar to modern sloths: both must be descended from a yet older type.

He began to think of branches of life, some improving, some dying out; a model that pulled all these sprawling thoughts together. Yes, this was what he thought. He sketched a tree of life, with irregular branches, terminal buds dying as new ones grew. Types shared a common structural plan, but each animal had the tendency to change, and that change was not the result of will but of laws of adaptation. There were no ordered hierarchies – the thought of some animals being 'higher' than others was absurd. There was no grand plan, just an endless, irregular, sprawling growth.

On and on through the summer months in his study at Great Marlborough Street, he wrote, page after page. By the time that the Whig government returned to the House of Commons in August, re-elected but with a much slimmer majority, Charles Darwin had covered more intellectual ground than he had done during the entirety of his four-and-a-half-year voyage. And as these thoughts took form, he began to feel their weight. He began to feel the strain of the exertion of getting them out of his mind and into the world.

As he scribbled on in private, his public plans progressed rapidly too. He had the final proofs of his *Beagle* journal now, and heard that he had been awarded the Treasury grant to publish his zoological findings as well. Leading a double life might have been the only solution he could see to meeting his twin desires of outward respectability and intellectual freedom, but it was tiring. His stomach was troubling him. Then, one day in September, he felt his heart beat so wildly that he feared it might leap from his breast. He summoned his doctor, who told him he must leave off his work. Darwin had Covington pack his

things, including his secret notebook. It was with no reluctance
that he shut the door on his study and went to the country for
some peace, quiet and fresh air. He was to stay with his cousins,
the Wedgwoods, at Maer. It had been an exhausting few months.

He might have been exhausted, but he hadn't finished. He was back
in London in late October and remained there for the winter,
one of the coldest anyone could remember. In private, cosseted
against the season and its smog in his study, his clandestine mental wanderings continued. In public, he continued work on his
geology book and commenced the series of publications on the
zoology of his great voyage. Each part was to be written by the
experts who had been helping him make sense of the different
specimens he had amassed: Gould for the birds, Waterhouse for
the Mammalia, Owen for the fossil Mammalia, Thomas Bell for
the reptiles, and Leonard Jenyns for the fish. Darwin oversaw it
all, chivvying the already busy men, trying to keep to the publication schedule. Gould's contributions were of particular
concern, for he had announced that he was soon to be leaving
the country. He was going to Australia. It was not sufficient for
the ornithologist that he was publishing a series on the birds of
that country, he wanted to go on a collecting mission himself.
Darwin could hardly complain. He could only hope he would
get all he needed from the man – including the fifty illustrations
he'd agreed – before he quit these shores.

Things began to progress. In the first icy days of the new
year, with the Serpentine frozen and covered with skaters, Darwin was indoors, working slavishly. He wrote to the Council of
the Zoological Society enclosing a prospectus of the forthcoming work, asking that it be sent out with future numbers of the
Proceedings of the Committee of Science and Correspondence.
Although officially he was still only a corresponding member of
the Society, they agreed. By February, when the first part of the

series appeared, Owen's on the fossil Mammalia, Darwin's musings had filled the notebook he had begun the previous summer.
He commenced a second, focused on more specific questions:
how adaptations in species might occur, how certain characteristics were passed from one generation to the next.

This time he turned not to his own exotic specimens but to
the more mundane: pedigree dogs and birds. He wondered if a
better understanding of how inheritance was manipulated by
man might help him to unlock the laws of it in nature. He chris-
tened his new notebook with questions about pigeons: *How are
varieties produced? By picking offspring?* Once again, it was the
experts of the Zoological Society to whom he looked for the
answers – though, of course, they did not know the real question, the underlying question.

In the bitter early months of 1838, Darwin spent many hours of
many days at 28 Leicester Square. He called upon Mr Yarrell's
expertise again. Yarrell was a keen hunter, and he asked him about
dog-breeding and pigeons, of the 'monsters' and 'mutations' and
'adaptations' that could and were produced by breeding, thinking
privately of how varieties might be preserved in nature over the
ages, how new species were created. He spoke to Gould about
inherited characteristics in birds. He focused on questions of hered-
ity, of how species were changed, and he started to use the term
'descent' in place of 'transmutation'. His appetite for literature was
voracious: he read the publications of the Society and the works in
the Library, Sir Stamford Raffles's and Dr Thomas Horsfield's
works on Java among them. In his mind he travelled the world all
over again, as he sat out of the cold in the Museum on Leicester
Square or in his study a short walk away. And with every answer
came another question. He listened on. He scribbled on.

Once the weather had warmed a little, and the first notes of
spring were discernible in the smoke-choked air of the city,

Darwin decided to venture further afield, to the Zoological
Society's second establishment in the Regent's Park. He'd been
before his voyage and recalled that he had immensely enjoyed it.
He had been meaning to revisit for a time now, especially since
an orang utan had arrived at the end of last year. One mild
Wednesday morning in late March, the weather finally permitted it. For some time he had eschewed social invitations so he
could focus on his work, but this was not an entirely frivolous
outing.

He rode his horse through the bustle of Regent Street to the
haven of the park at its tip. Riding in the metropolis could not
compare to the open-country riding he adored, the thrill of the
hunt and fresh cold air on his face, but it was pleasant enough
today, he thought. He felt healthy – he had been putting on
weight. He rode along the park's eastern edge in the spring sunshine, passing the Colosseum (which was advertising astronomy
lectures, featuring a large orrery) and the imposing classical terraces, resplendent in the morning light. The grand edifices had
clearly not been immune to the city smog: they were no longer
the gleaming white he remembered.

He followed the Outer Circle into the park, not yet awoken
from its winter slumber but showing the first signs of doing so.
He liked the sense of promise in the buds he saw. At the carriage
drive on the Outer Circle, adjacent to the Zoological Society's
Gardens, he dismounted, with a sense of anticipation. He was
glad he had found the time to come. He left his mount with the
horse-holder, alongside a carriage and a couple of other beasts,
patiently waiting, and gave his name to the money-taker at the
entrance lodge: Charles Darwin. As a corresponding member, he
was allowed access to the Gardens, though he supposed he would
have to become a Fellow at some point. He was now Vice-President
of the Entomological Society and Secretary of the Geological
Society: he should at least be a Fellow of the Zoological. His

name duly recorded, he passed through the turnstile. That was an innovation since his last visit, a sign of the changing times, perhaps. As with all the reform that had been wrought while he was away – the abolition of slavery, the regulation of factories and poor relief – another sign that England was advancing.

It was the first warm day of the season. Quite a few people had taken advantage of the sudden good weather as many other visitors were in sight, but the Gardens he now found himself in were peaceful yet. He could hear as much birdsong as he could human conversation. The grounds had been extended westwards since the last time he was there; sheep and a calf were grazing on the new land. It felt very spring-like. He walked on along the terrace, which afforded him a fine view over the lawn and ponds beneath on the eastern side, and the Gardens beyond, much expanded since his last visit, with the fine little buildings dotted around the ornamental grounds. It was a far cry from the city that met his gaze in the southerly direction. On a day like today, London was not so bad. He had been wondering, lately, where his future would take him, and thinking of marriage, but he envied his Cambridge friends their peaceful rectories and their wives. He did not want a city life where he was bound eternally to rake through the same material: he wanted to be free to make new observations. He could not do that in this man-made metropolis. In time he would find himself his country retreat.

He carried on to the bear pit, which he remembered vividly from his last visit. Here he lingered awhile, watching the entertainment, but he made his way quite swiftly past the other main attractions of the South Garden: the camels in their fine little house, the twittering, vividly adorned macaws, the grizzly bear beneath the terrace, the antelopes and zebra, the llamas, the sloth bear, the monkeys in their crowded house, making mischief on their poles. He stopped longer with the less exotic residents: the hybrid birds and dogs he had spoken and thought about so much of late. As he wandered the paths, he thought, too, of the man he had been last time he was there. That was seven years ago. Now he had seen many such creatures in their native lands. As he watched the kangaroos move about their paddock, he recalled how two years ago, when he was in Australia, he had looked at marsupials in wonderment. So different were they from mammals it seemed that two Creators had been at work. But he had also seen antlions there, using exactly the same bizarre method of catching prey – creating a slide of sand – as their European relatives. That had reassured him, implying as it did that there was indeed One Hand at work throughout the universe. Now he dared not think too much about the Creator. He had given up any idea of repeated divine *personal* interventions, and did not believe God had created anything more than the laws that determined what happened on earth.

It was the North Garden that held the real attractions for him and it was not long before he found himself in the elegant tunnel that led to them. When he had been there last, there had been little to see on the other side, but now he was met with a number of structures. The elephant and rhinoceros were both new additions, as far as he was concerned, and as he approached the solid timber building, with separate enclosures in which the two beasts were kept, he was greeted by the remarkable sight of the rhinoceros running at great speed around its yard. Remarkable, yes, even by the standards of a man who had seen so much, and he laughed out loud when he saw it, rushing to the bars. Standing alongside a few other visitors, he was treated to the spectacle of the huge, inelegant beast galloping from one end of the enclosure to the other, kicking and rearing as it did so.

Darwin, ever-inquisitive, beckoned to the keeper and demanded to know the cause of what could only be interpreted as the beast's pure joy. *It's his first time in the paddock this year*, was the man's answer. *Jack seems as surprised as you, sir*, the keeper continued, gesturing to the elephant paddock adjoining, where the yet larger creature watched intently, pressed right up against the wooden palings. Darwin laughed, as did his fellow observers, as Jack, having seen enough, turned and, in a feeble imitation of his neighbour, trotted across his own yard, trunk and tail lifted. What luck, he thought, to see this! How interesting to see two creatures of the Pachydermata side by side, to compare the more intellectually developed elephant with the galloping rhinoceros! He recalled Lyell's remarks in *Principles of Geology* that an elephant has the sagacity to understand a contract: a promise from his keeper of a reward for a task.

In buoyant mood, he continued through the North Garden to the Giraffe House at its western edge. It was in this large, stable-like building, a handsome construction with oversized doors, that the most celebrated attraction in the Gardens was kept. Not the giraffes, not any more. The giraffes were old news now. The Nubian attendants were long gone, and one of the giraffes, too, had been lost (Owen had spoken to Darwin of its dissection last year). For Darwin, however, the giraffes were novel yet, and he stopped to watch them in their area of the large, heated interior. He marvelled at their impossible, unique proportions, ruminating on Lamarck's theory that their necks had been elongated because individual giraffes had actually stretched them in the process of reaching up for food on tall trees, and then passed on their longer necks to their offspring. He had been devouring Lamarck's works of late. In private, of course. He believed much of what he argued, certainly that habits did sometimes go before structure. But the idea that an animal's actions were sufficient to cause a development like the giraffe's magnificent neck? It did not quite satisfy him. He thought of his discussions with Yarrell, the peculiarities produced by breeding. Then he turned his back on the giraffes, moving instead towards the railed-off section of the building. Where the orang utan was kept.

Here she was: Jenny. The first such creature he had ever seen, not in the lush jungles he had trekked through or tropical islands he had landed upon, but in the middle of London. An orang utan, dressed in smock and trousers, in an area furnished with a carpet and an armchair, in addition to a few sorry-looking 'trees'. Here she was, on the other side of a barrier, made of a bamboo lattice, before him. Darwin was enraptured. Seated on her rear on the carpet, hairy hands with their elegant fingers clasping the bamboo, she was looking intently towards the keeper, who was talking to a departing visitor on the other side. On seeing Darwin peering so intently at his charge, the keeper greeted him. Jenny followed the keeper's every movement with her large, dark eyes. Darwin followed Jenny's with his own. She did no more than glance at him.

He asked her keeper if she knew him; recognized him. He laughed. *Yes, sir, you ought to see what happens when I try to leave!* The man turned to her now and removed an apple from the pocket of his uniform jacket. Jenny leaped up – she stood about three feet tall – and lunged for it, at which the keeper withdrew it through the bars. She stopped. Waited. He proffered it again, but withdrew it again. Jenny was incensed. She threw herself onto her back, kicked her feet and wailed in despair. Precisely like a naughty child! She writhed and kicked her long limbs, and then she sulked, then kicked and wailed again! Staring all the while at the cause of her misery, her lower lip protruded, she whined loudly in his direction. Finally, the keeper said to her, *Jenny, if you will stop bawling and be a good girl, I will give you the apple.* The whining immediately diminished, though it did not cease. The keeper repeated his entreaty. The whining diminished again, and she moved gingerly towards him. He said it again, and this time she stopped, looking up at her tormentor with hopeful eyes. The keeper handed Jenny the apple. Taking no chances she grabbed it and ran with it to her

chair. Darwin was duly amazed. *Does she . . . understand you?*
The keeper smiled and nodded. *It seems so, sir.*

Darwin could hardly believe what he had just seen. He had
watched savages behave with less humanity than the ape. She sat
before him in her little armchair, eating her apple, utterly content. Darwin's mind was sparkling as he stepped into the light of
the day outside. He made his way to the turnstile exit, not notic-
ing the dens and cages he passed but lost in his thoughts.
Emerging into reality, on the public drive, he met Professor
Owen, with a couple of other Fellows from the Zoological Society Council, on their way in through the entrance directly
opposite. They were on good terms now (Owen, recently promoted to Hunterian Professor at the Royal College of Surgeons,
was a very useful acquaintance) and greeted each other warmly.
Darwin told him excitedly of what he had just witnessed. Owen
said it was nothing unusual: *Jenny was quite a character and adored
her keeper − and he adored teasing her.* Owen changed the subject,
going on to talk of his own visit to the Surrey Zoological
Gardens a few days earlier, to see a much-feted fire balloon
show. *The crowds had attacked Mr Cross and torn the balloon to shreds
when it had failed to rise. Oh, how uncivilized man could be!* They
parted, Darwin going to fetch his horse.

Darwin knew how uncivilized man could be. He had seen
the wretched savages of the Tierra del Fuego, would never forget their painted, distrustful faces, their nakedness, their
inarticulate language, their cannibalism. But he had not known,
until this very day, how *civilized* apes could be. He could not get
the image of Jenny from his mind: an intelligent being, com-
municating her passions and feelings to her keeper, a man she
obviously cared for. An ape, as civilized as some men he had
seen; more so? Darwin had lost the conviction of his peers that
man was elevated from the rest of the Animal Kingdom, hand-
crafted in his perfection by the Creator. Mankind was, he was

sure, just another branch of his tree of life. He thought of Jenny. He thought of the first fossil monkeys, discovered the previous year. He thought of Lamarck's belief that the human had evolved from the chimpanzee, refuted by Lyell and his new set. Why was it so wrong to think of man among the monkeys as the elephant among the Pachydermata, the most developed species emerging from a particular branch of life? The different races of mankind, then differently developed in turn?

Darwin paid the boy and mounted his horse. He set off for home. The day he rode into was bright and full of possibility. Yet the thought that Professor Owen or any of the others might read his mind passed over him like a cold shadow. The anxiety of exposure was growing in equal proportion to the exciting conviction that his thoughts were leading him somewhere remarkable.

John Gould quit the employ of the Zoological Society in April, to make final preparations for his forthcoming expedition to Australia. He had not completed his work on the birds of the *Beagle*'s voyage for publication, and Darwin was left to finish it himself. Though unhappy at the unwelcome additional workload, he could not but wish Gould luck. He had immensely valued his collaboration with the man. After all, it was his minute observations that had unlocked the secrets his specimens held and set his thoughts in motion. Darwin sent Gould a parting gift, an engraved silver compass. Gould, clearly not as touched as its sender intended, wrote to thank him for a dram-bottle. He did not seem to share the sense of import of what he had unleashed, of the momentous content of their 'pleasing chats', as Gould had put it in his letter (in the hand of his secretary, Darwin noticed). Or he did, and wanted nothing to do with it. Gould and his entourage, which included his wife and John Gilbert, his erstwhile assistant at the Museum, set sail for the distant, wild lands of Australia in the middle of May.

Darwin was busy that spring and early summer, with Geological Society meetings, social calls with the Owens and his other scientific associates, dinners with his brother Erasmus and his circle of reforming Whigs, and visits from the family. His cousin Emma Wedgwood came to London from Maer, and he spent time with her, which he much enjoyed. He even managed a trip to Cambridge, where he still hoped to live permanently. Primarily, he was busy with his publications; the geology of the voyage was moving along nicely, and the first of Waterhouse's *Mammalia* was released too. He chased Gould's secretary, Prince, for the details he needed to finish the volume on birds. Privately, he continued to fill his notebooks with his gleanings from his researches into domestic breeds, his observations from the books he was devouring and of the animals at the Zoological Gardens. He had been thinking a great deal about how thoughts and instincts were passed from one generation to the next. Was desire hereditary, a result of the structure of the brain? Was thought a function of that organ as bile was a function of the liver? He could only see it as such.

Oh, you materialist! he chided himself, in his private world of the page; a denier not only of free will but, worse, of a soul. In troubled times like those he lived in, such unchristian arguments were considered disgraceful. He was increasingly anxious about his own thoughts, worrying about how he could defend them to his peers when the time came. How would he tell them what he confided to his notebooks, that when they smiled at him he now saw the residue of mankind's origin as a monkey, a baboon with giant canines? His health was troubling him again, and it grew worse as spring turned to summer. His stomach was not right. At the end of June, in desperate need of a break, he left the stifling city, which was in the throes of preparation for the young Queen's Coronation, and set off to Edinburgh by steamer, from there to Glen Roy. To focus on his other, much less contentious, passion: geology.

He returned to London via Shrewsbury, to see his family at the home his father had built, The Mount. He should have rested, but he did not. Instead, he started not one but two new secret notebooks. He was still preoccupied with how instincts and desires were inherited as a result of brain structure, and quizzed his doctor father for hours about the many patients he had treated over the years, covering pages of his notebooks with anecdotes on insanity, memory, dreams, deformity, inherited characteristics and character, thoughts on pleasure and happiness, instincts and emotions. He was not feeling as well as he ought, and he often woke in the night in a state of fear. On the other hand, he felt that his senses were more alert than they ever had been. He saw questions and puzzles everywhere around him, in the family dogs and cats, the singing birds in the garden. Could dogs feel shame? Were cats practising abstinence when they did not eat the young birds in a nest until they were big enough to truly enjoy? He found himself referring often to his grandfather's work. He confidently believed in fixed laws of nature and, more than ever, that emotions, instincts and talents were inherited, in man and beast. He was questioning the existence of free will. Did all animals – from an oyster to a man – have it? Or did it all come down to hereditary disposition and instinct? Was a man just the product of his parentage? He wondered what it meant that his handwriting was so similar to his grandfather's . . .

That summer, Darwin also sought answers to more immediately pressing questions, more personal questions. Again he turned to his father's experience for help. He had been back in England for almost two years. With his work on the 'species theory' he had found his occupation, or it had found him. But as a man now approaching thirty he had his personal life to consider too. He wondered whether he ought to marry. He visited his cousin Emma Wedgwood while he was at home. Their families were very close – his sister had already married Emma's brother – and he was growing fond of Emma. As a logical man, a man of science, Darwin thought through the arguments for and against marriage, weighing up the financial obligations and commitments of his time (he might even have to work for a living) against the comforts a wife and family would offer, noting them on a scrap of paper. His father, furnishing an additional consideration, warned that Emma's religious zeal might be incompatible with his son's enquiring, doubting mind.

It was a pivotal few weeks Darwin spent at The Mount that July of 1838. A moment for the young man to reflect. On the 1st of August, he left the peace of his family home behind and, for the first time, boarded a train. The railways had reached the Midlands. When he had left on the *Beagle*, there had been only the thirty-mile Liverpool–Manchester line, just built. Since then it had been linked to Birmingham by the Grand Junction Railway, finished last year, and that to the capital by the brand-new Birmingham–London line. How quickly things had changed, he marvelled! As his carriage pulled out of the station, in a cacophony of steam, whistles and clanging doors, he reflected on how things would, he hoped, soon change for him. In his time at home he had become convinced of two things. First, that he should propose marriage to his cousin Emma. Despite the disadvantages of marriage, he had ultimately decided in favour of 'a nice soft wife on a sofa', as his scribbled list of 'pros and cons' had put it, concluding: 'Marry, marry, marry, QED.' Second, he was more convinced than ever that his clandestine work, now sufficiently developed that he thought of it as a theory, was of real significance. As such, it was weighing heavily on him. How nice then, to be looked after, to have companionship and affection in place of the solitary existence of the worker bee that the train was returning him to. And a wife was better than a dog, his list reminded him.

As the train chugged onwards towards London, it began to rain. Darwin was disappointed that his first personal experience of the railway, so celebrated as the travel of the future, was in reality rather a chore. The journey was rough and noisy, and he had endless changes to negotiate (and the London–Birmingham line, though supposedly opened for the coronation of the Queen Victoria in June was still not quite complete: he boarded a stage-coach for part of the route). He hoped that his own future, now that he had decided on one, might run a little more smoothly.

Back in London, Darwin continued his work. He was starting to realize the mammoth scale of the task he had undertaken and the excessive labour of the inventive thought, as he termed it, demanded. He was suffering from headaches. He often ventured to the Regent's Park, hungry for respite from the grimy city and his mental efforts. Its greenery and the scent of beasts were a welcome reminder of the country home he pined for, of the family home at The Mount with its geese and ducks. He found the scenery particularly soothing at this time of year. As the softer light of autumn began to mute the bright glare of summer days, he passed many enjoyable, instructive hours in the Zoo-logical Gardens.

Darwin was getting to know the animals and their keepers, whom he mined for information about the animals' behaviour, responses and expressions. In September of 1838, he was trying to understand how such things fitted into his theory: if and how man's descent from monkeys had shaped his emotions and pas-sions. He spent time outside the bars of the Monkey House, watching how the mischievous creatures inside interacted with the visitors and with each other. He studied the expressions of the different species and groups. He listened to the noise of the baboon and compared it with that of a human expressing pity. *Do monkeys cry?* he wondered. He observed the postures of the cats. He stood on the lawns watching the birds, monitoring the movements of the vicious black swan the keeper had to arm himself against (when the female was sitting) and before the kennels where the chained dogs were housed, watching how they competed with each other for scraps of food.

Everywhere he looked he saw comparisons with man. And not just in the monkeys' behaviour and face-pulling. He saw in a dog barking, a horse yawning or even the chin of a bull similarities with the habits and expressions of his own species. Seeing a dog, a horse and a man yawn was evidence to him of the similarity of the structure all animals are built on. He thought it remarkable that involuntary sounds, like whining and growling, were common to *all* animals. He saw the world through different eyes, his senses taken up with his one grand idea. He couldn't even take a carriage without minutely observing the behaviour of the horses, or ride his own horse without wondering whether it, too, enjoyed the wide prospect of the park (he believed it did). He could not smell the last summer blooms without thinking that he must enjoy the scent because man's parent had been a fruit-eater. It fatigued him, keeping his idea before him, day and night.

On his trips to the Zoological Society's Gardens he spent many hours in the heated, carpeted division of the Giraffe House that was the orang utan's den. It had become doubly exciting of late, for Jenny had been joined over the summer by a companion, a young male orang utan known as Tommy, after the chimpanzee he had succeeded. It gave Darwin the opportunity of making observations on a subject that was on his mind: sexual attraction. He was working up to making his proposal to Emma. He studied Jenny and her new companion, fascinated by how they interacted, by their understanding of their sexual difference, by the power relationship between the larger, yet still young, female and the new little boy who had joined her. Now, she often bit and hurt him for his attention. He had been told that when Jenny had first met Tommy she had carefully examined him, touching and smelling his genitals. He had questioned Mr Youatt, the Medical Superintendent, when he found him in the Monkey House, as to whether the monkeys knew the difference between men and women. He said they certainly did, and demonstrated it, often.

On the first weekend of September, Darwin had been permitted to conduct some experiments with the orang utans, and entered the bamboo walls of the enclosure to join Jenny and Tommy. He knew that Jenny understood language: he had seen it for himself a number of times now and had just watched her keeper comb her unruly red hair: she stood still when she was told to do so. Now he wanted to know what else she was capable of. He had brought a few things with him to try out on her. Jenny was not really interested in people other than Goss, her primary keeper, and Hunt, another who attended to her, but when Darwin produced two handkerchiefs from his pocket she clutched at them. She didn't pay him much attention, but he watched her intently as she played with them, just like a girl with a shawl! Darwin was vaguely aware of other visitors watching them both, remarking on what they saw: a well-dressed gentleman, sitting in the cage like a beast himself. But Jenny had his full attention. Darwin wanted to move on with his experiments, but when he tried to retrieve his handkerchiefs she was furious. He put them into his pocket and stood up, but she followed him. After failed attempts to pick his pocket, which had the onlookers giggling, she took more drastic measures – and bit him. A quick show of the whip by Goss, though, had her cowering in her box in the corner (where the pair both slept, apparently snoring loudly). Jenny knew what the whip meant: another sign of her understanding, Darwin eagerly noted, filing it in his mental cabinet.

He left her alone a moment. Slowly, she peered out and, realizing the danger had passed, began to play with the straw she sat in. Little Tommy sat nearby, less active than his older friend. Darwin watched her from the other side of the cage. She arranged the straw in careful rows, then stuffed it through the bamboo bars like a bored child. Next she played with the sticks in the den. Darwin enquired of Goss as to what else she was capable of handling. *She has even taken a whip to one of the giraffes when we let her near them! She will seize anything she can when she sees a dog, to better defend herself against it.* He told Darwin that *she had even beaten the men with a stick,* nodding to where she sat now, playing idly with one. Darwin observed how she used her hands, just like he might himself. She used foreign objects just like man did, for her own ends.

Darwin had brought with him a looking glass, and now he took it from his pocket and approached Jenny warily. He got down to her level and, a little cautiously, brought it towards her with the glass facing in her direction. She started when she saw her own reflection, visibly, almost comically, shocked. She looked over to Goss, who nodded at her, reassured her, and then she grabbed the glass from Darwin. The next few minutes were wonderful to watch. She looked at it in every possible way, before reaching her lips to the glass in a kiss. Darwin wanted to see how little Tommy reacted, too, and asked Goss to bring him to them. Goss did as directed, and ushered Tommy next to the bigger orang utan. Tommy had obviously been watching Jenny because he, too, kissed the glass! Darwin clapped his hands, startling them both, but soon they returned to their new toy. Tommy pouted at himself – out of displeasure? Not unlike when man was dissatisfied, Darwin thought. Jenny was visibly trying to work it out, putting her hand behind the glass to see where the trick – or perhaps the orang utan – was. After many minutes of such exploration, she dropped it to the floor in frustration. Darwin was jubilant.

And he had thought he could conduct experiments only if he moved to the country! That evening, he recorded his observations of the remarkable day with the orang utans, and musings on what he had learned of them thus far. Not only could the ape understand spoken language, it could use tools, and attempt to understand a puzzle. Yet man boasted of his own pre-eminence! In his notebook Darwin dared his critics to compare the savage Fuegians with the orang utan and find a great difference. In public, he did not challenge the beliefs of his peers, but he was arming himself with arguments for when the time came that he would.

Over the month of September, collected on numerous visits to the Gardens, Darwin's observations of the orang utans and other creatures filled many, many pages of his notebooks. With the descent of man the question now uppermost in his mind, he interrogated the Superintendent, Mr Miller, on the behaviour of the monkeys. Miller gave him the tantalizing piece of information that behaviour and expressions were unique to each monkey group. Hunt, a keeper Darwin liked a great deal and who was clearly a thinking man (unlike some of the others), told him that he had noticed the American monkeys showed no interest in women visitors, whereas a green monkey would put his head on the ground to look up petticoats. Darwin saw Tommy use a stone to pound the earth. He saw Jenny untie a knot and play the harmonica he had brought to her. He listened to the animals' noises, he watched their faces, and he recorded it all when he got home. So captivated was he by the wonderful laboratory on his doorstep, and the vast pool of knowledge of its staff, that he wrote to the Council requesting that he be allowed access to any written records kept at the Gardens, too. The Council agreed. He was pleased. He knew he could find much of value there, much by way of the evidence which he would need if he was to persuade his reluctant contemporaries of his theory.

'Origin of man now proved,' he wrote in his notebook. He was unequivocal now. He had taken the idea of transmutation to its much-feared conclusion. He knew what heretical waters he had waded into. He was thinking deeply about religion at this time. After all, he was working up to propose to a woman whose Christianity was not just in keeping with the age but was stricter and more traditional. He wondered why his peers were so unwilling to accept the idea of a Creator governing through laws, why they so admired a view of the world in which each object was formed by an act of separate creation. He thought it must be because it was comparable to the state of their own minds. He wondered, even, if the very idea of God arose from a confused idea of 'ought'. He did not set limits on his thoughts – he would not – but he was increasingly troubled by vivid dreams, and his headaches were still bad.

That autumn, Darwin passed his evenings as a bachelor. He had not yet set in motion his decision to marry. He had joined a club in the summer, the Athenaeum, and most evenings he dined there, alone. He enjoyed being part of this esteemed world, enmeshed in the comfortable web of respectable London society. It was such an elegant building – designed by the Zoological Society's own architect, Mr Burton, he had been told – in a newly developed, fashionable part of London. Darwin had been gratified to be elected a member on the same day as Mr Dickens, no less, a great man to whose works he was most partial as welcome distraction from the burden of his thoughts. Darwin always looked out for the author of the words he so enjoyed when he walked the mosaic floor of the vast lounge, hoping he might have cause for an introduction.

Darwin passed many hours after dinner in the beautifully appointed library, which had an unparalleled supply of the latest periodicals and publications, or he sat reading by the fire with a glass of the fine wine that filled the cellars beneath him. In late September, he was reading a copy of Thomas Malthus's *Essay on the Principle of Population*, a sixth edition he had picked up. He was familiar, of course, with the arguments about the inevitability of population growth and the equal inevitability of it being kept in check by the limit of resources. Malthus's ideas were decades old now, and what man of his social class and political persuasion did not know them? Malthus was the darling of the Whigs, who used his arguments to support their own revision of the Poor Laws. Competition, they argued was everything: no longer could the poor rely on handouts, only the last resort of the workhouse. The poor were compelled to try harder, to compete.

Reading Malthus's famous work again now, in the Athenaeum, in the light of his own obsession, Darwin suddenly saw it differently. He had long ago lost his faith in the natural theologian's vision of a perfect world of nature, where every little thing lived together in happy harmony. Now he saw the true savagery of the reality; of populations in competition not just with other species but with *each other*. Far more individuals were born than could be sustained by the environment. Only the strong, best-adapted individuals would survive to breed. Little variations – a heavier coat, a slightly longer stride – could make all the difference, and over time, small adaptations could add up to create a whole new species. So his finches and mockingbirds had adapted from their South American parent species to become one that was more suited to their new island homes. So, in time, monkey had become man.

He already knew that species were not immutable, that new branches sprang from each other in an organic tree of life. Now, he saw *how* this had happened; he saw the mechanism behind it. Now he had the final piece of the puzzle.

It was good timing. His days as a bachelor were numbered and his quiet, cogitative evenings at the Athenaeum doomed to extinction. He proposed to Emma in the middle of November and she accepted. An additional task was added to his workload: finding somewhere for himself and his future wife to live. Darwin did not want to quit London yet, not until he had secured his place in scientific society, so he looked for a suitable house to rent in the capital. In early December, Emma travelled to London to help, staying with her brother. They spent their days travelling the city streets in omnibuses and public coaches, searching out their first home like geologists scouring for fossils, planning their future together.

On the 19th, while his wife-to-be was still in town, Darwin attended the monthly meeting of the Geological Society, of which he was the Secretary. Dr Grant was presenting his theory that the jawbones of 'the world's oldest mammal' actually belonged to a reptile. Mammals as old as those bones were believed to be, unearthed in rocks in Oxford, did not fit into his view of the development of species from the simplest to the most complex forms. Grant was torn apart by the others present, men with more conventional Creationist views, who had organized their attack in advance of the meeting. Darwin watched as his old mentor was ridiculed and mocked in front of the great and good of the geological world. They wanted Grant silenced. It was done. It was emphatically done.

Darwin did not share Grant's simplistic view of the progressive development of life: he was far beyond that now. He had total confidence in his own theory. Yet as he watched the entirety of those assembled turn on Grant in choreographed unity, he saw what virulent opposition he, too, would inevitably face if ever he were to share it. In the troubled times he lived in, heterodoxy of any sort was not permitted. This stark warning came at a moment when he was more sensitive to it than he might otherwise have been, at a moment when he had more than his own reputation to think of. He had tentatively confessed some of his doubts about the Christian understanding of the world to Emma. Devout, lovely Emma. She had been shocked, and confessed in turn that she feared for his immortal soul. She had directed him to the Gospel: 'I am the Way, the Truth and the Life.' Those who did not accept Jesus would be cast into the fire. As he left the victory dinner that took place after the routing of Grant, Darwin saw now that that would be his fate in this life as well as the next, if he were to share his secret theory. At least, if he did so before he was sure that it was completely, utterly irrefutable.

On the first day of 1839 Darwin, aided by Covington, moved his many possessions – his now numerous secret notebooks, his heavy crates of geological specimens – to his new home on Upper Gower Street. A gaudily decorated terraced house that he and Emma referred to as Macaw Cottage, it was to be their first home together. They were married in Emma's village, Maer, on the 29th of January and returned to Macaw Cottage the following day. Darwin was now thirty years old, Secretary of the Geological Society, a recently elected Fellow of the Royal Society, member of the Athenaeum Club. He was a respectable married man. A wealthy one, too, thanks to Emma's dowry and a generous allowance from his father.

He was a respectable married man with a secret obsession. Privately – though Emma had some idea of the nature of his work, which was a source of great anxiety to her – he continued to work at his theory, to add ballast to it. His preoccupation with breeding and sexual attraction was more relevant than ever. During his courtship with Emma he had scribbled in his notebooks on kissing, blushing and blood flow. In the first months of his marriage, he focused on reproduction. Nature, he had now concluded, was not so very unlike the breeders he had spoken to, selecting, in its own brutal way, those adaptations that allowed an advantage over competitors. He opened a new notebook, which he entitled 'Questions and Experiments', and launched into detailed investigations of the breeding of plants and animals, sending long lists of questions to endless correspondents, which would continue for many years to come. He was no longer looking for theories: he was seeking only evidence. And he would take it from anywhere: from the behaviour of orang utans to the distribution of pollen, and the length of the intestine of a Persian cat.

He turned to the statistics of breeding in the Zoological Gardens, now that he had been permitted full access to the Society's records. He wondered why so few wild animals were propagated there. It was a subject of some concern to the Society, and of much interest, not least to its President, Lord Derby. A Breeding Committee had been established for at least a decade, and although the farm – intended as a place for breeding and rearing young – was long gone, experiments with inter-breeding and efforts to encourage it had continued. A register had recently been started of all the animals born in the menagerie. They had not had much success in reproducing their big attractions: the young of carnivores never survived long. Darwin's questions touched on a sore subject, one on which he had his own concerns. His sister, married to Emma's brother, had lost her first baby just a few days after Charles and Emma's wedding. Both couples were first cousins.

Perhaps because of the ongoing use the Society was proving to be, and to guarantee his access to the wealth of evidence and knowledge it contained, in the spring of 1839 Darwin joined as a full Fellow. He was elected to the Council during the anniversary meeting at the end of April; another prestigious appointment to add to the list. It was not an easy time to be taking it up, those at the meeting learned. Expenditure was soaring, despite the substantial cost-cutting measures that had been introduced of late, which had ranged from substituting cheaper foodstuffs in the elephant's diet to the reduction of staff and asking the Crown for a diminution of the rent. Worryingly, the Society's income had fallen, too. The number of visitors to the Gardens had peaked in the summer of 1836 with the arrival of the giraffes, when 260,000 visitors had come there. That number decreased by 90,000 the following year, and numbers were low this season too. The economic depression was largely to blame, of course, but it didn't help that there was nothing really exciting to draw the crowds in, now the novelty of the giraffes had worn off. An orang utan was not quite enough, not now.

On the 1st of June, Darwin left Macaw Cottage and made his way to Leicester Square for his first Council meeting. The meeting had been convened to discuss the tenders for the building of a new Monkey House, which, it was hoped, might check the rates of mortality among the animals. But it was another mortality that dominated the conversation in the meeting room and Library at the front of the first floor, at least before official business commenced. Jenny had died a few days previously. Tommy had already been lost, as winter had set in at the end of last year, but Jenny had always been the star of the two, and her death was a real blow to the Society at a time when visitor numbers were in decline. It was a blow also to Darwin, who was saddened by the news. He felt somehow that it was the end of an era for him. Jenny was not the only loss to the Society that month. She was followed by a baby giraffe, born just a week earlier, whose corpse went under Professor Owen's knife.

It was a wet and unsettled summer for Britain. The Whigs' reforms of recent years had bitterly disappointed the working classes – not only were they still not able to vote, they were now penalized for their poverty in the hated workhouses – and they were taking matters into their own hands. On the 14th of June, the Chartists – so-called because of the People's Charter they had devised the previous year – presented a call for universal suffrage to Parliament, with more than a million signatures. That type of unrest was deeply worrying to most of the respectable gentlemen of the Zoological Society Council, its newest member included. It increased his loathing for the city. Darwin's attraction to the scientific community that necessitated his residency there seemed also to be paling. And vice versa. His journal of the *Beagle*'s voyage had finally been published, and the reviews were decidedly mixed. The *Athenaeum*, published the day after the Chartists had taken to the streets of the capital, criticized Darwin's attempts to generalize, the lack of minute evidence for his theories. It was another reason not to publish his species theory before he was convinced his arguments were watertight, his evidence irrefutable: he lived in an age that valued detail above all else.

The city felt increasingly hostile. Darwin was beginning to turn inwards, away from the world outside, to focus instead on his own family. And a family he and Emma were soon to be: she was three months pregnant.

The Darwins' first child was born in the last days of the decade, a boy, William. He was a healthy babe, who made his parents very happy. Darwin now had his own little monkey to conduct his experiments on. He spent many hours observing him, his every movement, his every expression, just as he had Jenny. He repeated the same experiments, even, all of which confirmed his conviction of the similarities between man and the orang utan. A second child, Annie, was born in early 1841. As his family grew, Darwin increasingly withdrew from his metropolitan associations, from the scientific coterie among whom he had once cared so much about winning a place. He did not agree with their views, and he knew they would not agree with his.

What he wanted now for himself and for his family was peace
and quiet. That was what Emma wanted for him, too. She worried about her husband in this life as well as the next. His health
went from bad to worse in the first years of their marriage, with
his headaches and stomach troubles ever present, though quite
what was the matter no one could determine, not even his father.
He seemed better, and they were all happier, in the seclusion of
the country. Staying at The Mount in the summer of 1841,
Darwin persuaded his father to buy his growing family a country house of their own. He had spent many happy days among
the flowers of the gardens over the previous summers and had
all the subjects of study he needed there, with the plants, the
fowl, the cattle, children and dogs. He could continue his work
from the isolation of his own country home, he decided, where
his health might improve.

In the summer of 1842, Down House in Kent came up for sale:
unpretentious, two hours out of London, in a quiet village on
the bleak North Downs. The Darwins visited it in the middle of
July. Charles negotiated a good price and the deal was done.
Emma, pregnant again, spent the following weeks packing up
the family's life in London. They were glad to be leaving. They
had enjoyed another summer in the country, Darwin filling his
'Questions and Experiments' notebook with thoughts about the
plants that surrounded him there, and working on experiments
with his father's gardener. The city they had returned to felt
more dangerous than ever. Troops and demonstrators flooded
the streets not far from their home on Upper Gower Street. The
wage cuts and unemployment of the ongoing depression had
caused much unrest. There was a national general strike, organized by the Chartists, whose calls for more dramatic political
change had gone unanswered. There was rioting in the north,
which it was feared would soon spread to the capital. It was time

for the Darwins to leave all this behind. Emma busied herself preparing her family for their new, more peaceful life.

She and the children left London on the 15th of September. Charles spent a few last days packing his own things. Among them was a document he had written during that turbulent summer. As men had clashed on the streets, he had sketched out his vision, for the first time in full, of the war taking place in nature. His species theory, the theory he had developed, piece by piece, since his return from the voyage almost six years previously. A thirty-five-page document, scribbled in pencil: an outline of the theory of descent by means of natural selection. Thirty-five pages of heresy, he packed it away with his secret notebooks into the box on his desk.

As he did so, he thought of the people who, unwittingly, had helped him develop it. He thought of those he was leaving behind, but whose friendships and associations were captured in the incendiary little document. He thought of Professor Owen, whose work on fossils had shown him the similarities of species over time, a man who had become his friend. He thought of John Gould, whose labours had shown him how species were determined by geographic distribution and had lit the flame of thought in his mind. Returned from Australia, Gould was a great celebrity now. His wife had died last summer, a few days after the birth of their eighth child. (How sad it had been for her to survive Australia only to die in her own bed.) He thought of Mr Yarrell, Lord Derby, and the breeders at the Zoological Society who had helped him understand how nature worked at selecting characteristics, just like they did. He thought of the keepers at the Gardens, who had helped him understand animal behaviour. He thought of Jenny, of course. But he seldom went to the Gardens now. He had heard that things were going down-hill there, that the financial problems had worsened. A symbol of the entire city, he thought. The recession was deepening. He did not need to be there any longer. He had left his old London life behind him, in his heart, long ago. He could, he would, correspond with all of those people, from the comfort and seclusion of Down House.

Darwin called his servant to fetch the boxes, now filled with his most precious possessions. It was not Covington who arrived at the door to the study. Covington had left him after he had married Emma, joining the masses exchanging the poverty and chaos of this country for the opportunities of Australia. Darwin watched his replacement lift the heavy box from the desk. He was not sorry to see his study emptied, abandoned. He turned, closed the door, and followed his man downstairs.

He had taken what he needed from London, and it was coming with him; his grand theory, the work of so many years and so many sleepless nights, now properly committed to paper. He was finally going to claim the quiet country life his family had long imagined for him. But how different from the old dream reality was! He was not a contented academic and cleric. It was a godless parish for which he was leaving, and he was an ill man, bearing the burden of a secret.

7. The Earl and the Hippopotamus

The 13th Earl of Derby, President,
1847–51

May 1847. It had been twenty years since the first plot of land in the north-eastern corner of the Regent's Park had been given over to the Zoological Society of London. Twenty years almost to the month. He well remembered, earlier still, when Sir Stamford Raffles had first written to him of it in 1825, of his plan for London's very own Jardin des Plantes. He had embraced it, of course: natural history was already his great passion, if not yet his life's work. He had been one of the Society's first supporters. That had been before he had developed his own private menagerie, when the prospect of putting together a collection he could study and experiment with had been thrilling indeed. How curious to recall a time when this place had been but a dream. Here, with the Gardens before his very eyes and twenty years' worth of memories of it committed to his brain. His intellectual capacities had, so far, been spared the ravages that the

passing of the years had wrought on his body, and he could vividly remember so many of the beasts that this patch of land had
accommodated. What a great pity, he thought, that Sir Stamford had been denied the pleasure of witnessing his vision
realized. Especially in its heyday. Little Tommy, the chimpanzee, in the keepers' kitchen; the crowds pouring in to see the
giraffes, and Jenny alongside them in Mr Burton's elegant barn.
It had all been so promising, for a time.

He had been the President of the Zoological Society of
London for more than fifteen years now, and had seen it in good
and bad times. Now the truth must be told, unwelcome as it
was: its best days were in the past. A little like himself, he
mused. Lord Derby had just turned seventy-two. He was an
elderly man, confined to a Bath chair. As a manservant pushed
his much-diminished figure around the elegant curves of the
Gardens' walkways, he recalled the tall, slim man he had once
been. It seemed not so long ago, though it was already almost
a decade since the seizure that had reduced him to this state. It
was not vanity that made him think of his former self but
frustration at being unable to bound up to the enclosures, cages,
kennels, pits and ponds, as he had once done. As he still wished
to do. Now he had to be content to watch them roll by, as life
seemed to sometimes, at least when he was in London.

The passage of the Bath chair, with its attendant pedestrians,
was relatively unimpeded. There were not the same great
numbers of visitors choking the pathways as Lord Derby remembered. His memory was not failing him: he had heard the
reports, at the Anniversary Meeting just last week, of the dramatic reduction – yet again – in the numbers of people passing
through the gates, despite all they had done in recent years to
entice them. The Promenade days, when a military band had
entertained the visitors (albeit a decade after the suggestion had
first been made to engage one); the poultry exhibitions, an

attempt to woo expert and amateur breeders with monetary prizes and medals; the grand new Carnivora Terrace . . . None of it had been enough to entice them. People bewildered him, truly. The glorious attraction of the globe's finest creatures in such a pleasant setting was waning, while Mr Cross's Gardens at Newington were as popular as ever – people flocked to see *his* spectacles; all fireworks and acrobats. This year, he had been told, the summer show was to be a representation of the British triumph at the siege of Gibraltar, complete with the sinking of the battleships! He did not understand it. But, then, there was much he did not understand, these days.

The buildings, it must be said, were a little tired. Though the new dens for the Carnivora, on which the Society had expended a great deal a few years ago, were still rather fine, he thought, as he was wheeled past. An elegant parade of open-fronted dens, beneath an extension of the terrace, they were much along the lines of the original design by Mr Burton. Strange how things came around if you waited long enough. Burton had left before they were realized, gone to work his magic at Kew Gardens. There weren't many left who remembered the early days now. No, the problem was not the terrace, rather that the beasts its dens now held were not worthy of it. They had lost a tiger and a puma when they had moved them in, both killed by their companions, the puma partly eaten. (The fresh air had indeed restored the animals' spirits, though not quite in the manner they had intended.) A lion had died not long afterwards. Now, as he was pushed past the row of dens, a rather sorry-looking bunch of creatures was pointed out to him, not the big, ferocious beasts the visitors seemed to adore and that the grand Carnivora Terrace was intended to house.

The party clustered around the President in his Bath chair made its slow way onwards, past the old Llama House with its clock tower, the aviaries and the Monkey House, all a little worn, then disappeared into the tunnel and popped up again in the North Garden. Here the new Museum greeted them, constructed a few years ago. The centrally located premises at Leicester Square had not corrected the low visitor numbers, as had been hoped. Neither had moving the collection to the Gardens. The Museum Establishment was diminishing all the time. The people were not interested in the preserved specimens, it appeared, many of which had been sold over recent weeks. The Council had been much criticized by some of the Fellows for allowing this branch of the Society to suffer at the expense of the crowd-pleasing living beasts. The President well understood their frustrations, shared them, in fact. But what was to be done when the people did not care for bird skins and butterflies as they did giraffes and lions?

Mr David William Mitchell, the new Secretary to the Society, was among the party that slowly snaked its way onwards. He was delivering a rather bleak report to the President as they went. A zoologist in his mid-thirties, he spoke, almost without interruption, on the grave situation they now faced. They passed the Elephant House and paddock. *Jack the Elephant was often shut away from the public now, his temper worse than ever.* They moved on to the Giraffe House at the far west of the North Garden. *At least ten years old now, but in a more acceptable state than many of the other structures.* It was noticeably cooler in there since they had discontinued the artificial heating a year or so ago. The same had been done across the Gardens – only open fires were used in the coldest winter months now – with noticeable improvements in the animals' health, particularly that of the monkeys. They were finally working out what conditions suited them, after much trial and error.

Yet they still had so little success with the orang utans. The inner room that Jenny had inhabited (and then her replacement, another Jenny, and then her replacement, a chimpanzee called

Susan) was now filled with smaller monkeys. Mr Mitchell led the party past and no one paused to look at them. Lord Derby did not like to see the race of monkeys confined to cages, and even less so the bigger ones. It made him uncomfortable. They stopped before the elegant giraffes. *They had lost the largest one this past winter.* The remainder – even the young that had been born there – were not the draw they had once been. *Novelty was what the people wanted.* As Mitchell spoke, Lord Derby thought how melancholy a giraffe could look.

As they came to the end of the tour, Mr Mitchell was explaining to the President that desperate times were upon them. Quite unnecessarily: Lord Derby could see the decay of this place for himself. But the Secretary clearly wanted to make sure that the President, in his Bath chair, did not miss the point. The group continued on its way through the half-deserted Gardens. Gardens that Lord Derby had helped to build. Gardens that, he was now being told, *might not exist for much longer. Unless they could put a stop to this gradual decline, unless they could turn the tide somehow.*

Mr Mitchell was the reason that Lord Derby had made the long, tiresome journey to London from his estate at Knowsley, near Liverpool. The new Secretary had been in the post for just three months, replacing Mr Ogilby, an Irish landowner, who had had to return home to deal with the crisis of the Famine. Mitchell was the first Secretary to be paid a salary, in recognition of the weighty task ahead of him: saving the Zoological Society of London, no less. President and Secretary had been corresponding regularly since Mitchell's appointment in February, and Mitchell had requested, rather firmly, that Lord Derby preside in person over the Anniversary Meeting. He had hated to leave Knowsley Hall now, especially to face such a bleak task, but finally he had agreed. It was an important meeting, after all, and only appropriate that the President oversaw it from the chair.

Overseeing it was all, in truth, that he had done. He was not the most engaging speaker, never had been, and now he could hear so little. But it was symbolic that he was present on that important occasion, just as he had been present at the very first meeting of the nascent Society more than twenty years ago. For the most significant change in its history, proposed by the auditors and encouraged by the new Secretary, had been put to the membership: the proposition that the Gardens be opened to the public two days in the week, upon payment of a shilling, without the necessity of an order of admission from a Fellow. There had long been debate over making the collection more accessible, as there had been debate over admission to many public institutions during the past decade, from St Paul's to the British Museum. And though the Society had acknowledged some years ago that it would no longer be wise, given the changing political climes, to be quite so vigilant over their own entry policy, they had not revised it. Now it had become a matter of expediency, indeed of urgency. The number of visitors to the Gardens in the previous year had been just 94,000: the lowest in its entire history. Funds had never been in a worse condition. So it had been agreed: the gates were to be thrown open to the general public on Monday and Tuesday of each week, and all week at Easter and Whitsun.

With that decision made, a Council meeting and his visit to the Gardens behind him, Lord Derby returned home as quickly as he could. How things unfolded he could learn by letter. He preferred it so: when he was shut away at Knowsley Hall, the world could come to him, if necessary. He had all he wanted there: his family, yes, but also the birds and beasts – from toucans to turkeys, llamas to lemurs – of his personal menagerie (though he didn't call it that: he thought the word too foreign). He had spared no expense in making the hundred acres of land and water he inhabited into a little slice of Paradise, his own private zoological gardens. There, he did not have to share the pathways with anyone else or concern himself with popular tastes, only with what was most useful and interesting. He permitted visitors, by appointment, but he limited the numbers most carefully. He wanted the beasts to be largely undisturbed; he knew that was what they required to breed. He had become an expert in the delicate science of it, equally passionate about perfecting breeds of bloodhound and chicken as he was about more exotic species. His careful attention meant that he had successfully reared several species in captivity for the first time, from the ostrich to the Stanley crane named in his honour.

It was late in the day when he approached the Hall on the last leg of his return journey from London, much wearied by it. He found travelling more exhausting and uncomfortable than ever now. He was too old for it, he had decided many times on the way. Now, as the carriage rattled along towards the sandstone wall around the park (ten miles of it, which he had constructed to protect his beloved beasts), his spirits began to lift. Fleetwood emerged from Huyton Lodge to greet the carriage with a doffed hat and a warm *Good evening, my lord* as he opened the gate to the grounds within. Lord Derby's fatigue faded even as they passed through it to the tree-lined drive. Once they were clear of the dense plantation of fine oak trees to the left, he cherished the first glimpses of the familiar beloved landscape between the trunks. There! He spotted a small group of Cape eland, a species he had been first to import into England, horned heads down, grazing on the summer grass. He was home. The Hall came into view as the carriage clattered along: the imposing red-brick façade of the east wing, with the older south wing in red sandstone to one side. His ancestral home, not perfectly beautiful but perfectly familiar.

He wondered if he was up to a quick visit to the New Aviary, to see the birds and beasts housed there before the light went, or if he should wait until the morning. Perhaps he would content himself with a report from Thompson, his Superintendent, for now. His bones were aching and dinner would soon be served. A flock of geese flew overhead, destined for the lake, White Man's Dam, with its lovely boathouse. One thing he was sure of: he would not leave home again, not for as long as he could possibly help it.

He could dispatch his duties as President of the Zoological Society very well from Knowsley. Where he could forget what an old man he had become, where the world still made perfect sense to him, where he could enjoy his days as he had always done (Bath chair aside). After prayers, he breakfasted with whichever members of the family happened to be at the Hall. His wife had died many years ago, but his sons and daughters and brother-in-law were often there, and usually a handful of grandchildren, nieces and nephews, great-nieces and great-nephews besides; he never had to dine alone. After this warm and sociable start to the day, he retired to his private suite of rooms at the north end of the Hall, where he could work in peace at his correspondence. The walls around him were hung with the Old Masters his forefathers had gathered, as in the rest of the house, but in here his own additions to the family collection hung alongside: mementos of his enduring passion. Liverpool Academician Richard Ansdell's *Zebras* adorned the library, his *Brahman Bull Cow and Goats* and his *Antelopes* the main sitting room. In the bedroom, Lord Derby had hung his personal favourite, which he woke up to every day: *Head of Master Thomas Chimpanzee from the Zoological Gardens, Regent's Park* by Benjamin Waterhouse Hawkins. Poor old Tommy. He lived on, in a way, here at Knowsley Hall.

From these comfortable rooms, his private sanctuary, Lord Derby could reach out across the globe to a network of animal traders and experts on natural history built over a lifetime. He could travel the world from his desk. There, he felt no less a man than he had ever been. His useless legs were unimportant as he went about his business, watched over by the beasts depicted in the paintings on the walls, surrounded by the many living creatures in the grounds beyond them, some of which he could hear, even now. He wrote to animal dealers in the capital, to men like Mr Jamrach, who specialized in the import and export of live beasts, and Mr Gould, who always knew of birds and bird skins on the market all over the world. He wrote to experts and amateurs further afield too, men who collected on his behalf. Like Edward Blyth at Calcutta, the Curator for the Asiatic Society of Bengal, and the Reverend John Fry at the Cape, both of whom sent shipments of birds and beasts to him regularly. When he had a particular interest in a part of the world that was not adequately covered already, he sent men on special collecting missions, organized from the seclusion and ease of Knowsley.

His rooms were in the part of the Hall nearest to the New Aviary, while the brew-house ponds, stables and animal pens were close indeed. As he worked at his letters, he liked to listen to the birds. He could identify them all from their calls and he knew exactly what each species would be doing as he heard it: he knew their habits minutely. It was May: the mating season was over and the nesting season under way. It was one of his favourite times of the year, so full of promise, neither its treasures nor its disappointments – useless eggs and dead chicks – yet revealed. Listening to the birds at their labours beyond his window, he worked hard too, enquiring, organizing. This was how he had built up his extensive collection of both living and dead animals. It had all started, he supposed, with the usual aristocratic interest in ornamental game-birds and hunting dogs, and had grown from there into the finest collection anywhere, he liked to think, and had often been told. Finer even than that of

the Zoological Society, constrained as it was by the need to satisfy the curiosity of amateurs.

He might seldom venture to its meetings now, but he was still
very much a participant in the business of the Society he had
presided over for the best part of two decades. Many of his own
animals had spent periods at the Gardens for breeding purposes,
and vice versa, and he often tapped into and shared the Society's
networks. It was a mutually beneficial arrangement, for they
were each other's biggest competitors when it came to the market for exotic birds and beasts. In the late spring of 1847 Lord
Derby was working particularly hard on the Society's account.
Mitchell's warnings on his recent visit had not been lost on
him. Not long after his return home, the Council accepted his
offer of a pair of lions, a sale he had negotiated. He hoped they
might do justice, long overdue, to the Carnivora Terrace.

Lord Derby was also working on a rather more complicated
plan on the Society's behalf. The President and Secretary were
conspiring on it together: a plan to satisfy people's desire for novelty, for large and terrifying beasts. They had been corresponding
privately since April about a collecting mission to North Africa.
Mr Warwick had offered to go on the Society's behalf. The Society had had a fraught relationship with him over the years – he
had once worked for them, but left in acrimonious circumstances, then had brought back the giraffes for Mr Cross to rival
their own. Lord Derby was not concerned with his history, only
whether or not he was up to the job. And a big job it was. Warwick's proposal to Mitchell and Lord Derby – as yet a secret from
the Council – was that he would obtain for the Society a creature
so mysterious, so wonderful, that it would reverse their fortunes
at a stroke. He was to capture and bring back a beast that had
never before been seen in this country. He was going to go to
North Africa to get them a . . . *hippopotamus*!

*

Mitchell came up in person to discuss the proposition. It was a chance, too, to better acquaint himself with the President of the Society for which he daily toiled. The Secretary had taken the daily train from Euston station and arrived at Huyton Gate on the evening of the 3rd of June. The guards were more used to unloading crates of animals at this rural station than to greeting disembarking passengers. The carriage awaited him there to take him the short distance on to Knowsley Hall.

Mr Mitchell spent a pleasant few days there, as most did who were accommodated in one of the many bedrooms on the guest floor above the family's living quarters. It was a most impressive house, always filled with the family and their guests, there for the shooting or to see the Earl's collection, or just to enjoy Knowsley hospitality. Lord Derby was a generous host and his extraordinarily large domestic staff made him a very good one. He enjoyed sharing his life's work with fellow natural historians, more so than ever now that he was at such an advanced stage with it. Mr Mitchell was a younger man, in his thirties, a collector of skins and eggs. He was the perfect interested guest as Lord Derby was pushed alongside him through the library rooms on the first floor that made up his Museum. The Earl had accumulated thousands of preserved specimens, buying up other museum collections and specimens, and preserving the animals that died on the estate – his extensive staff even included an animal stuffer – and the glass cases of the Museum now covered specimens of every taxonomic group, every type of bird and mammal.

The real highlight of life at Knowsley for a naturalist was the daily excursion around the grounds. Lord Derby liked to embark on it at midday, to work up an appetite for lunch. The frail, white-haired Earl was helped into the waiting carriage by the footman, and was usually followed by one of his sons or daughters. On this day in early June, it was Mr Mitchell who sat

in the seat beside him as the horses pulled the carriage away
from the entrance. They set off alongside the red-brick frontage
to the grounds to the north. It was a dry day, and the warm
breeze carried the scent of grass and manure to them. Lord
Derby wanted his guest to enjoy it. *It was a world away from the
smoke and filth of London, was it not?*

They came first to the new stables, the latest addition to the
grounds by the current Earl. A large, modern complex of buildings to accommodate all the horses he loved. They made good
use of the hunting season here. Opposite was the brew-house
pond and the Old Aviary, where the noise of its feathered
inhabitants – a constant presence anywhere in the grounds –
was thrown into loud, crisp definition. Lord Derby had overseen the birds kept there since he was a young man, the parrots
and song birds, game-birds and guans; he had much improved
the accommodation in the Old Aviary more than forty years
ago, and had redesigned the pond to better suit the waterfowl.
But it was only when his father had died in 1834 that he had been
able to turn over much more of the family's extensive grounds
to the birds and beasts he adored. He had built an entire New
Aviary complex. That was where the carriage was headed now,
continuing beyond the walled kitchen gardens – *Designed by
Capability Brown*, the Earl explained to his guest, as they passed.

The New Aviary was a fenced enclosure of ten acres, containing a huge array of structures for the different birds and beasts
that resided there, from paddocks to dens to glasshouses. No
expense had been spared in its construction – *he had had four hundred labourers at work on it!* Neither was it spared today. He had a
permanent staff of thirteen men working exclusively with the
animals there, with many more called in when needed. The
running costs were six-fold the expenditure on the maintenance
of the estate grounds. The elderly Earl was told, often, by his
land agent that it was a luxury he could not afford. His son and

heir, styled Lord Stanley, as he himself had once been, increasingly echoed those concerns. Lord Derby's partial deafness was convenient during those conversations. He refused to be told what he could and couldn't afford when it came to his animals. It was not his frivolous hobby: this was his life's work. It was important work, scientific work. He was advancing knowledge about the practices of breeding animals in captivity, hybrids and pure species alike; animals he hoped might be useful for mankind – or, at the very least, ornamental. His own objectives were similar to the original ones of the Zoological Society, and those put into action at the Society's farm, in which he had been very involved. It was a shame that that side of the establishment was long gone now. But he had all he needed here.

Thompson, the Superintendent of the living collection, came out of his home to meet the carriage, which had now drawn to a stop on the drive that cut through the centre of the sprawling complex. Thompson had once worked at the Gardens in the Regent's Park but had been at Knowsley for at least a decade now. He knew Mitchell, for he was often in London on Lord Derby's business, collecting specimens and overseeing the transport of animals between Knowsley and the Regent's Park, and greeted him warmly now. Thompson lived and breathed alongside these creatures, in a house, The Nest, within the New Aviary, and gave Lord Derby a report each day on what had mated, what had died, anything of note. He now joined the footman in assisting his master down from the carriage. The Bath chair was brought to the Earl and he was helped into it. Mitchell jumped down, eager to inspect the delights on offer here.

There was a huge wired structure for smaller birds of all kinds, from parakeets to thrushes, in front of The Nest, with glass-roofed houses at its rear for pheasants and turkeys. Then there were arched dens and terraces along the eastern side for smaller Mammalia: beavers, porcupines, hares, armadillos and lemurs. Then there were countless enclosed paddocks and buildings for larger creatures: ostriches, antelope, kangaroos and zebra. Thompson led the way. When they had finished there, they would continue about the grounds where other animals roamed free, such as the countless species of deer: muntjac, Savannah, Barbary, wapiti, sambur (most of which had been bred at Knowsley), cattle and sheep. Then, perhaps, they would go on to White Man's Dam to see the black-necked swans, the ducks, coots, geese, cormorants, kingfishers, oyster-catchers and herons. If they had time, they might make a visit to the kennels in the far north of the grounds to see the deerhounds and bloodhounds.

He had everything a naturalist could dream of, a lifetime's worth of study, within his walls! He did not keep larger carnivores, which held little interest for him and posed too great a danger, and the higher orders of primate he avoided, too: he could not bear to see them, so sad, in confinement. Those omissions aside, he had a private, perfect little world of nature here, all the wonders of God's Creation represented. He would show Mr Mitchell as much of it as he could. Then the hour for lunch would be upon them.

By the time he left Knowsley Hall, Mr Mitchell had been suitably impressed. Who could not be, with so many different species, all so carefully accommodated, so intimately studied and understood? It was quite remarkable that this was the work of one man. The purpose of his visit, however, was connected with Lord Derby's public rather than personal endeavours and far more difficult to celebrate at this present moment. The President and Secretary of the Zoological Society had spoken at length about the immense challenges currently facing the Society. They seemed to be mounting all the time, despite Mr

Mitchell's best efforts. The letter he sent to thank Lord Derby for his hospitality a few days after his return to London contained yet more depressing news. Jack the elephant had died. (He apologized for the delay in writing, but he had been much occupied with organizing the dissection.) Lord Derby decided he would send Thompson to London with a donation from his own collection. He could not replace the elephant, of course, but Mr Mitchell had expressed an interest in a Stanley crane: the beautifully elegant, blue-coloured crane that Mr Nicholas Vigors had named after him back in 1826, and that he had gone on to breed (for the first time) in captivity. He must see what he could do about that. It might soften the blow of the loss of the elephant, a little at least.

The next day's post brought more disappointing news. It was a letter from Devereux Fuller, erstwhile head keeper of the Gardens, dismissed for misconduct a few years ago. (Lord Derby had wondered if it had been more a matter of expediency: there had been a rather ruthless cull of the keepers and other staff and cutting of salaries at that time. Mr Youatt had lost his position too, the Medical Superintendent dispensed with altogether; the Superintendent Mr Miller's salary had been cut. Those had been dark days indeed.) Lord Derby had decided to give Fuller a job, for he had seemed competent enough, and had dispatched him, in March last year, on a collecting mission to Calcutta. Now his lordship received a letter in Fuller's hand from London. He was back, and due to get the earliest second-class train from Euston on Sunday with his haul. He asked for Thompson to meet him with the horse and cart at the station. Not that it sounded as if it would be too difficult to transport what he was bringing with him. Fuller had been away for more than a year, and Lord Derby had entertained high hopes of the mission, which had cost him a great deal. Yet the letter before him now stated that he would be arriving at Huyton Gate with the 'few birds' he had successfully brought back alive. It had been a waste of money, by the sound of it.

The disappointment made him more aware than ever of the risk of the mission he and Mitchell were hatching for Warwick: it was so exceedingly difficult to get anything here alive! Yet it was becoming ever more vital that something on that scale was attempted, for the Society's fortunes worsened further still over the summer. The Promenade days and poultry competitions stuttered on (at the latter of which the President ensured the Knowsley menagerie was well represented), but the public was not taking advantage of the new admission policy as hoped, and another large deficit had been forecast for the year. A special meeting was called to make the reductions in expenditure necessary to deal with it. The possibility of getting rid of the Museum altogether, to save money, was raised, giving the collection to the nation in exchange for reduced rent from the Crown. Before a final decision was made, the Museum staff was reduced to just one. The role of Assistant Secretary and the architect's yearly retainer were also dispensed with. It all made the President's heart sink. What else could he do? He sent down another donation care of Thompson, in July: some toucans.

What the Society really needed was money. In this time of hardship, there must be an incentive for the public to pay their shilling admission fee and the Fellows to pay their annual subscriptions. It had to be a real draw; something that showed the Society remained a scientific pioneer. Like the giraffes had done a decade ago. Toucans would not be enough. Another chimpanzee or an orang utan would help, but the Society had such a poor record of keeping them alive and, besides, they were not the novelty they had once been. A hippopotamus, though . . . no one had ever seen a hippopotamus in this country before. It could change everything, the President and Secretary agreed.

At the Council meeting on the 21st of July, Mitchell finally put Warwick's proposal to the assembled men: this was the chance to reverse the decline of the Society. They referred it to the Committee for the Purchase of Animals. Professor Owen and Mr Yarrell were the only members besides the Secretary and their decision was unanimous: the possession of a hippopotamus would be of the greatest possible service to the Society. The agreement with Warwick should be entered into without delay. Now Lord Derby could work out of the shadows. From his desk over the warm weeks of August, as the harvest was brought in from the miles of his estate that surrounded him, and deliveries of animals arrived (including a boatload that Mitchell had inspected for him and sent up with a keeper, Hunt), Lord Derby helped to draft the agreement for the mission to Upper Egypt. Everything was falling into place. It had to for, as one of the many letters from Mitchell that passed over his desk that summer said, the prospects for the Society were 'as bad as possible'.

In the first days of September, news reached Knowsley Hall that Warwick had suddenly called off the agreement. The President's work during that summer and his hopes of saving the Society's fortunes vanished in the space of the few seconds it took him to read the opening lines of a letter. Lord Derby could not rescue the agreement. He did the only thing he could and sent some more donations to Regent's Park: rats, genets, birds and deer from his grounds. Of course such animals were no substitute for a hippopotamus, even he knew that, much as he loved all of God's creatures. The sudden collapse of what had seemed the best chance to save the Society was a blow he felt keenly.

More than that, he felt it personally. That autumn was a time of much reflection for the seventy-two-year-old 13th Earl of Derby. As winter fell on Knowsley, robbing him of his view of the grounds beyond his window a little earlier each day, and as

another year of dawns and dusks drew to its close, he was thinking of his own end. It felt as if the time had come, was long
overdue in fact, to acknowledge the ebb of vitality from his limbs,
leading to its inevitable conclusion. He was thinking of what he
would leave behind him, as every man does at such a time. It was
a sorry situation, in that this was the moment that the Society he
had helped to build began to crumble. No longer was it the valuable legacy he had long envisaged it would be, no more the living
monument to the pursuit of natural history, which he had cham-
pioned all his life. His public work might come to naught.

He had long wondered, too, what would become of his own
collection after his death. Of course he had, yet the time had
never seemed quite right to make the necessary arrangements
for it. The truth was that he had not wanted to look so directly
at the painful fact that his menagerie would not long survive
him. He could not bear to think that even the memory of it
would in time be erased from the Knowsley landscape. His son
and heir was a politician. A much better one than his father, and
now for another party, too. He had changed sides and become a
Tory. Lord Derby had never really understood politics' twists,
turns and manipulations. He preferred the ordered beauty of the
Animal Kingdom: fixed, understandable, willingly revealing its
secrets to those who had the careful patience to study it. He yet
harboured a secret hope that his son might maintain the menagerie, but he was not a fool and knew it was probably futile. He
had not passed on his love of natural history, much as he had
tried. So painstakingly assembled, over a lifetime, his collection
of birds and beasts would surely be broken up, too enormous to
be bestowed in its entirety on anyone else.

His preserved collection, of which he was also justifiably
proud, he believed he should pass on to the nation. It was of
immense scientific value. He began to consider to whom he
would entrust it. It was unfortunate timing that the Zoological

Society's Museum was in a poorer state than ever, and now possibly destined for dispersal itself. It would be folly indeed to donate it to the Society, at least in its entirety. The British Museum Lord Derby considered too. He wondered if the solution might be to split it between the two. Among the usual correspondence with Mr Mitchell that October, about the birds he was hoping to buy, borrow or lend, Lord Derby's letters contained his musings on the eventual destination of his Museum collection. In the strictest confidence, he mentioned to Mitchell the arrangement he was currently considering.

In the regular letters that flowed between them over the autumn, Lord Derby closely monitored the Society's fortunes. A pair of aurochs had arrived in October from Memel in East Prussia, truly valuable zoological specimens donated by the Emperor of Russia, but they had failed to capture the public attention. Mitchell wrote of the possibility of procuring chimpanzees, and yet entertained hopes of obtaining a hippopotamus. Lord Derby doubted that he himself would survive long enough to see it, even if the Society did. And he doubted that now, too. He tried not to dwell on it. He focused on his Aviary: he and his keepers had had some successes and some failures, as ever, over the year that was now coming to a close. They had not managed to breed the Honduran turkeys as hoped, but they had succeeded with the beautiful Impeyan pheasants, which had bred for the first time in captivity. He had also produced a hybrid between the common black and common white swan. This was a legacy he had no anxiety over: such scientific breakthroughs would outlive him. It was the physical things and where they would go that continued to trouble him.

By November, Lord Derby could delay no longer in committing his last requests to paper. On the second Saturday in November, he sat at his desk looking out of the window over the grounds. He had spent so many hours like that, over so many

years. Thompson and Shaw, the deer keeper, had turned the
deer out last month and he watched a small group of them moving idly in the distance. He turned to the paper in front of him,
and wrote, 'Memo for my Will'. Beneath, he began, with a
heavy heart: 'In the event of my successor not desiring to keep
up and continue the menagerie and museum which I have established at Knowsley, it is my wish that the following arrangement
should take place . . .'

He wrote a letter to Mitchell containing his decision at the
end of November. Then, in the last days of 1847, he sent the
document to London for his son to inspect. Lord Stanley replied
on the first day of the new year: he hoped that it would be a long
time before he had to look at his father's will again. But he did
not query his decision. He did not say that he would take over
the menagerie.

The months seemed to pass quicker than ever now for the Earl.
Another inevitability of old age, it seemed, and all the crueller
now that time was at its most precious. The shooting season was
over, the mating season's colourful and entertaining displays
had passed in an instant, the birds already taking to their nests.
With that, the Anniversary Meeting was suddenly upon him
again. Mitchell's letters entreated him to preside over it this year
as he had done last. The Earl, blessed with seeing another spring
on his estate, had much to keep him at home. The deer had come
through the winter in fine form, and the Anatidae had been
breeding well. Most excitingly the pair of *Melopsittacus undula-
tus*, the budgie birds that Gould had procured for him from
Australia, had bred – for the first time ever in captivity. Louis
Fraser (an erstwhile employee of the Society, who had more
recently undertaken collecting missions for him) had approached
Lord Derby for employment, complaining of the hard times,
and had been put to work on a catalogue of his preserved

specimens. Lord Derby welcomed the chance to see exactly what he had accumulated over the years. He was looking into converting part of the old stables into a new museum for some part of the collection too. (This went against the advice of his agent, Earle, who spoke far too much about the cost of the thing. He did not seem to understand that the estate would always provide.) Yes, he had much to keep him here, yet he had resolved that go to London he must, however begrudgingly. The Society needed him.

The situation it was in remained bleak. It was not for want of effort on Mitchell or the Council's part. In February, a committee had been appointed to investigate how the Society might be reinvigorated, in all of its branches. Works were proposed, including a building specifically for the display of reptiles (a novelty indeed), a structure for demonstrations and musical performances and a new entrance gate. Other efforts to increase the scientific appeal of the Society included lectures and new publications – there had not been an updated guide to the Gardens for some years now. Lord Derby was sorry, and somewhat mystified, to learn that the annual summer poultry exhibition would not be continued. He had always taken it seriously. Thompson had returned with three first prizes last year. (His wild turkey in particular was much admired by the judges, and the potential value of a cross with the domestic breed acknowledged.) The biggest change that had been introduced, however, was the reduction in the price of admission to the public. Already allowed into the Gardens on any day without an order, now on Mondays the entrance fee was reduced from a shilling to sixpence. There were concerns, naturally, among some of the Fellows about the sort of character it might permit into the Gardens, but the Society had had little choice.

In addition to his usual reluctance to leave Knowsley for the capital, there was a further concern this time about Lord

Derby making the tiring and unwanted journey south. Mitchell warned him that he might find disturbances in the capital: another petition was due to be presented by the Chartists. Lord Derby supported minor reform, but trouble like this was a different matter altogether and he did not sympathize with it, not at all. He had seen such disturbances so many times in his life and it saddened him to see it again: the bloody revolutions and civil wars of his infancy, in France and the Americas; Peterloo, on home soil – thirty years ago now – when he had been incensed by how the militia had been treated for merely doing their job in protecting order! Order must triumph against insubordination. Then, more recently, the disturbances of 1842, where there had been such trouble up here again – he hoped things would not become as bad they had then. The revolutions that were now sweeping the Continent were a terrifying example of how things could end. What had happened to the times when everyone was contented with their God-given lot? The correct order of things had been so horribly disrupted of late, the world of mankind such a stark contrast to the minutely ordered natural world . . .

He arrived, exhausted, in a tense capital. At the station, his party was met by the staff of his London household in Grosvenor Square. Tired as he was, Lord Derby noticed something as he was escorted to the waiting carriage: an advertisement of the new admissions policy to the Gardens of the Zoological Society of London. The Society was setting much store by the cheaper fee. As he was helped into the carriage, its President earnestly hoped it would work, that in such troubled times it would not simply degrade the establishment further. He knew that there was not much more that could be done. Except, of course, to procure a hippopotamus, and that seemed nigh on impossible, now.

Lord Derby did not venture down for the Anniversary Meeting the following April. He had decided he would stay in his peaceful little Paradise. From now on, friends and scientific associates could come to him.

In July of 1849, he welcomed back a man who was both: Edward Lear, just one of the artists who had been employed at Knowsley over the years, to record the Earl's collection. (He often had his animals painted upon their death, so they could live on his walls, or at least in the albums and portfolios of his library.) Lear had become a friend of the whole family. He had spent these past years in Italy, at Lord Derby's expense, for reasons of health as well as the desire to develop his skills as a landscape painter. His eyes were too poor for the close work of natural-history illustrations now. A great shame, as far as his patron was concerned, though the patronage continued: two of Lear's landscapes hung in the entrance hall among the more traditional Old Masters, as the guest was exceedingly pleased to see upon his arrival. Lear had quit Rome at the beginning of 1848 when the rumblings of revolution had reached it. (Things seemed to be fizzling out on the Continent now, thank God, and the Chartist threat had died down here. Perhaps these troubled times were passing, the Earl liked to think.)

After a lengthy tour of the Mediterranean and then Egypt, Lear had returned to England only the previous month. Bursting with stories of his adventures, he was not at all sorry to be back at Knowsley in the full bloom of summer. Neither was Lord Derby sorry to welcome him there once more. Lear had visited most recently in the summer of 1841, but it was of the years he had passed there in the 1830s, living almost as one of the family, that they both had such fond memories. Lear had been employed as an artist, and had initially lived below stairs. He had, however, earned his place among the family by entertaining the children with his wonderfully amusing drawings and nonsense rhymes. He was an odd fellow, who had then had little experience of high society and its etiquette, yet at

Knowsley he had become a much-loved face around the large
dinner table.

On the first evening of his guest's stay, the Earl was prepared
for dinner by his valet. He sat, helpless as ever, on a chair in his
wardrobe room as he was put into his evening dress. 'Master
Thomas Chimpanzee' looked on as the old man was helped
through his bedroom and along to the dining room. As the huge
floor-to-ceiling oak doors were parted for him, to reveal the
lavish dining room his father had built, Lord Derby was happy
to see Lear among his family once again. Here were so many
people dear to him: his brother-in-law, Mr Charles Hornby, and
numerous other members of the Hornby and Stanley families,
united by his own marriage and his sister's. He greeted them all
warmly, and it was reciprocated. He allowed the bubbling chatter to wash over him. Anything other than direct conversation
was nigh on impossible for him now, but he was happy to watch.
Lear looked much older than he remembered, though yet a
young man compared to himself. He must be in his late thirties.
The children he had entertained were now fully grown. His
'Nonsense' was no longer the exclusive delight of the Stanley
family, either: he had published two volumes of it not long ago,
much of it inspired by his time and the creatures here. Lord
Derby could not help but taste sorrow as he sipped his wine.
How quickly the years had gone by.

The dining-room walls were covered with portraits of his
forefathers. There was his father, the 12th Earl, a politician and,
more famously, a man of society, remembered by the horse races
he had established, the Oaks and the Derby. His own son was so
like his father, a lover of animals only when sport was involved.
His horse was due to run at Goodwood next week. His grandfather, his great-grandfather . . . They were all here, all looked
down on him every evening. The question that often forced its
way into his mind – more so than ever, in recent months – did

so now: how would he, the 13th Earl, be remembered? He looked to his children and grandchildren, sitting around the candlelit table, talking, smiling, laughing. They would long thrive after him, even if his beloved collection did not. He thought of all the creatures that surrounded them, out of sight. The kangaroos and the alpaca, the deer and antelopes. The swans and the vultures. The beavers and foxes, jerboa and owls, only now, in the darkness, coming to life.

He looked at Lear, who had helped to preserve his birds and his beasts for posterity: for his descendants and for science both. Lear had done many of the drawings for the zoological work Lord Derby had had printed and distributed privately a few years ago: *Gleanings from the Menagerie and Aviary at Knowsley Hall.* John Edward Gray, keeper of Zoology at the British Museum, had edited it, and Gray was now working on a second volume on hoofed quadrupeds. Lord Derby hoped to see it published soon. He had reconciled himself with the fact that *this* would be his legacy: the records of the work he had done. He knew that his son would not upkeep the menagerie to which he had dedicated himself, and he could accept it, now, albeit with some disappointment. His son had to be free to live his life as he saw fit. It helped, immensely, that he now had restored faith that the Gardens of the Zoological Society would serve as his living monument, when he was just a portrait on this wall and the Aviary beyond it was no more. Things had improved there over the past year. So he had heard, anyway.

Mr Mitchell had sat at the dining table at Knowsley Hall earlier in the year and the news he had brought with him of the Society's fortunes had been good, for a change. Very good, in fact: the new admissions policy had been a resounding success. From 1847 to 1848 there had been the greatest annual increase in visitors in the Society's history. (Excepting, of course, the year

when the giraffes had arrived.) By the summer of 1849 the Reptile House had been completed, and new wings to the Giraffe
House and the Ostrich House were under way. A batch of new
animals had just arrived, a lion, giraffes, ostriches and antelopes,
which helped to keep the new visitors interested. (They had
been gifts from the late Ibrahim Pasha of Egypt, keen to impress
the nation that had granted him the hereditary governorship
only fairly recently.) Lord Derby had done his bit, of course. He
had helped to arrange a selection of fowl that had been sent to
the Pasha in return for his gifts, and had himself donated two
harnessed antelopes, three Demerara sheep, a jungle cock,
twenty-four Senegal pigeons, eight passenger pigeons and a
jaguar.

The lack of big carnivores was still, sadly, a concern. Losses
had continued, too: the aurochs had died suddenly over the
winter, as well as the male giraffe, both from inflammation of
the lungs, the old curse of the Gardens. Mitchell was only cautiously optimistic. Yes, things were much improved but he knew
the pressure was on to keep the public interested. He despaired
of ever getting a hippopotamus – an agent in Egypt had offered
to attempt to capture one, but at two thousand pounds, plus the
cost of the fifty men he said he required for it, they could never
afford even to try. Lord Derby allowed himself to be pleased
that things were improving for the Society. It was a huge weight
off his mind.

That summer, he continued to follow the Society's progress
remotely, and do what he could, when he could. But he was free
also to enjoy his many other passions. Though popular tastes
and pursuits had moved on, he still cared immensely for the
detail and the less spectacular subjects of natural history. He and
Mitchell corresponded on topics as endlessly fascinating as the
distinction between quails and partridges, as well as rather
bigger matters, like a possible joint collecting expedition to

Singapore. Lord Derby also enjoyed a very full correspondence with the Reverend Mr Edmund Dixon, an expert on domestic and ornamental poultry breeding, which might no longer be deemed fashionable by the Zoological Society but remained a great interest of his. Mr Dixon had travelled to Knowsley from his parish in Norfolk to see Lord Derby's collection. In July, in a letter predominantly about the japanned peafowl and its characteristics, Lord Derby read with interest of a discussion Mr Dixon had had with Charles Darwin. He had met him at Malvern, where Mr Darwin was undergoing water therapy for his chronic illness. Apparently, he had expressed a belief that 'new species do, at intervals, show themselves in the midst of our fauna'. Lord Derby knew Darwin, of course – he had helped him to fund his work on the zoology of the *Beagle*'s voyage and had shared his knowledge on breeding with him at intervals over the years. Derby respected him generally, but cared not for the idea of the mutability of species – such a radical one! Mr Dixon agreed.

Rather suddenly, in September, as the air began to cool for another winter, so, too, did the enthusiastic tone of Mitchell's regular letters. Among the news of eggs laid and tigers wanted, he reminded Lord Derby of the money he owed the Society for the various animals sold to him and purchased on his behalf (including one of the leucoryx donated by the late Pasha of Egypt: a beautiful white horned oryx). The Secretary was under pressure to settle accounts. Cholera had hit London again – with greater ferocity than before – and anyone who had enough money and sense seemed to have left the capital. The receipts at the Gardens' gates had plummeted. Not long afterwards, the rhinoceros died. (The dissection had revealed a broken rib and injured lung, which some put down to Jack the elephant, his erstwhile neighbour.) As the nights fell earlier, bringing as always a sense of endings – and this time a decade was drawing to a close too – Lord Derby saw why Mr Mitchell had been only cautiously optimistic about the fate of the Society. Perhaps he should have exercised the same caution himself, he thought, looking out on the falling darkness of a winter's dusk.

In the very last days of the year, Mr Mitchell was confined to his home in Russell Square, unwell. He had not contracted the cholera as thousands of others in the capital had done over recent months, probably thanks to his address in a good neighbourhood. (It was now thought that poor sanitation was the cause of the disease.) His complaint was rather more mundane: Mr Mitchell had had surgery on his leg and was housebound. When correspondence reached him there, from the British Consul in Egypt, he deemed it so urgent he called the Council to his home to discuss it. The Viceroy of Egypt's successor, his nephew Abbas I, now wanted to make a donation of animals to the Society. It included an animal captured near the island of Obaysch in the Nile: an infant hippopotamus.

Mitchell, incapacitated at home, dashed off a letter to Knowsley. A suitable gift to exchange in return was needed. His predecessor had been most gratified with the fowl sent out to Egypt to thank him for the last generous donation, but this time something rather more spectacular would be necessary. Colonel Murray, the British Consul, had suggested some greyhounds. Lord Derby's help in the matter was urgently sought. His expert knowledge of a subject all too often considered mundane, even *passé*, these days, was suddenly desperately required. Who knew better the breeds and breeders who would deliver the necessary prestige? The President gladly offered to take charge of the matter.

The first month of 1850 was very cold. There was ice on the Thames, and two hundred miles north, the landscape that the Earl of Derby looked out upon was white. The men of the shooting parties who rode out from the Hall on those mornings returned red-cheeked and hungry. Lord Derby heard the occasional shot as he sat at his desk. Today, he was glad he was not among them as he had once been: he was doing what he did best now. He knew exactly who to approach. He was a most enthusiastic keeper of hounds and had annotated a painting of a hunt from Knowsley, which adorned a wall downstairs, with the names of his own favourite hounds. Though he could no longer accompany the young men who rode out with them, he still knew what a man looked for in his hunting dogs. Only the very finest specimens would do for His Highness, of course, and they had to be the perfect mix of animals for breeding to maintain the stud. Lord Derby had to take into account not only the Pasha's desires but also the conditions and climate in which they would run in Egypt. Apparently the Pasha had had a lot of deerhounds and foxhounds last year, sent from France, but they had failed. Thus the President's work was not straightforward. Yet Mr Mitchell, confined to his sofa for most of the month, and the anxious Council he was reporting to, could have every confidence that the job would be done to the Society's credit.

On the 20th of February, the gift for His Highness Abbas Pasha was dispatched onboard a steamer from Southampton to Cairo, care of the Peninsular and Oriental Company (the same that had transported the giraffes over a decade earlier; having expanded its operations and been incorporated by Royal Charter, it had changed its name). The four brace of greyhounds and two of deerhounds, with their keeper, had first been displayed at the Gardens for two days. For the greyhounds, Lord Derby had turned to his friend Lord Sefton, the most successful winner of prizes in the north. The animals he sold to the Society – Speaker, Superfine, Sergeant at Arms, Saxon Lass, Sire and Madam – had many victories to their names. They were accompanied by

additional greyhounds purchased from Mr Ralph Etwall, plus
one pair of deerhounds each from the keeper at Richmond Park
and from the deer-park keeper to the Duke of Bedford. All were
acquired for £121, which was a snip of what they were actually
worth, thanks to Lord Derby's intervention. The keeper who
was to have charge of them was Lord Sefton's very own trainer,
no less, Henry Beale (who also had a list with him of animals
that the Knowsley Aviary would be glad to acquire, if the
opportunity arose). Lord Derby's work was done and it was well
done.

That day, the Council received a full report on the matter
from the Secretary, now able to attend in person again, and Mr
Yarrell, who had also been helping with it. On the proposal of
Professor Owen, it was resolved unanimously that the sincerest
thanks of the Council be returned to their President for all he
had done. Now they could only wait. Wait and see what, if anything, arrived in return.

The flow of letters from Knowsley Hall did not slow as the winter mellowed and the first blossoms graced the trees beyond the
Earl's windows. The shooting season was over and his lands, so
full of promise in their spring clothes, were quiet, once again the
preserve of the beasts, not accosted by man. Lord Derby's hours
spent at correspondence were undiminished. In addition to the
long letters exchanged with his usual correspondents – Gould
on hummingbirds, Dixon on poultry – he wrote much on the
hippopotamus. Lord Derby kept in contact with Henry Beale,
who had gone to Africa with the hounds, and with Colonel
Murray, the British Consul in Cairo, who was overseeing the
exchange of gifts. Beale had concerns about the hounds out in
Egypt, which he passed on to the Earl. The letters written by the
Secretary of the Society brought better news: the hippopotamus
was in good health. Yet Mitchell was, as ever, only cautiously

optimistic. He knew all too well, as did Lord Derby, that shipping animals across the world was no simple matter. Especially not when it was one as huge, as strange, as a hippopotamus.

In April, as reports came in from Thompson that the birds in the Aviary were beginning to nest, news reached Knowsley from much further afield that the hounds had been delivered. In letters from Murray and Beale, he learned that the Pasha was pleased, despite Beale's concerns. Then word came from Mitchell in London that preparations were under way for the sending of his gift in return. The newspapers picked up on the story of the creature's imminent dispatch from Egypt and of the preparations that were being undertaken. The Peninsular and Oriental's steam packet, the *Ripon*, was to transport it. Currently docked at Southampton, it was undergoing alterations to render it suitable for the strange cargo it was to return with: a 400-gallon iron tank was being fitted by the P. and O.'s workmen, for the animal to bathe in. It was a massive and expensive undertaking – one with no guaranteed returns. Though if they succeeded in this endeavour the rewards would be great indeed. The almost mythical creature had already captured the public's attention, and the newspapers began to publish snippets of information about 'the Nile Seahorse', dubbed an 'improbable monster'. Stories ran of the ten gallons of milk required daily by the young and docile creature, 'as tame and playful as a Newfoundland puppy'. It was beginning to cause much excitement, of course: it would be the first hippopotamus to reach Europe alive, at least since Roman times.

It reminded Lord Derby of the giraffes that had been sent over, nearly fifteen years ago now. He hoped fervently this mission would end as well as that one had. The *Ripon* left Southampton at the end of April. The President did not go to the capital for the Anniversary Meeting that took place not long afterwards. No, he would not make that trip again. He learned remotely the contents of the twenty-first Annual Report delivered to the assembled membership in London. Despite the impact of the cholera, it had been another good year overall and receipts on the gate had increased again. They had just received a gift from Her Majesty the Queen of a lioness, a leopard, two ostriches and a gazelle that had been presented to her by the Emperor of Morocco. The hippopotamus would secure what had now been in progress for nearly two years: the rebirth of the Zoological Society's Gardens as, the Council claimed, the 'finest public Vivarium in Europe'.

That was if it survived the journey. The five-hundred-pound beast had been transported from Cairo, where it had spent the hot season, to Alexandria, ready for embarkation, along with its Arab attendants and its food supply: rice, and fresh milk, in the form of a small herd of cows. The other donations destined for the Regent's Park from Abbas Pasha and Her Majesty's Consul General, including a lion and a leopard, were also ready and waiting. There were twenty-one cases of animals, birds, lizards and snakes in total. The latter came with its own 'Arab boy' to attend to them. Getting them all onboard – not least the ten-month-old hippopotamus – was no simple matter. There had already been one unfortunate mishap during the transport of this special cargo, when a young giraffe had fallen into the canal at Alexandria and died. The hippopotamus, however, was loaded onto the *Ripon* without incident.

A hundred and one first-class passengers, sixty second-class passengers and the crew under Captain Moresby also boarded. His Excellency General Prince Jung Bahadur, the Prime Minister and Commander-in-Chief of Nepal, and his train were among them, visiting Britain on a historic diplomatic mission. Eighteen bales of silk, eleven packages of elephants' tusks, ten bales of senna and ten of tobacco were loaded into the hold of the 230-foot-long vessel, alongside the crates of animals. The

Ripon sailed from Alexandria on the 9th of May. The Zoological Society and its friends had done all they could.

Lord Derby was distracted from the tension of the countdown by the usual hum of life on his Knowsley estate and keeping up with his network of correspondents. He was helping Gould with his latest undertaking, *The Birds of Asia*, and sent him a specimen of Nectariniidae. And he was distracted by more unusual events: four of his keepers were attacked by a large gang of poachers and seriously injured. Over the middle days of May, Lord Derby was kept informed of his servants' progress as well as that of the steamship that made its way across the Mediterranean, via Malta and Gibraltar, and into the Atlantic. He was most gratified to learn that its journey proved perfectly uneventful.

The *Ripon* steamed into Southampton on the 25th of May. A crowd had gathered to see the doubly unusual cargo: the first Hindoo of high caste to visit the country – his exquisite costume and jewellery were much remarked upon – and then, of course, there was the young hippopotamus and *his* suite. A cheer rose up from the onlookers as the creature was disembarked – alive! They had been the lucky ones: they had caught the first ever glimpse of such a beast in Europe. But a glimpse was all they got for it was immediately loaded onto a specially adapted train carriage and whisked away to its new home at the Regent's Park. The people who flocked to stations along the way, desperate for a passing sight of such a monster, were disappointed. They saw only the beast's Arab keeper's head occasionally emerge through the roof of the carriage for a breath of fresh air.

By the 29th of May, 1850, the hippopotamus was on display at the Gardens. He had been named 'Obaysch' after his faraway homeland, an island in the Nile. Advertisements announcing his hours of display, between one and six o'clock each day, were placed on the front pages of London newspapers. The crowds did not need much persuading: they poured in.

The President of the Zoological Society of London, who had done a great deal to make it possible, was not among them. He learned of it all from Mr Mitchell, who wrote him letters aglow with the furore the beast was creating. London had gone wild for the hippopotamus! Ten thousand people came each day to see him; hippopotamus memorabilia were sold on the streets; a polka was composed in his honour. Such a furore indeed that he was sure to return the Society to fortune, if he lived. If he lived: there was some concern over his health initially, but that seemed to be resolved fairly quickly, and by the time the Queen and her family visited him in the middle of July, he was in hearty health. He had grown a little more than half a foot in length since his arrival, under the good care of Hamet, his Arab keeper, who remained with him. The other new animals, too, had been a great success with visitors. Lord Derby read the letter reporting the Royal Visit not without emotion. It was, in a sense, an expression of the security of the Society's future. His legacy in the Regent's Park, his gift to the nation, was secured. It was a shame, he thought, that he would probably never see the beast but he contented himself with Mitchell's letters, and the comfort they brought. All of his recent concern vanished.

In early 1851, Lord Derby was corresponding with Mitchell about some mandarin ducks he wanted in time for the breeding season; with Gould about some ring-necked pheasants that he was after for a scientific study; with a dog-breeder, Brierly, about a particular specimen he had concerns about; with the Reverend Mr Fry at the Cape about a possible shipment of cattle back to Liverpool by steamer; with a local surgeon about an operation on one of his antelopes, which was suffering from cataracts. The elderly Earl was perfectly content to follow the rhythms of his studious life at home.

That was until a letter arrived from Mitchell at the beginning of February. It contained the news that the Council had made a rather exciting decision. The coming summer, the much-anticipated Great Exhibition of the 'Works of Industry of All Nations' was to take place in Hyde Park, organized by the Prince Albert. An incredible glass palace was being built to house the magnificent display. But Lord Derby knew all about that. The Society, Mitchell wrote on, had agreed to a proposition from Mr Gould that they do something rather special in their own grounds too, to mark a summer of such import and festivity in the capital. Gould had proposed, and they had agreed, that they put on an exhibition of his hummingbirds. This was news to the Earl, most interesting news. Gould always seemed to know where public tastes were going and his *Monograph of the Trochilidae* had been a huge success. Mitchell wrote of a huge display of two thousand specimens of at least three hundred species of the beautiful little birds, impossible to bring here alive but preserved and arranged by Gould. Lord Derby was sorely tempted to go and see it himself. Sorely tempted.

He thought about it over the next few days. The letter sat on his desk. This summer would mark, he realized, twenty-five years since the Society had held its first meeting. For a quarter of a century he had been part of this endeavour. Could he really forgo the opportunity to see it in all its newfound splendour? The first ever hippopotamus to have been brought into the country – a feat he had had a hand in himself – and now one of the most magnificent preserved displays of natural history there ever was? London in the year of the Great Exhibition might be worth the trip, he began to think. By the end of February, he had determined to go and see it for himself, even if it killed him.

★

How London has changed in just a few years. What a different expression the city wears now. It is almost a stranger to him. Perhaps he is to it, also. A shadow of the man who once passed through these streets and sat in its Parliament (though he has outlived the building he sat in: its magnificent, Gothic replacement is still being built). As his carriage tries to find a pathway through the chaos, Lord Derby cannot escape the feeling that the great, sprawling metropolis he finds himself in is out of control. Like a beast, unchained and angry. With its omnibuses everywhere, its train tracks crisscrossing the streets, its tunnel under the Thames, even! Its millions of people! And he knew it long before there were any of these things.

Now, too, it has this glittering temple to modernity, this Palace of Glass – 1,851 feet long, no more no less – filled with the wonders of this stinking, modern world. He thinks it a little like Burton's Palm House at Kew, only bigger. So much bigger! Taller than the trees, even. In its cavernous interior he sees the diamonds from India, the silks and porcelains of France. He sees, in the Fine Art Court, John Gould's illustrations of the Trochilidae – he is showcasing his invention, the new gold-leaf technique he has used to capture some of the magnificence of the little birds. All these things possess a beauty, a majesty that he well understands. But he sees much he cannot really comprehend: the massive tools of modern industry – steam-hammers and hydraulic presses and printing presses, adding-machines and reaping machines, human-powered two-wheeled velocipedes and steam-engines. He sees daguerreotypes, too – people, so eerily captured on paper! Frozen in time. So cold, so different from Gould's subtle, living illustrations. Tens of thousands of people flood into Hyde Park each day to see such wonders, to marvel at the grandeur and might of Britain under Queen Victoria, at the wonders of the world in 1851. He is glad he has been one of them. But it is not the only purpose of his visit to London.

On the 12th of May, the President of the Zoological Society of London arrives at the entrance to the Gardens he has watched grow in the damp north-eastern corner of the Regent's Park over a quarter of a century. He is much changed since he first stepped onto its clay soil, when it was but a dream and a few of Burton's markings on the ground. He is not much changed, though, since his last visit, despite how he may feel, despite how overwhelmed he is by all he has encountered in the capital this time. He is still an old man in a Bath chair. A little thinner, a little frailer, a little deafer, but still an old man, pushed around the elegant curves of the Gardens' walkways.

Oh, but the Gardens! The Gardens of the Zoological Society of London are changed. They are changed indeed. Mr Mitchell, the man who has overseen so much of their transformation, is once again delivering a report to the President as he is wheeled alongside him. This time it is a glittering one: income in the previous year was double what it had been in 1847, when Lord Derby had seen the establishment from the chair he sits in now, had seen it in decay, near-deserted, at its lowest ebb. Mitchell goes on: visitors last year were double what they had been the year before – 360,000, their highest ever number. But Lord Derby is not really listening. He has almost completely lost his hearing. He is also much distracted: he is marvelling at all the people, at the new buildings, at the spectacular scene laid out before him. The crane enclosure right by the entrance, complete with a Stanley crane. The Carnivora Terrace, now filled with lions, tigers, jaguars, leopards and pumas – all that it was meant to contain.

It is quite remarkable. There are animals from every single corner of the globe: they are the real, enduring wonders of the world, made of fur and feather and bone. So unlike those man-made wonders, built of iron and steam and sweat, displayed in the glass palace two miles away. There are giraffes

from the Pasha of Egypt, a tree-kangaroo from the Governor of
Singapore, ostriches from the Emperor of Morocco, an infant
elephant from India, grizzly bears from the Americas, deer from
Colombo, bison from Bombay, monkeys from Gambia, marsupials from Australia . . . There is another orang utan on the way
too, Mitchell tells him, from Borneo. If it survives the passage,
they will truly have the greatest collection of living creatures
anyone could imagine.

For once, Lord Derby is as interested in the humans he sees in
the Gardens as the animals. There are hundreds here today – it
will be well over a thousand by the time the sun is set, so Mr
Mitchell tells him. He has chosen to come on a Monday, the day
of reduced-price admission, to see the people who have rescued
the Society he presides over. They are not like him or the gentlemen of the Council or those who attend the scientific meetings.
They are clerks and servants and other workers. These are the
people who crave the carnivores, the big and ferocious beasts,
the tricks of the snake charmer. Let them! In this man-made city
of factories and railways and slums, they are here to see the wonders of the natural world. They are here, not at the taverns and
gin palaces he has seen in the stinking city to the south of him.
They are here for the love of natural history. He could not have
asked for more. He thinks of Raffles with sorrow: not even Sir
Stamford's children have lived to see this. He is glad, painfully
so, that he has seen this day.

The Hummingbird Exhibition is not yet open to the public,
but Lord Derby is wheeled into the building constructed specifically to house it, in the South Garden, behind the Carnivora
Terrace. It contains twenty-four custom-built, revolving cases.
In these are the thousands of specimens of Trochilidae, expertly
mounted by Gould on invisible wires. They seem to be alive,
hovering over the mouths of the flowers in the displays, the
lights perfectly directed to shine on, to magnify the luminosity

of their wings, like tiny gemstones. Lord Derby drinks in this Paradisiacal picture of nature, perfect in all its minutest detail, the glory of Creation so evident in this tiny, resplendent species. The people will come to see this when it is opened at the weekend; Mr Mitchell is confident of that. Yes, the President agrees, *this is all that he had hoped, all that he had expected from John Gould.*

They venture through Burton's tunnel into the North Garden. Here are the serpents and lizards in their new house, the first of its kind, erected solely for these strange, cold creatures, where Mohammed, one of the Arab boys who came on the *Ripon* with Obaysch, did his tricks with the cobras, captivating the crowds. The Reptile House shares the plot of the Museum, on the site of the old Carnivora House. The Museum is the first disappointment the President encounters on his tour of the Gardens. The single member of staff who remains here now spends most of his time with the reptiles next door. Already so much reduced, Mitchell tells him that it is only a matter of time before this branch of the establishment is eradicated altogether. The people do not care for it, not here. They still hope to present it to the nation. But the love of preserved specimens will not be lost altogether, he consoles himself: he knows the public will be enraptured by Gould's masterpiece.

Finally, the President is wheeled to see Obaysch, in his home at the far north-western corner of the Gardens, in a wing of the Giraffe House. Lord Derby's chair is pushed through the noisy crowds that surround the enclosure and pond. The President deserves a close look at his prize: the hippopotamus that he has read and written so much about from his desk at Knowsley; that he has worked so hard to bring here over these years past. Finally it is here before him. He laughs. It is like a huge prize hog! With its tiny legs and its grotesque, enormous head, rolling like a porpoise in the water! A platform is being built nearby, from which the crowds will be able to look down on the beast in its bath. For now, Lord Derby must content himself with a view through the railings, like everyone else. It is more than good enough to see Obaysch. Obaysch, grotesque and wonderful.

He laughs. He thinks, *I have seen it all, now. Truly, I have truly seen it all.*

'Death of the Earl of Derby, KG, FLS', *Sherborne Mercury*, 8th July, 1851

We regret to announce the decease of the Rt. Hon. The Venerable Earl of Derby, which took place at his seat, Knowsley Hall, Lancashire, on Monday last, in the seventy-seventh year of his age. A few weeks ago, his Lordship determined upon attending the Great Exhibition in Hyde Park, and from the fatigue of the journey he never recovered. Previously, he had been in a very infirm state, suffering from an attack of paralysis, which commenced about a dozen years ago.

Epilogue

On the 9th of July, 1851, the funeral of *the 13th Earl of Derby* took place at Knowsley Hall: he was buried in a coffin made from his favourite oak tree on the estate. The contents of the Aviary were sold at auction in October. As per the instructions of the late Earl's will, the Zoological Society of London and the Queen Victoria had each already selected a gift from it. Mr Mitchell of the Zoological Society of London chose the herd of Cape eland. In May 1852, an Act was passed to establish a new museum at Liverpool for the 13th Earl's preserved collection, to be opened to the public at least four days a week with free admission. It is still in operation today, known as the World Museum.

Prince Albert succeeded Lord Derby as the President of the Zoological Society of London. The *season of 1851* was the most successful in the history of the Gardens up until that point, with more than 650,000 people visiting that year.

In 1851, *Devereux Fuller* was working as a porter and living in Richmond Place, Marylebone, with his wife, Sophie, his eldest daughter, Eliza (soon to go into service), his eldest sons, William and James (working as errand boys), and his four little children. It is not known if he worked with animals again. He died in 1858, at the age of fifty-three.

By the end of 1851, 75,000 people had visited *John Gould*'s Hummingbird Exhibition (including the Queen Victoria and Charles Dickens), making him a profit of at least £1,500. Gould continued to produce hugely popular works of ornithology. He distanced himself from any association with Darwin's ideas when they were finally published. When he died in 1881, at the

age of seventy-six, he was a rich man. In his lifetime he had produced more than 3,000 coloured plates and identified 377 new
species of bird – a figure none of his rivals had come close to.

In 1852, *Decimus Burton*'s Waterlily House was unveiled at Kew
Gardens, where he had already designed the largest (at the time)
greenhouse in the world, the Palm House. Both survive today –
as do the Llama House and clock tower, the Giraffe House, the
Raven's Cage and the tunnel he designed for the Zoological
Society of London. He never married. He retired in 1869 and
died in 1881, at the age of eighty-one.

In 1853, *Charles Spooner* was promoted to Principal Professor
at the Veterinary College, where he had previously taken up the
post of demonstrator of anatomy in 1839. He had reached the
pinnacle of his profession. He was a fierce opponent of vivisection all his life, an early advocate for the use of chloroform in
veterinary surgery and a council member of the Society for the
Prevention of Cruelty to Animals. He lived in the college with
his wife, Marianne, with whom he had eight children, until his
death in 1871 at the age of sixty-five.

In 1854, *Edward Cross* died at the age of eighty. Two years
later, the Surrey Zoological Gardens were closed, and a music
hall opened on the site. The only remaining Zoological Gardens
in the capital were those at the Regent's Park. Visitor numbers
there remained high over the 1850s, an average of 350,000 a year.

In 1854, a female hippopotamus was brought to London as a
mate for *Obaysch*. The first baby hippo was born in 1871, but did
not survive. Two more were born the following year, one of
which, Guy Fawkes (subsequently discovered to be a female),
was the first captive-bred hippo to be reared by its mother; she
lived for thirty-six years.

In 1855, *the Museum of the Zoological Society of London* was closed,
its collection transferred to the British Museum where, the following year, Professor Richard Owen was appointed to look

after the Natural History Department. In 1881, a dedicated Museum of Natural History was opened in South Kensington. It is not clear if Tommy, Jenny or John Gould's giraffe made the move with the collection. The Natural History Museum is now visited by more than five million people each year.

Lady Raffles was the last surviving member of her family. She had lost her daughter Ella in 1840, when she succumbed to tuberculosis shortly before she was due to be married at the age of nineteen. Lady Raffles lived on alone at Highwood (which she had been unable to sell after her husband's death, and she kept as a shrine to him) until her death in 1858, aged seventy-two.

In 1859, *Charles Darwin* published *On the Origin of Species*. Its critical reception was initially hostile, but it received a great deal of popular attention. Essentially, it legitimized the concept of evolution, though it was not until 1871 when he published *The Descent of Man* that Darwin dared to discuss human evolution. In that book he referred to many of the observations he had made of Jenny. Darwin died at Down House in 1882 at the age of seventy-three, by which time the theory of evolution was already known as Darwinism. He was buried in Westminster Abbey, taking his place alongside that other great scientific pioneer Isaac Newton (and not far from a bust of Sir Stamford Raffles, which Lady Raffles had commissioned).

By the 1870s, *the Gardens of the Zoological Society of London* had become one of the most popular attractions in the capital (after 1864 visitor numbers did not drop below half a million for the rest of the nineteenth century). The Zoological Gardens began to be known simply as 'the Zoo' after a popular music-hall song, 'Walking in the Zoo', used the word for the first time.

Though its popularity continued to wax and wane in the twentieth century, *London Zoo*, the first 'zoo' in history, now attracts well over a million visitors a year – still located on its original site in Regent's Park.

Select Bibliography

The following sources were referred to throughout the book:

From the archives of the Zoological Society of London

Annual Reports, April 1829 onwards
Correspondence of John Gould
Daily Occurrences, February 1828 onwards (1832 is missing)
Early prospectuses and press clippings, 1820s
Inventory of Fixtures, Furniture &c. belonging to the Zoological
    Society of London at 33 Bruton Street, December 1834
Minutes of the Committee of Science and Correspondence, July 1830
    onwards
Minutes of the Council, May 1826 onwards
Minutes of the Garden Discipline Committee, 1838
Minutes of the Museum Committee, 1836–7
Museum Report, 1833
Proceedings of the Committee of Science and Correspondence of the
    Zoological Society of London, July 1830 onwards
Staff records, various, 1830s
Surgeon's Journals, 1829–31 and 1833–4

Newspapers

Bell's Weekly Messenger
Brighton Gazette
Chester, Cheshire and North Wales Advertiser
Evening Mail

Examiner
Hull Packet
Literary Gazette
Mirror of Literature, Amusement, and Instruction
Morning Advertiser
Morning Post
New Monthly Magazine
Public Ledger and Daily Advertiser
Saunders's Newsletter and Daily Advertiser
Sherbourne Mercury
Southern Reporter and Cork Commercial Courier
Standard
The Times
Waterford Mail
Western Flying Post
Yeovil Times

Published works

Akerberg, Sofia, *Knowledge and Pleasure at Regent's Park: The Gardens of the Zoological Society of London during the Nineteenth Century* (Department of Historical Studies, Umea University, 2001)

Baratay, Eric, and Elisabeth Hardouin-Fugier, *Zoo: A History of Zoological Gardens in the West* (Reaktion Books, 2002)

Barber, Lynn, *The Heyday of Natural History* (Jonathan Cape, 1980)

Barrington-Johnson, J., *The Zoo: The Story of London Zoo* (Robert Hale, 2005)

Blunt, Wilfrid, *The Ark in the Park: The Zoo in the Nineteenth Century* (Hamish Hamilton, 1976)

Chalmers Mitchell, P., *Centenary History of the Zoological Society of London* (Zoological Society of London, 1929)

Cowie, Helen, *Exhibiting Animals in Nineteenth-Century Britain: Empathy, Education, Entertainment* (Palgrave Macmillan, 2014)

Donald, Diana, *Picturing Animals in Britain: 1750–1850* (Yale University Press, 2007)

Holloway, Sally, *The London Zoo* (Michael Joseph, 1976)

Inglis, Lucy, *Georgian London: Into the Streets* (Penguin, 2014)

Ito, Takashi, *London Zoo and the Victorians, 1828–1859* (Royal Historical Society, 2014)

Porter, Roy, *London: A Social History* (Penguin, 2000)

Ritvo, Harriet, *The Animal Estate: The English and other Creatures in the Victorian Age* (Penguin, 1987)

Scherren, Henry, *The Zoological Society of London: a sketch of its foundation and development, and the story of its farm, museum, gardens, menagerie and library* (Cassell, 1905)

Summerson, John, *Georgian London* (Yale University Press, 2003)

Thornbury, Walter, *Old and New London, Volume 4* (Cassell, Petter & Galpin, 1878)

White, Jerry, *London in the Nineteenth Century* (Vintage, 2008)

Zuckermann, Solly, 'The Zoological Society of London, 1826–1976 and Beyond', *Symposia of the Zoological Society of London*, No. 40 (1976)

1. The Ark in London

Bastin, John, *Lady Raffles: By Effort and Virtue* (National Museum, Singapore, 1994)

Bastin, John, 'The first prospectus of the Zoological Society of London; new light on the Society's origins', in *Journal of the Society for the Bibliography of Natural History* (5), October 1970, pp. 369–88

Bondeson, Jan, *The Feejee Mermaid and Other Essays in Natural and Unnatural History* (Cornell University Press, 1999)

Cross, Edward, Proprietor, *Companion to the Royal Menagerie, Exeter 'Change, containing concise descriptions, scientific and interesting of the curious foreign animals now in that eminent collection* (Tyler & Honeyman, 1820)

Desmond, Adrian, 'The Making of Institutional Zoology in London, 1822–1836, Part 1', *History of Science*, xxiii (1985), pp. 153–85

Elmes, James, *Metropolitan Improvements, or London in the Nineteenth Century* (Jones and Co., 1827)

Fosbroke, Reverend T. D., *A picturesque and topographical account of Cheltenham, and its vicinity, etc.* (Cheltenham, 1826)

Glendinning, Victoria, *Raffles and the Golden Opportunity* (Profile, 2013)

London Scenes: A Visit to Uncle William in Town, containing a description of the most remarkable buildings and curiosities in the British metropolis (John Harris, 1824)

Noltie, H. J., *Raffles' Ark Redrawn: Natural History Drawings from the Collection of Sir Thomas Stamford Raffles* (British Library and the Royal Botanic Garden Edinburgh, 2009)

Papers of the Royal College of Surgeons Archives, including letters between Sir Stamford Raffles and Sir Everard Home

Raffles Collection, British Library

Raffles, Lady Sophia, *Memoir of the Life and Public Services of Sir Thomas Stamford Raffles* (with an introduction by John Bastin), (Oxford University Press, 1991)

Rush, Richard, *Memoranda of a residence at the Court of London, comprising incidents official and personal from 1819 to 1825* (Philadelphia, 1845)

Statement of the Services of Sir Stamford Raffles (with an introduction by John Bastin), (Oxford University Press, 1978)

Wurtzburg, C. E., *Raffles of the Eastern Isles* (Hodder & Stoughton, 1954)

2. The Gardens Grow

Arnold, Dana, *Rural Urbanism: London Landscapes in the Early Nineteenth Century* (Manchester University Press, 2005)

Arnold, Dana, *Re-presenting the Metropolis* (Routledge, 2000)

Burton, D., *Design for the Garden in the Regent's Park, belonging to the Zoological Society* (Zoological Society of London, 1827)

Burton Papers, Hastings Museum

Colvin, Howard, *A Biographical Dictionary of British Architects, 1600–1840*, 4th edn (Yale University Press, 1995)

Davis, Terence, *The Architecture of John Nash* (Studio Books, 1960)

Graves, Algernon, FSA, *The Royal Academy of Arts: Complete Dictionary of Contributors and their Work, from its Foundation in 1769 to 1904* (reprinted ed. 1970)

Guide to the Gardens of the Zoological Society, March 1829 (Richard Taylor, 1829)

Hobhouse, Hermione, *Regent Street: A Mile of Style* (Phillimore, 2008)

Miller, Philip, *Decimus Burton 1800-1881: A Guide to the Exhibition of his Work* (Building Centre Trust, 1981)

Papers relating to the refurbishment of the Geological Society's rooms in Somerset House (GSL PLAM/1/1, SGM/2/2, Council Minutes and Correspondence), Archives of the Royal Geological Society

A Picturesque Guide to the Regent's Park (London, 1829)

Smith, H. Clifford, *Buckingham Palace: Its Furniture, Its Decoration & Treasures* (Country Life Limited, 1931)

Summerson, John, *The Life and Work of John Nash, Architect* (George Allen & Unwin, 1980)

Whitbourn, Philip, *Decimus Burton Esquire: Architect and Gentleman (1800–1881)*, (Royal Tunbridge Wells Civic Society, 2003)

Williams, Guy, *Augustus Pugin versus Decimus Burton: A Victorian Architectural Duel* (Cassell, 1990)

3. The Solitary Surgeon

Collier, George Frederick, *A translation of the New Pharmacopœia of the Royal College of Physicians* (Highley, 1837)

Cotchin, Ernest, *The Royal Veterinary College London: A Bicentenary History* (Barracuda Books, 1990)

Desmond, Adrian, *The Politics of Evolution: Morphology, Medicine and Reform in Radical London* (University of Chicago Press, 1992)

List of the Animals in the Gardens of the Zoological Society, with Notices respecting them and a plan of the Gardens, June, 1833 (Zoological Society of London, 1833)

Owen, Richard, *The Life of Richard Owen* (John Murray, 1894)

Papers of the Royal College of Surgeons Archives, including Richard Owen's notes on dissections performed at the ZSL

Papers of the Royal Veterinary College Archives, including library catalogues, 1793 and 1893; monthly abstracts of the proceedings of the Veterinary Medical Society; papers discussed at the Veterinary Medical Society; notes on veterinary lectures delivered by Professor Coleman in 1829 by R. Pritchard

Pattison, Iain, *The British Veterinary Profession 1791–1948* (Hyperion Books, 1983)

The Picturesque Companion to the Regent's Park, Zoological Gardens, Colosseum and Diorama (Kidd, 1832)

Pugh, L. P., *From Farriery to Veterinary Medicine* (W. Heffer, 1962)

Robinson, Phillip T., *Life at the Zoo: Behind the Scenes with the Animal Doctors* (Columbia University Press, 2004)

Rupke, Nicolaas A., *Richard Owen: Biology without Darwin* (University of Chicago Press, 2009)

Smith, Major-General Sir Frederick, *The Early History of Veterinary Literature and its British Development* (J. A. Allen, 1976)

Surgeon's Journals, 1829–31 and 1833–4

The Tower Menagerie, Comprising the Natural History of the Animals Contained in that Establishment, with anecdotes of their characters and history (Robert Jennings, 1829)

The Veterinarian, A Monthly Journal of Veterinary Science (London), various editions, 1829–33

White, James, *A Compendious Dictionary of the Veterinary Art* (Longman, Rees, Orme Brown and Green, 1830)

Wilkinson, Lise, *Animals and Disease: An Introduction to the History of Comparative Medicine* (Cambridge University Press, 1992)

Woods, A., and S. Matthews, ' "Little, if at all, removed from the illiterate farrier or cow-leech" ': the English veterinary surgeon, c.1860–1885, and the campaign for veterinary reform' in *Medical History* 54, 1, pp. 29–54

4. *The Business of Bird Skins*

Barber, Lynn, *The Heyday of Natural History* (Jonathan Cape, 1980)

Catalogue of the Animals Preserved in the Museum of the Zoological Society of London, April 1829 (London, 1829)

Gould, John, ALS, *A Century of Birds from the Himalaya Mountains* (London, 1832)

Grant, Robert E., MD, *Outline of a Course of Lectures, on the Structure and Classification of Animals, to be Delivered to the Members of the Zoological Society of London, in their Museum, to Commence on Tuesday the 15th of January 1833 and to Continue on the Succeeding Tuesdays and Thursdays, at Half Past Seven o'Clock p.m.* (London, 1833)

Jackson, C. E., *Bird Illustrators: Some Artists in Early Lithography* (Witherby, 1975)

McAllan, I. A. W., and M. D. Bruce, 'Systematic Notes on Asian Birds. 27: On the dates of publication of John Gould's "A Century of Birds from the Himalaya Mountains" ' (http://repository.naturalis.nl/document/46275)

Morris, Patrick A., *A History of Taxidermy: Art, Science and Bad Taste* (MPM Publishing, 2010)

Noakes, Vivien, *Edward Lear: The Life of a Wanderer* (William Collins, 1968)

Obituary of John Gould, in *Proceedings of the Royal Society of London*, 33 (1881)

Ornithological Correspondence of John Gould (correspondents include Charles Darwin, Lord Derby and Professor Owen), in the archives of the Natural History Museum

Papers in the Linnean Society Archives, including certificates of John Gould's membership

Papers of the Royal College of Surgeons Archives, including letters and papers relating to museum business

Sauer, Gordon C., *John Gould: The Bird Man, a Chronology and Bibliography* (Henry Sotheran, 1982)

Swainson, W., *Taxidermy with the Biography of Zoologists* (Longman, 1840)

Tree, Isabella, *The Bird Man: The Extraordinary Story of John Gould* (Ebury Press, 2004)

5. Gifts from Afar

'Account of the Habits and Illness of the Late Chimpanzee by W. Youatt Esq.', in *Lancet*, vol. 2, 1835–6

Bartlett, A. D., *Wild Animals in Captivity: Being an Account of the Habits, Food, Management and Treatment of the Beasts and Birds at the Zoo* (Chapman and Hall, 1898)

Bennett, Edward Turner, *The Gardens and Menagerie of the Zoological Society Delineated* (Zoological Society of London, 1835)

Bostock, Frank C., *The Training of Wild Animals* (Century, 1903)

Broderip, W. J., 'Observations on the Habits &c. of a Male Chimpanzee, Troglodytes niger, now living in the Menagerie of the Zoological Society of London', in the Proceedings of the Zoological Society of London, 27 October 1835

Broderip, W. J., *List of the Animals in the Gardens of the Zoological Society, with Notices respecting them and a plan of the Gardens* (Zoological Society of London, 1836)

Collection of programmes, plates, cuttings from newspapers and magazines, pamphlets, etc., relating to the Surrey Zoological Gardens, 1831–61, in the British Library

Gerhold, Dorian, *Bristol's Stage Coaches* (Hobnob Press, 2012)

'A Letter from the Chimpanzee', *New Monthly Magazine*, vol. 46 (1836)

Lynn, Martin, 'British Business and the African Trade: Richard and William King Ltd. of Bristol and West Africa, 1822–1918', *Business History*, vol. 34, October 1992, no. 4

Owen, Richard, *The Life of Richard Owen* (John Murray, 1894)

Scott, Matthew, *Autobiography of Matthew Scott, Jumbo's keeper* (Bridge-port, 1885)

The Tower Menagerie, Comprising the Natural History of the Animals Contained in that Establishment, with anecdotes of their characters and history (London, 1829)

Warwick, J. E., *Description and history, with anecdotes, of the giraffes (Camelopardis giraffa, Gmel.) now exhibiting at the Surrey Zoological Gardens, with an account of their capture and voyage* (J. King, 1836)

Wise, Dorothy (ed.), *Diary of William Tayler, Footman* (Westminster City Archives, 1998)

6. From Mockingbirds to Man

Barrett, Paul H. (ed.), et al, *Charles Darwin's Notebooks, 1836–1844: Geology, Transmutation of Species, Metaphysical Enquiries* (Cambridge University Press, 1987)

Bennett, Edward Turner, *The Gardens and Menagerie of the Zoological Society Delineated* (London, 1835)

Broderip, W. J., *List of the Animals in the Gardens of the Zoological Society, with Notices respecting them and a Plan of the Garden* (Zoological Society of London, 1836)

A Calendar of the Correspondence of Charles Darwin, 1821–1882 (Darwin Correspondence Project, 1985)

Chaplin, Simon David John, 'John Hunter and the "museum oeconomy", 1750–1800', Department of History, King's College London. Thesis submitted for the degree of Doctor of Philosophy of the University of London (May 2009)

Darwin Correspondence Project, https://www.darwinproject.ac.uk/

Desmond, Adrian, and James Moore, *Darwin* (Penguin, 1992)

Desmond, Adrian, *The Politics of Evolution: Morphology, Medicine and Reform in Radical London* (University of Chicago Press, 1992)

Sulloway, Frank J., 'Darwin's conversion: the *Beagle* voyage and its aftermath', *Journal of the History of Biology*, vol. 15, issue 3 (1982)

Sulloway, Frank J., 'The Legend of Darwin's Finches', *Nature* (June 1983) (http://www.nature.com/nature/journal/v303/n5916/abs/303372a0.html)

Tree, Isabella, *The Bird Man: The Extraordinary Story of John Gould* (Ebury Press, 2004)

Ward, Humphry, *History of the Athenaeum, 1824–1925* (William Clowes, 1926)

Waterhouse, G. R., his papers in the archives of the Natural History Museum, including: Manuscript Reports of the Curator of the Society's Museum 1836, and Waterhouse, G. R., Notes and Memorabilia relating to his employment at the Zoological Society of London

Wyhe, John van (ed.), *The Complete Work of Charles Darwin Online* (http://darwin-online.org.uk)

Wyhe, John van, and Peter C. Kjærgaard, 'Going the whole orang: Darwin, Wallace and the natural history of orangutans', *Studies in History and Philosophy of Science Part C: Studies in History and Philosophy of Biological and Biomedical Sciences* (June 2015)

7. The Earl and the Hippopotamus

Archival material at the World Museum, Liverpool (National Museums and Galleries on Merseyside), including Museum Reports from Knowsley in 1849 and 1851, and the journal of Thomas Moore

A Catalogue of the Menagerie and Aviary at Knowsley, formed by the late Earl of Derby, K. G., President of the Zoological Society, which will be sold at auction by Mr J. C. Stevens, on the premises, Knowsley Hall, near Liverpool, on Monday, 6th October 1851

A Catalogue of most of the Pictures in the principal rooms at Knowsley Hall; the Seat of the Right Honourable Edward Smith Stanley, XIIIth. Earl of Derby; K. G. taken in September MDCCCXLVI (1846)

Correspondence of John Gould regarding the hummingbird exhibition in the archives of the Zoological Society of London

The Derby Correspondence in Liverpool Record Office, including letters to and from the following correspondents: D. W. Mitchell, D. Fuller, Rev. E. S. Dixon, Rev. John Fry, Henry Beale, John Gould, J. E. Gray, Edward Lear, Louis Fraser, James Brearly, William Broderip, Colonel Murray, Hugh Neill

Fisher, Clemency (ed.), *A Passion for Natural History: The Life and Legacy of the 13th Earl of Derby* (National Museums of Merseyside, 2002)

Lloyd, Stephen (ed.), *Art, Animals and Politics: Knowsley and the Earls of Derby* (Unicorn Press, 2015)

Noakes, Vivien, *Edward Lear: The Life of a Wanderer* (William Collins, 1968)

Noakes, Vivien (ed.), *Edward Lear: Selected Letters* (Clarendon Press, 1988)

Ornithological Correspondence of John Gould (correspondents include Charles Darwin, Lord Derby and Professor Owen), in the archives of the Natural History Museum

Papers held in the archives at Knowsley Hall, including papers connected with the establishment of the Derby Museum, personal correspondence of the 13th Earl of Derby (correspondents include Edward Bennett, John Warwick, Richard Yarnell, Edward Wilson, Rajah Rajendra Mullick and Edward Blythe); notebooks on the menagerie, April and May 1839

Plan of the Gardens of the Zoological Society in the Regent's Park (1851)

Sauer, Gordon C., *John Gould: The Bird Man, a Chronology and Bibliography* (Henry Sotheran, 1982)

Tree, Isabella, *The Bird Man: The Extraordinary Story of John Gould* (Ebury Press, 2004)

Woolfall, S. J., 'History of the 13th Earl of Derby's menagerie and aviary at Knowsley Hall, Liverpool (1806–1851)', *Archives of Natural History* (1990), 17 (1), pp. 1–47

Notes on the Use of Sources

1. The Ark in London

Details of the establishment of the Society were taken from the prospectuses and early correspondence in the archives of the Zoological Society of London (ZSL) – and the excellent investigative work done by John Bastin organizes them into what I have taken to be the correct chronology. There were a few minor details that I couldn't pin down – for example, where the first ever meeting was held: I assumed the Horticultural Society's rooms, where later meetings took place (Joseph Sabine, the HS's secretary was already a subscriber to the ZSL). More significantly, there has been some debate over the extent to which Sir Stamford Raffles led events, rather than Sir Humphry Davy, but I have been guided by Bastin's analysis, which identifies Raffles as the driving force behind it, because it seems accurate. It certainly fits with my own understanding of Sir Stamford's character, which I have derived largely from his and Sophia's personal correspondence and her loving biography of him: it gives great insight into their thoughts and private world in this period but also into their pasts, which loom so large in this chapter. These sources provided me with the detail of their lives at this time, from their search for a new life for their family to his dispute with the East India Company. (John Bastin's interpretation of Raffles's 'statement' was very useful here too.)

I have pieced together the details of the young Society's development and the reaction to it from the Minutes of the Council of the ZSL (though these only began in May 1826) and from newspaper articles. The latter also provided much of the context and background colour to the period: the banking crisis, Chuny, the weather, the various schemes and businesses that were being developed and funded (including Sir Stamford's involvement with some of them). I have tried to be as accurate as possible in descriptions of London and Cheltenham at the time, and of the Jardin des Plantes, the Exeter 'Change, Highwood House, etc., which were informed by details from maps, guidebooks, newspaper articles and various other contemporaneous accounts. The same is true of descriptions of locations in later chapters; they have all been based on available records.

2. The Gardens Grow

Very little evidence survives of what Decimus Burton was actually like. I haven't found much, if anything, written by him, other than formal letters on business matters (though that perhaps says something in itself). I have based the personality I have drawn for him on accounts of his unfaltering professionalism (his obituary referred to his 'sound practical sense and good taste' as well as his 'self-negation'), the perfectionism of his intelligent designs, his love of Greco-Roman art and, above all, the fact that his clients were always satisfied. He was reliable and highly esteemed, if not adored. His rivalry with John Nash *is* exaggerated, but it is based on facts: Nash had not defended the young Burton's work on The Holme when it came in for criticism, and he did try to oppose his works at Regent's Park (the latter was uncovered by Takashi Ito in his marvellously detailed work on the history of the zoo at this period). Nash and Burton were also very different men – architecturally, and in terms of their personalities: Nash was far more frivolous. Burton's 'opinions' of Nash and his creations are drawn from others generally voiced at the time.

Unfortunately, Burton's various designs for the grounds and buildings of the ZSL in these years do not survive, as far as I know – aside from the one he drew up before any building commenced, in early 1827 (I uncovered it in the Maps Department of the British Library, rather to my surprise). From this it is possible to see his original vision for the site. Subsequent plans of the Gardens show what was *actually* built, a picture added to by records relating to building work in the Minutes of the Council and the Daily Occurrences. I have imagined and possibly exaggerated the 'thinking' behind Burton's designs for the zoo's structures but I have based it on the orders I know he was given, the differences between his original design and the realized buildings, and architectural ideas and mores of the time (gleaned from the work of architectural historians such as Dana Arnold). Conversations with working architects helped me to try to think like one. I also looked at other examples of Burton's work (designs and correspondence) held in the Hastings Museum and the Geological Society Museum.

The details of the layout and inhabitants of the Gardens at this time of their early development are drawn as accurately as possible from the plans, guides to the gardens, the Minutes of the Council and the Daily Occurrences. Nevertheless it was not always possible to work out exactly what was happening where, as animals and cages were very frequently moved around, but I have made guesses based on the available evidence (this is true for the other chapters too). The records in the Daily Occurrences at the menagerie, which commenced in February 1828 and detail the goings-on in regard to important visitors (including Mr Burton), building works and the animals, helped in this immensely.

The layout of 33 Bruton Street is based on an inventory of the building in 1834 (and there was indeed a mischievous infant wanderoo monkey in the ZSL offices in 1827, which liked to knock off visitors' hats, though I cannot confirm whether or not Burton was one of its victims).

The descriptions of Regent Street are based on records of the shops that were housed along it, and those of Burton's house are based on drawings of it, though I also used the Soane Museum for inspiration.

Finally it should perhaps be said that there remains some debate and confusion over the exact details of the gradual opening of the Gardens to the public: the Council seemed to change its mind quite frequently and it is hard to tell what regulations were put into place. I worked it out as best as I could from the Minutes of the Council (and the analyses of those who have attempted to do the same before me).

3. The Solitary Surgeon

I have based Charles Spooner's personality on various accounts of him, in which his quick temper, compassion for animals and surgical skill generally feature in equal measure. (A story I particularly liked was that he refused to get into a cab pulled by a lame horse, and was taken to court by its owner because Spooner would not pay him.) His correspondence with the Council is also revealing: he was clearly angry that he had been dismissed without warning. Some details of Spooner's life story seem a little confused in various other accounts of him (dates of his employment, his school of anatomy, details of his birth, etc.) but I hope, by going back to census records, details of his employment by the ZSL and snippets from contemporaneous veterinary journals, that I have clarified some, or at least made sensible guesses. The details of Spooner's relationship with Youatt remain a little hazy. I do know that Spooner helped in his school, that the men met regularly as part of the broader veterinary community, and that Youatt occasionally wrote about him in his journal.

The idea of his being a rival to Devereux Fuller is probably a little exaggerated, but it was based on the regulations that were laid out, after his dismissal, about the importance of a good working relationship between the head keeper and the new medical superintendent, which made me believe there had not been a good one previously. Conversations with vets about the differing interests of zoo veterinarians and keepers confirmed the plausibility of this. The personality of Mr Miller is based on his service history with the 3rd Foot Guards and accounts of his difficulties with the staff of the Gardens in the ZSL records. In terms of how the keepers handled the animals, I have based my descriptions primarily on those in Youatt's journals, which are much more descriptive than those of Spooner, and what I know of usual practice for animal handling at this time (see also '5. Gifts from Afar', page 173).

The illnesses of the animals, their treatment by Spooner and his feeding experiments were based on the records in the Daily Occurrences, the more detailed notes in the surgeon's journal (though there are chronological gaps in this) and the records of his experiments in the Proceedings of the Committee of Science and Correspondence. The details of where and how animals were cut up when his treatments failed were not always clear, other than in the case of the high-profile dissections reported in the newspapers or Proceedings of the Committee of Science and Correspondence. I have guessed that some of Spooner's dissections took place at the stables on Park Street at this time, as I know from Museum records that animals were macerated there so it seems logical that this might have happened, when a post-mortem was not a public display. I also used Richard Owen's dissection notes, in the Royal College of Surgeons' archives, to inform this.

Explanations of treatments and the understanding of veterinary science at this time were taken from a contemporaneous veterinary dictionary and Youatt's journal, the *Veterinarian*. I also consulted archival material in the Royal Veterinary College's library, which included notes made by a student from the course that Spooner had also taken. Bruce Vivash Jones helped me with the details of period veterinary equipment and practice. Adrian Desmond's book, *The Politics of Evolution*, provided much of the context of Spooner's work, as part of broader reform in the medical profession, and I have used Spooner as a conduit through which to bring some of these ideas to light. It is hard to say how much of a 'reformist' he was himself, though it seems he supported calls for reform in the college, for example, in the early 1830s, and was, to some degree, part of Youatt's set.

In terms of what was going on at the zoo at this time, I have pieced everything together as best I can from the ZSL archival records, as in the previous chapter. I have also drawn on Takashi Ito's research into access to the Gardens in the early 1830s, which reveals that the clientele were not always as genteel as the Council intended, and the debates that surrounded admissions policy. I have also used Spooner as a means to raise issues and concerns that were being articulated by Fellows such as Mr J. C. Cox (an ally of the radical Dr Grant) regarding heating and ventilation, in the broader context of animal health (which might well have been triggered by the leopard's death mentioned on page 125).

4. The Business of Bird Skins

Isabella Tree's lovely biography of John Gould was very helpful in getting a sense of his character and background. She, David Lowther and Clemency Fisher discussed (or, even, dissected) his personality with me, which helped me get to know him even better. I hope that the portrait I paint of him as an ambitious, clever man is an accurate one. His own letters, often written by his secretary, and with quite different tones depending on the recipient, seem to bear out that assessment. The letters have been painstakingly catalogued by Gordon C. Sauer, and I have read many of those that are held in the Natural History Museum and the ZSL archives.

Sauer's chronology of Gould's correspondence and publications has been incredibly useful in helping me to work out exactly what he was doing when, certainly with regard to his work outside the ZSL Preserving Department. In terms of what he was doing within 33 Bruton

Street, a very detailed, daily account of events in the museum is extant in the ZSL archives for 1833 (and there is also a later one, in London's Natural History Museum archives) from which I have also guessed at what happened in the years previously, combined with mentions in the Minutes of the Council, and the Proceedings of the Committee of Science and Correspondence. I do not know that Gould met Darwin before his trip but I do know that Darwin visited the Museum and consulted its experts; knowing what I do of Gould, I presumed he would have made himself known to him. It was also hard to pin down Gould's travels – Vivien Noakes and others have pointed out some dispute about dates of travels undertaken with Lear – but I have relied on his requests for leave from the ZSL, reported in the Minutes of the Council. These also document his promotion, the details of the staff working with him and so on.

The layout of Bruton Street and its contents were established quite accurately, I hope, from an inventory and ZSL Museum catalogues viewed alongside each other. I also used the Grant Museum as inspiration. I have taken the procedures, etc., detailed in the Museum reports as standard: the process of taxidermy, sending skins to tanners and skeletons to macerators. Patrick Morris and Clemency Fisher helped me with historical processes used in the preservation and setting up of specimens. The names and terms used at the time I have taken from the Proceedings of the Committee of Science and Correspondence, and the Museum catalogue. Many of these are out of date (for example, *Sarcoramphus californianus* and *Sarcoramphus papa*) but I wanted to reflect the state of knowledge in Gould's day rather than our own.

5. *Gifts from Afar*

There was very little evidence about Devereux Fuller to help me with this chapter – not even a single portrait of him that I could gaze upon for inspiration. I could find out very little about his past, or his employment previous to the ZSL; only the census records and minimal staff records give any information. The character and opinions I have drawn for him are inspired by memoirs of other animal keepers from this time, and from mentions of him in the Minutes of the Council. He did get into trouble for intoxication on the Windsor trip; it was a common problem among the keepers (as was running beer shops from their homes). The only evidence I have of anything written by Fuller are a few simple letters among the Derby papers, which do not throw much light on his personality but do perhaps indicate that he was not a particularly learned or expressive man. He was, however, a dedicated keeper – that much is clear from Youatt's accounts of him in his journal.

I have no evidence of Fuller's opinions on Edward Cross. His rivalry with Cross is a construct, but I based it on the genuine institutional rivalry that existed. The details of what was happening at the Surrey Zoological Gardens are drawn from a wonderful scrapbook of newspaper clippings, posters and advertisements in the British Library. Helen Cowie's book was very useful in providing the background to the menageries and animal shows that were commonplace in Britain at this time.

The details described of the capture, transport and sales of the rhino, Tommy and the giraffes are all based on accounts in newspapers (including shipping records) and in the Proceedings of the Committee of Science and Correspondence. Perhaps the most improbable of them – Tommy's story – is, I hope, pretty accurately told here, based on records in the ZSL archives of who sold him, where, for how much, his behaviour on board ship, research into the company Captain Wood worked for and where their warehouses were located, Bristol to London coaches and so on. There are a few references to Tommy being brought back on a night coach, sitting inside – for example, I found a mention of it in the *New Monthly Magazine* of 1836, and it is repeated in later accounts, such as Scherren's centenary history of the ZSL. Though the article of 1836 is not entirely serious, it does not seem improbable, given how tame Tommy was, and other accounts of the transport of apes. I've found no evidence that contradicts it, so I've

gone with this version of events. I have, of course, imagined some of
the other details of their trip (that Fuller brought a helper with him,
stayed in a certain inn and took a certain coach) but they are entirely
possible and based on what was available at the time.

Evidence of the practices and daily routine in the Gardens is taken
from the Minutes of the Council, Daily Occurrences, Spooner and
Youatt's journals, and from the Minutes of the Gardens Discipline
Committee (which, though later than these years, were very helpful in
terms of daily routine and management). Names of staff are accurate,
based on the Minutes of the Council and staff records, though sometimes it was hard to tell exactly who was involved in what – I have
made informed guesses where need be. Details of the rhino's and Jack's
behaviour are drawn from incidents noted in the Minutes of the Council and the Council's subsequent discussion of them, and the illnesses
and treatments noted in detail in Youatt's journal. The two beasts were
obviously a source of great concern to the keepers and the Society.
Drunkenness didn't help – Hacker really did allow the rhino to escape.

Details of Tommy's behaviour and personality, his illness and
death are based entirely on the very moving accounts written at the
time. Most mention his extremely close bond with his keepers, one
more so than the others, as well as the cook in the keepers' apartments. Mrs Williams was employed to work there at this time. I do
not know that John Foot was the keeper with whom he had a particular bond, but Foot was given a gratuity by the Council for his
'successful care' of the chimpanzee so I assume it was him (though he
gave notice to the Society a few months before Tommy's death, which
I can't help but think might have been a factor in Tommy's demise).

6. From Mockingbirds to Man

There has been almost too much written about Darwin. It is tough to
pick a line through it all, given differing opinions and theories drawn

from each and every bit of evidence that he left behind him. I have been guided largely by the work of Adrian Desmond as to his personality, motivations and the context of the wider scientific community in these years. (There are contrasting opinions about Darwin's anxieties over his work and the degree of hostility to his ideas from the wider scientific community.) I have also, of course, used Darwin's numerous and detailed personal papers – his notebooks and correspondence, primarily – to ascertain where he was, what he was doing, what he was reading and writing, what he was thinking, and I have used or paraphrased his own words where I could. I hope I have achieved a good degree of accuracy as there is plenty of material, all fantastically organized and available online at Darwin Online and the Darwin Correspondence Project.)

I have pieced together the layout of the second building to house the ZSL museum from plans of John Hunter's museum (featured in Simon Chaplin's thesis), combined with detailed descriptions of the building and its renovation/fitting out in the report of the Museum Committee of 1836. The Museum catalogue shows what was on display, and Waterhouse's report for 1836 (in the Natural History Museum archives) details what happened that year. Tommy's skeleton *was* being set up on the day that Darwin visited – though I can't vouch that he saw it. I like to think he did. I also refer back to the Bruton Street inventory of 1834, presuming, for example, that the books noted as being in the Library then would have been moved to the new premises.

The Proceedings of the Committee of Science and Correspondence were a very useful source for this chapter – Gould reported his findings to them, as did Darwin on occasion. The note I describe made by Darwin at his meeting with Gould is a wonderful artefact – it really does seem that this was the eureka moment. Isabella Tree's analysis of this was very helpful. The trappings of the meeting are imagined but, again, based on what I know of both men, the building and so on. Darwin's meetings and conversations with other experts of the ZSL are documented in his notes and correspondence.

The goings-on in the Gardens with Jenny were drawn from Darwin's own accounts. Particularly useful was a separate document he wrote in September 1838 about his visits to Jenny, but I have also trawled through all his relevant notebooks for comments on conversations and observations at the Gardens. These I viewed alongside the ZSL's Daily Occurrences, and guides and maps to the gardens. I have tried hard to paint an accurate picture of how it was at the precise period he was visiting. Darwin's involvement with the Society – his Fellowship and his time as a member of the Council – are recorded in the Fellowship lists and Minutes of the Council.

7. *The Earl and the Hippopotamus*

Dr Clemency Fisher's work on the 13th Earl of Derby has been extremely helpful in understanding and reimagining his living and preserved collections, his means of acquiring them from myriad different places and sources, his mode of keeping them at Knowsley Hall, and his ambitions for their care and breeding. The details and number of the animal inhabitants are drawn from the sales catalogue for the 1851 auction, and from various plans and accounts of the menagerie and Aviary in the Knowsley Hall archives, which Dr Stephen Lloyd furnished me with and Clemency Fisher's work explains. The journal of Thomas Moore, one of Lord Derby's keepers (which she kindly shared with me), was also very helpful in giving a picture of the daily running of the menagerie and Aviary.

The 13th Earl's voluminous collection of personal correspondence, largely held at the Liverpool Records Office but also in the archives at Knowsley Hall, makes it possible to put together with no small degree of accuracy the various breeding projects and collecting missions he was involved in at this time, the mode of transport used for acquisitions, visitors to the menagerie and so on. They also provided the basis for my portrayal of the Earl's personality, feelings and attitudes.

From these, I know that he disliked the idea of keeping monkeys in cages, that he was committed to providing optimum conditions in his menagerie and Aviary, and that he went to great lengths to keep his charges in comfort and the best of health, not just where breeding success was concerned. I do think he was quite modern in his thinking about animals. And although he was rather more of his time and class when it came to his views on people, he was surprisingly egalitarian in his range of correspondents. His commitment to natural history was astonishing, and he would discuss it with anyone who shared his passion. The newspaper accounts of his death and funeral also paint him as a popular man (as well as being the only source of information I could find on his paralysis, other than a reference in Moore's diary to him being pushed around in a Bath chair).

The many, many letters the 13th Earl received from Mr Mitchell are a wonderful source of information on the thinking inside the Society at this difficult period in its history, as well as the relationship of the President to the institution, and his involvement in various attempts to reverse its fortunes. The Minutes of the Council, the annual reports of the Society and accounts of anniversary meetings in newspapers were also much consulted here. Takashi Ito's research into the background to the changes in the admission policy was helpful, putting it within the wider discussion of access to all public institutions. The transport of the hippopotamus was based on the very detailed accounts of it in the press, also discussions of it in the Minutes of the Council. The events leading up to it (especially the dispatch of the dogs in return) are taken from Lord Derby's correspondence. Newspaper reports and the Society's annual reports paint a vivid picture of the ZSL's triumphant return to fortune. The details of Gould's exhibition at the Zoological Gardens was much documented in the press (Dickens's report of it in *Household Words* is particularly good) and also in correspondence between Gould and the Council of the ZSL.

Edward Lear's descriptions of family life at Knowsley Hall were the basis of my account of it here. He describes the daily routine, and a rather joyful, warm atmosphere. I used the census returns for Knowsley Hall and the surrounding properties for details of staff. Stephen Lloyd dug out a wonderful little document for me, a catalogue of the pictures in the Hall at the time, which detailed the layout of the rooms, and the paintings that hung in them. It made me very emotional to discover that a painting entitled *Head of Master Thomas Chimpanzee from Zool. Gardens Regent's Park* by Hawkins was hanging on Lord Derby's bedroom wall. Sadly, I have not been able to trace the painting.

Index